x

I0806791

ST. MARY'S COLLEGE
LIBRARY

FALLS ROAD

822·009

HIN

22088

GENERAL EDITOR: A. E. Dyson

Drama Criticism
Developments Since Ibsen

A CASEBOOK

EDITED BY

ARNOLD P. HINCHLIFFE

Selection and editorial matter © Arnold P. Hinchliffe 1979

All rights reserved. No part of this publication
may be reproduced or transmitted, in any form
or by any means, without permission.

First published 1979 by
THE MACMILLAN PRESS LTD
London and Basingstoke
Associated companies in Delhi Dublin
Hong Kong Johannesburg Lagos Melbourne
New York Singapore and Tokyo

Printed in Great Britain
by Unwin Brothers Limited
Old Woking Surrey

British Library Cataloguing in Publication Data

Drama criticism. – (Casebook series).
  1. English drama – History and criticism –
Addresses, essays, lectures
I. Hinchliffe, Arnold P   II. Series
822'.009   PR627

  ISBN 0-333-23472-3
  ISBN 0-333-23473-1 (PbK)

This book is sold subject to the standard conditions of the
Net Book Agreement.

The paperback edition of this book is sold subject to the condition
that it shall not, by way of trade or otherwise, be lent, re-sold,
hired out, or otherwise circulated without the publisher's prior
consent in any form of binding other than that in which it is
published and without a similar condition including this
condition being imposed on the subsequent purchaser.

CONTENTS

ACKNOWLEDGEMENTS

The editor and publishers wish to thank the following, who have kindly given permission for the use of copyright material: James Agate, review of *Macbeth* from *Amazing Theatre* (1939) and review of *St Joan* from *Red Letter Nights* (1944) by permission of George G Harrap and Company Limited; John Arden, 'Telling a True Tale' from *The Encore Reader* (1970) edited by Charles Marowitz, Tom Milne and Owen Hale, by permission of Methuen and Company Ltd; Harley Granville Barker, extract from 'Preface on Love's Labour Lost' in *Prefaces to Shakespeare* (1930) by permission of The Society of Authors for the Estate of Harley Granville Barker; Eric Bentley, 'What is Theatre? A Point of View' from *Theatre of Commitment* (1957) by permission of the author; Michael Billington, extract from *The Modern Actor* (1973,© 1971 by Michael Billington), reprinted by permission of Hamish Hamilton Limited; M C Bradbrook, extract from 'The Question of Characterisation' from *Elizabethan Stage Conditions* (1932) by permission of the author and Cambridge University Press; Peter Brook, extract from *The Empty Space* (1968) by permission of MacGibbon & Kee Limited/Granada Publishing Ltd; John Russell Brown, extract from *Theatre Language: A Study of Arden, Osborne, Pinter and Wesker*, (Allen Lane, 1972)© John Russell Brown, 1972, by permission of Penguin Books Limited; E Gordon Craig, extracts from *On the Art of the Theatre* (1956), by permission of Heinemann Educational Books Limited; T S Eliot, essay on 'Ben Jonson' from *T S Eliot's Volume of Selected Essays* (1919) by permission of Faber & Faber Limited; John Elsom, extract from *Post-War British Theatre* (1976) by permission of Routledge and Kegan Paul Limited; Tyrone Guthrie, 'Is There Madness in the Method' from *The Encore Reader* (1970) edited by Charles Marowitz, Tom Milne and Owen Hale by permission of Methuen & Company Limited; Andrew Kennedy, extract from *Six Dramatists in Search of a Language* (1975) by permission of the author and Cambridge University Press; G Wilson Knight, extract from *Shakespearean Production* (1964) by permission of Routledge and Kegan Paul Limited; Charles Marowitz, a review from *Confessions of a Counterfeit Critic* (1973) by permission of Eyre & Methuen; Bernard Shaw, extract from 'The Quintessence of Ibsenism' and 'Our Theatre in the 90's', by permission of The Society of Authors on behalf of the Bernard Shaw Estate; J L Styan, an extract from *The Shakespeare*

Revolution (1977) by permission of the author and Cambridge University Press; George Jean Nathan, extract from *The Critic and the Drama*, (1922) by permission of the editor and Associated University Presses; Kenneth Tynan, review of Paul Scofield's 'Hamlet' from *He That Plays the King* (1950) by permission of the author; T C Worsley, review of *Death of a Salesman* (1952) entitled 'Poetry Without Words' from *The Fugitive Art* (1952) by permission of the *New Statesman*; Katherine J Worth, extract from *Revolutions in Modern English Drama* (1972) by permission of Bell and Hyman Limited. Every effort has been made to trace all the copyright holders but if any have been inadvertently overlooked the publishers will be pleased to make the necessary arrangement at the first opportunity.

The editor is particularly grateful to his General Editor, A. E. Dyson, and his Publisher, Derick Mirfin. He would also like to thank Miss L. Kissell for typing the material.

VLADIMIR   Moron!
ESTRAGON   That's the idea, let's abuse each other.
            (*They turn, increase the space between them,*
            turn again and face each other.)
VLADIMIR   Moron!
ESTRAGON   Vermin!
VLADIMIR   Abortion!
ESTRAGON   Morpion!
VLADIMIR   Sewer-rat!
ESTRAGON   Curate!
VLADIMIR   Cretin!
ESTRAGON   (*With finality.*) Crritic!

For

DAVID and TONY

GENERAL EDITOR'S PREFACE

The Casebook series, launched in 1968, has become a well-regarded library of critical studies. The central concern of the series remains the 'single-author' volume, but suggestions from the academic community have led to an extension of the original plan, to include occasional volumes on such general themes as literary 'schools' and genres.

Each volume in the central category deals either with one well-known and influential work by an individual author, or with closely related works by one writer. The main section consists of critical readings, mostly modern, collected from books and journals. A selection of reviews and comments by the author's contemporaries is also included, and sometimes comment from the author himself. The Editor's Introduction charts the reputation of the work or works from the first appearance to the present time.

Volumes in the 'general theme' category are variable in structure but follow the basic purpose of the series in presenting an integrated selection of readings, with an Introduction which explores the theme and discusses the literary and critical issues involved.

A single volume can represent no more than a small selection of critical opinions. Some critics are excluded for reasons of space, and it is hoped that readers will pursue the suggestions for further reading in the Select Bibliography. Other contributions are severed from their original context, to which many readers will wish to turn. Indeed, if they take a hint from the critics represented here, they certainly will.

A. E. DYSON

INTRODUCTION

> . . . and there is no new thing under the sun

A Biblical text carries less weight than it used to, but the idea, surely, is unexceptionable. It suggests why the title of this Casebook does not with entire accuracy apply to the collection of essays here presented. The title looks like a sensible description of what we might find, particularly since Ibsen is, with some justice, regarded as the father of modern drama and his work coincided, naturally, with the rise of the producer or, as he is now called, the director. Until the nineteenth century, production had been co-ordinated or directed by the dramatist or the leading actor – stock companies and the simplicity of stage machinery making any other supervision unnecessary. But the improvement of stage lighting and machinery, naturalistic plays and the consequent under-acting, made rehearsal more important, and the actor-manager was gradually replaced by the director. But it is only a shift in emphasis rather than a development: performance is replaced by production.

But I keep the title because over the years Dramatic Criticism has developed within its many varieties; it has grown more serious and more seriously concerned with fusing the demands of the drama and those of the theatre. For drama still stands on a different basis from the novel or the poem. For Aristotle and the Greeks, all the arts received public, or at least oral, performance: the epic was recited, while elegiac and iambic poetry were accompanied by the flute, melic poetry by the lyre. Today we read the novel and poetry mainly in private; but drama still requires a mixture of talents: it is both literary and spectacular. So, while the critic writing about a novel or a poem can express a point of view which will differ from others, the thing reviewed will remain the same. But drama lacks this fixed quality. There is, it is true, the text (words on a page), but performance is, even in a long run, a 'one-off' thing. The drama critic, therefore, must decide what he is criticising as well as how to criticise it.

It is one solution to suggest that dramatic criticism is written in the study with the text in front of you, while theatre criticism looks at performance. But such a division is arbitrary and confers more upon a text that recent writers would allow. Stanley Wells, in his introduction to *English Drama: Select Bibliographical Guides* (Oxford, 1975), comments

that readers will probably not need reminding that theatrical experience is fundamental to the study of drama (p. viii); but in a later
essay in the same volume Allardyce Nicoll can write, unblushingly, that
his bibliography is 'of course, concerned specifically with drama, not
with theatre' (p. 279). Peter Thomson, in the first essay on bibliography, lists ten areas of dramatic criticism: Dramatic Theory;
General Studies; Origins of Drama; Dramatic Genres; Reference Books;
Theatre History; Stage Design; Theatres; Directors and Directing; and
Actors and Acting – none of which actually includes the dramatist.

Recent criticism has tried to fuse these many parts into a whole.
Thus, Martin Esslin, in *An Anatomy of a Drama* (1976, p. 14), points out
that drama means action. It is not simply a form of literature, although
the words used when written down can be treated as literature: 'What
makes drama drama is precisely the element which lies outside and
beyond the word and which has to be seen as action or *acted* – to give the
author's concept its full value.' Raymond Williams, in *Drama in
Performance* (1972, pp. 3–4), writes:

We can study a written play, and state a response to it, and that statement is, or
is intended to be, literary criticism. Alternatively, we can study an actual
performance of a play, and state a response to that; and that statement is, or is
intended to be, theatrical criticism. For legitimate purposes of emphasis, the
study of a text may fail to include any detailed consideration of the way in which
that text would be performed, as the author intended it should be performed.
Similarly, the study of a performance may isolate the details of performance
alone, without particular consideration of the play. These methods have their
uses, but, ultimately, dramatic criticism must proceed beyond them.

In recent years it is that journey which has preoccupied critics, resulting
in studies like that of J. L. Styan – significantly called *Drama, Stage and
Audience* (1975) – where he insists (p. vii) that

drama is not made of words alone, but of sights and sounds, stillness and motion,
noise and silence, relationships and responses. Yet: these relationships and
responses are not those between characters, rather those between actor and
audience. Drama study insists, therefore, that we think of a particular social
situation, a here-and-now or (imperious demand!) a there-and-then recreated
in the imagination to be here-and-now.

One factor in this critical effort must be the development of Departments of Drama. Until recently, plays were taught in departments of
literature, and criticism of plays was written either by playgoers or by
critics used to writing about texts who saw no reason to distinguish

between novel, poem and play. Theatre history has a long tradition, dating back to Juba II, King of Mauretania in the time of Augustus. But criticism learned outside departments of literature is very recent. It was not until 1901 that Max Herrman began his lectures and seminars on the theatre at the University of Berlin, working outside the traditional framework of literature departments. The development has been very slow – understandably, because there is some doubt about what, precisely, a Department of Drama should be doing in an academic context (as opposed, for example, to a School of Acting). But at least drama as both a literary and a theatrical experience struggles more legitimately when it is under the aegis of a centre of study called (as it is at Birmingham) the Department of Drama and the Theatre Arts. Yale has a professorship of Playwriting and Criticism, the University of California at Berkeley has one of Dramatic Art, while at the University of Indiana there are professors of Theatre and Drama. But even this confusion directs attention away from the dramatist (something, incidentally, which Ibsen deplored) and reminds us that performance or production involves an audience, a social context, the box office (or subsidy) and a collection of talents.

It also reminds us that, if drama is permanent and universal, the essence of theatre is its transitoriness. A text remains – but as literature, not drama; it is only *potentially* dramatic. Dramatic criticism – which, like all criticism, is a parasitic art – is thus less certain of what it feeds on and what it illuminates; and this is its fascination. The purpose of this anthology must be to suggest dramatic criticism as an art rather than to bring together critical judgements on works of literature or performances. The art of selection – always the science of rejection – becomes less important; more crucially, the reader must constantly be encouraged to think, not how true this piece is about X, but how interesting that treatment of what happens to be X, but could be anything else, actually is. The first part of this Casebook, therefore, is not a comprehensive survey of dramatic criticism up to Ibsen, but rather a collection of comments by writers who will be familiar in themselves but whose opinions can now, we hope, be seen as examples of the methods and subjects available in dramatic criticism.

The earliest dramatic criticism seems to have concentrated mainly on the morality of acting. The basis of characterisation is a moral concept that goes back to Aristotle's *Poetics* and rests upon the idea of the individual as a moral being. On the opposing side of the argument was Plato, who saw dramatists as imitators of imitations, and therefore producing copies which were 'third in descent from the sovereign and the truth' (*Republic*, 597). Plato was also inhibited by his concept of justice: doing what you were best at and thereby contributing to the social whole. To act was to pretend to do, and often involved pretending to do bad things, like imitating women or slaves. He allowed the poets the right to argue (in verse) for their inclusion in the well-ordered state only because he personally enjoyed the theatre so much. The Christian Fathers, who thought Plato divinely inspired, adopted much of Platonic thought into their attitude to the theatre, as St Augustine illustrates; and their antagonism led, eventually, to the secularisation of the theatre and to its doubtful moral reputation. (A certain way to Hell lies through the door of a playhouse.)

In England dramatic criticism naturally centres on Shakespeare who was regarded, in his own time, as the greatest of all dramatists: a view never seriously challenged in the seventeenth century. But criticism – the criticism that organises and evaluates – only becomes systematic after Dryden. Ben Jonson was probably the first Englishman with a critical temper, but he contributes no single original idea to criticism. His attempts at practical criticism are always interesting but the methods and language are usually borrowed. It was Dryden who reviewed the problems forced on dramatists since the death of Shakespeare. There were unShakespearean methods used in France and Spain, while some scholars – like Milton and Thomas Rymer – believed that better models could be found in such ancient writers as Aeschylus and Sophocles. The stage itself was different, since it had, after the Restoration, movable scenery, and women instead of boys playing the female roles. So it was necessary to test Shakespeare's genius against these new ideas and conditions. Much emphasis was laid on the Rules, but it must be remembered that the seventeenth-century inherited these Rules rather than invented them. The classical injunction to follow Nature meant Nature defined in the mechanical universe of Hobbes and Locke; hence critics were asking only for the same order in literature as was exhibited in life. It is also true that Dryden – and Addison and Pope – agreed that genius which ignored the Rules was better than a second-rate talent which observed them. Dryden's *Of Dramaticke Poesie*, part of which appears in Part One, was described by Samuel Johnson as a 'model of encomiastic criticism', and it was a model which Johnson followed in his famous Preface of 1765 to the works of Shakespeare (also used here). But Dryden's dramatic criticism is often very untheatrical. For theatrical criticism the reader is advised to consult Thomas Rymer, who accepts that plays are intended to be acted and should, therefore, be looked at in connection with the

stage and its actors. For this Castelvetro was responsible. Aristotle insists
in at least four places (*Poetics*, vi, 19; vii, 6; xiv, 1, 2; and xxvi, 3) that plays
should be criticised primarily without reference to stage representation.
Castelvetro, one of the commentators on Aristotle, founded in 1750 a
theory of dramatic criticism which rests on the physical conditions of the
theatre. Nevertheless, it is Dryden who stands as the first great modern
critic.

When we turn to Samuel Johnson we find little that is new. His
Preface rehearses the arguments about Shakespeare's irregularities.
Johnson's own play, *Irene* (1736), was as regular as it was possible to be,
and even with Garrick must have been faultlessly dull. But Johnson can
see both sides of the argument and represents the last statement in the
judicial manner. The Preface, as a balanced estimate by a wise and
shrewd mind, cannot be surpassed.

A new direction came with the Romantics, as suggested by Coleridge
and confirmed by Hazlitt in his *Characters of Shakespear's* (sic) *Plays*
(1817). Hazlitt's was the first *book* in which nineteenth-century criticism
speaks clearly and confidently, but Coleridge had already been
lecturing on Shakespeare for some time. Unfortunately, Coleridge
never collected or collated his work on Shakespeare (part of which is
reproduced here) in any systematic manner. It remains in note form
(for oral delivery in the lectures given between 1808 and 1819) or is
mentioned in letters or reported secondhand from dinner tables or in
newspaper reports, or in occasional jottings in his commonplace books.
Even so, there is no question of the powerful impression made by
Shakespeare on Coleridge's mind and transmitted by him to his
contemporaries. For Coleridge Shakespeare was an unprecedented
phenomenon: a poet and a dramatist, and both simultaneously. Much
influenced by German scholarship, Coleridge insisted that it was
Schlegel and the German critics who first taught Englishmen to admire
Shakespeare *intelligently*. The Romantics felt they were discovering
Shakespeare for the first time. They no longer had to admit his faults
before admiring his merits; they simply sought to explain those merits.
Their aim, then, was interpretation, not judgement. The plays were
real life and the characters human beings of whom the plays remained
the only record. A. C. Bradley's *Shakespearean Tragedy*, although not
published until 1904, is probably the last great representative of this
tradition.

Such imaginative freedom was exciting and full of insights, but it was
also dangerous. And it overlooked one aspect that both Dryden and
Johnson recognised: that the genius Shakespeare was a man with a
living to earn. At the same time, it was Coleridge who outlined a

programme for historical criticism (the need to know the manners, language and sources of Shakespeare), and whose attention to the text anticipated modern symbolist criticism. And we remember Coleridge as preoccupied with a central problem: the nature of dramatic illusion, summed up in the famous phrase from *Biographia Literaria* concerning the willing suspension of disbelief for the moment, which constitutes poetic faith.

Also included in Part One are some direct accounts of great performances – although Henry Morley's review of Kean is more concerned with the scenery and the production. Such statements could be multiplied into several volumes, but they would only add up to the kinds of dramatic criticism available. The section closes with Ibsen's famous letter to Lucie Wolf announcing the prose play, and therefore laying some kind of foundation for the modern theatre.

Part Two is the core of the selection, and is divided into three sections. Once again Shakespeare looms large in one form or another. But it must be remembered that the intention is not to illuminate Shakespeare as such but to demonstrate the ways of looking at him: ways which can be exercised on more recent drama in the final section of Part Two. The inclusion of one of our most distinguished modern critics, T. S. Eliot on Ben Jonson, will help to keep this in mind.

Henry James sets the scene. He was, of course, never a dramatic critic; and some say that he was never a dramatist either, although he aspired to be one and wrote eighteen plays. *The Scenic Art* collects articles he wrote on the theatre, mainly for American journals, and is a sort of playgoer's diary. He much preferred the French theatre, but he is nonetheless an intelligent reporter of the English scene and it is possible that he saw Ibsen's achievement more clearly than Shaw. The latter's *The Quintessence of Ibsenism* is, after all, more of a guide to Shaw's own values and practice than to Ibsen's; it claims Ibsen as an ally for Shaw. James, on the other hand, though speaking of Ibsen as 'massively common and middle-class', recognised that beneath these surfaces there was both independence and intensity, 'the hard compulsion of his strangely inscrutable art'.

But the two obvious champions of Ibsen in England were also the two best dramatic critics of the time, Shaw and William Archer. Shaw's views on Shakespeare are very well known. Archer, an example of whose writing on Ibsen is reproduced here, produced in *English Dramatists of Today* (1882) what Michael Booth has described as 'the most thorough review of the state of contemporary drama written at any time in the nineteenth century' (*English Drama: Select Bibliographical Guides*, p. 219). And Shaw's work, collected in the three volumes of *Our Theatre in the Nineties*, reminds us that much of the best dramatic criticism was journalism – a tradition continued by James Agate. It was, according to Agate, the articles signed GBS in *The Saturday Review* which made him decide to become a dramatic critic; and his *Red Letter Nights* (1944) – a survey of post-Elizabethan drama in actual performance on the London stage between 1921 and 1943 – makes us aware that Agate had seen between four and five thousand plays in those twenty-two years.

T. C. Worsley's collection of reviews (1952) is well-named *The Fugitive Art* for not only is the performance transitory but so also is much of the contemporary criticism. What is interesting in Worsley's review (presented here) of Miller's *The Death of a Salesman* is his opposition to the replacement of words by other theatrical devices. A misplaced faith in words alone produced a brief resurgence of verse drama under T. S. Eliot and Christopher Fry (to name but two notable exponents). Yet this approach overlooks the fact that theatre language does not consist of words alone. Moreover, as has been pointed out by Gareth L. Evans in *The Language of Modern Drama* (1977), theatre language is now 'a vast apparatus identified separately from the language of drama', and it is at the command of the director, not the dramatist.

In recognising this, it would have been interesting, if space had been available, to have material from or about, say, Richard Wagner, Artaud, Brecht and many more who have fertilised the theatrical compôte. But basically our policy is to include critics who have assimilated the theories of such seminal minds into the English theatre. And these have been particularly directors. For, alongside critics who were sometimes journalists, sometimes dramatists (like Shaw and Eliot), sometimes academics (as was A. C. Bradley), the directors were beginning, in this century, to write criticism. Harley Granville-Barker began his famous Prefaces to Shakespeare's plays in 1930, much influenced by William Poel and by A. C. Bradley; and he tries to have the best of both worlds! If his first preface, included here, is not his most exciting one, it does ask the key question of why we should bother to produce such a play as *Love's Labours Lost*, and sends us constantly back to the play with its insights.

In the academic field, too, the emphasis on character was being challenged. In 1932 M. C. Bradbrook published *Elizabethan Stage Conditions* (part of which is reproduced here) in which, after reviewing the dramatic criticism of Shakespeare in the eighteenth, nineteenth and twentieth centuries, she showed how the attitude to character had been established by Coleridge and Hazlitt and reduced to absurdity by A. C. Bradley, whose character studies were, she suggested, little more than 'thinly disguised gossip about the private lives of the dramatis personae'. This method of attack was continued in L. C. Knight's famous essay, 'How Many Children Had Lady Macbeth?' Yet the study of character, either in the text or on the stage, seems central and inescapable. Dramatic criticism remains, surely, a study of the dramatist's ability to create, and an actor's ability to recreate, roles?

In *He That Plays the King* (1950), Kenneth Tynan records an era of heroic acting and hero-worship of the actors who created such giant performances. We reproduce here an account of Scofield's Hamlet, part of the whole study written out of *enthusiasm* because Tynan felt that contemporary criticism had 'taken a wrong turning into imperturbability and casualness' (p. 23). Tynan remains enthusiastic, though his enthusiasm is now focused on different matters. In 1958 Charles Marowitz came to Britain from New York, and has since become well-known (or notorious, according to taste) for his collages of Shakespearean plays. He started with *Hamlet* in 1965: a play which he admits he hates! In *Confessions of a Counterfeit Critic* (1973) he reprints reviews from 1958 to 1971, with comments on what he thinks of them and their subjects now. We reproduce here his account of the Richardson–Williamson *Hamlet* of 1969 (which, incidentally, was thought by Harold Wilson to be the best presentation of the play in this century, and he strongly urged President Nixon to go and see it). Michael Billington's *The Modern Actor* (1973), from which we reproduce another view of that performance, complements Tynan's book of 1950 by showing that acting is no longer heroic; but it also reminds us that since 1950 the cinema and, increasingly, television have offered alternative employment for the actor. Thus no actor is now confined to one medium (and the theatre is probably now the least available, and certainly the least lucrative). Similarly, the playwright has other opportunities for exercising his craft than the theatre. This may be the most significant development of our time. If so, it is a technical one, replacing even the director by a cameraman and gaffer.

The Granville-Barker tradition was carried on by Wilson Knight, and later by Tyrone Guthrie and Peter Brook. Granville-Barker wrote his Prefaces after he had left the theatre, but the connection between play and performance is clear, and Wilson Knight, although dedicating *Principles of Shakespearean Production* to H. Beerbohm Tree and Leslie Harris, was greatly indebted to Granville-Barker. Both Guthrie and Brook are known as brilliant and inventive directors – and the adjective 'inventive' is not entirely flattering. Guthrie's attack on a school of

acting, 'The Method' (reproduced here) arose from his conviction that
it was the actor's business to make the audience feel emotions, not enjoy
them himself. He objected that The Method made the thing real and
true for the actor but not necessarily for the audience. Peter Brook,
meanwhile, has become more and more involved with methods from
the Continental theatre, and particularly the ideas of Artaud. Artaud
saw the stage as a space to be filled: a process in which language would
play only a very minor role. Hence Brook's study (an excerpt of which is
reproduced here) was called *The Empty Stage*, and he has shifted from
brilliant interpretation of the text to the elimination of the text in favour
of non-verbal language – which makes performance even more ephemeral than usual. Moreover, and ironically, it reflects the ideas, not
only of Artaud, but also of Gordon Craig, whose *On the Art of the Theatre*
(part of which appears here) was published as long ago as 1910. Craig's
attitude was summed up by Agate in *Buzz Buzz* (no date, p. 50), where
he remarks that when Craig produces Shakespeare he feels himself to be
as much an artist as Shakespeare and has no intention of being
subordinate: 'When we listen to Shakespeare's verses we are to feel in
terms of Shakespeare; when we look at Mr Craig's settings we are to feel
in terms of Mr Craig. And never the twain shall interpret one another,
though you put them on the stage together, and with every pretence of
mutual support.'

But so-called academic writing on drama was also accepting the
challenge of the theatre. Barrett H. Clarke's study of modern drama,
published in 1936 and incorporating editions of 1925 and 1928 (his
essay on *Candida* is reproduced here) is written very much as an
academic history with bibliographies. But it asks the kind of question of
the reader which shows that performance was always in mind. The idea
that British Theatre changed overnight with *Look Back in Anger* in 1956
is simply not tenable. But new dramatists, new acting styles and new
kinds of production – reflecting first Beckett, then Brecht, and finally
Artaud as influences – not only made T. C. Worsley's complaints of
1949 out-of-date: they stimulated a flood of theatrical criticism, of
dramatic criticism. Fundamentally, there was a new question posed:
What *is* dramatic criticism? In *Effective Theatre* (1969), John Russell
Brown advanced the view that dramatic criticism was a matter of
solving 'the important problem of how to be intellectually responsible' –
which means attention to theatre language as a whole, not just words.
He explores this attention in *Theatre Language* (1972) – part of which is
reproduced here – focusing on Arden, Osborne, Pinter and Wesker.
This kind of exploration is continued in Andrew Kennedy's *Six
Dramatists in Search of a Language* (1975) in which (as the excerpt

included here shows) it proves possible to revalue such earlier
dramatists as Shaw. This kind of revaluation occurs also in a history
such as K. J. Worth's *Revolutions in Modern English Drama* (1972), where
the revolutions are both cyclic and revolving, and where (as the extract
presented here shows) we can reassess T. S. Eliot as something more
than part of a minor vogue for verse-drama. Similarly, John Elsom's
Post-War British Theatre (1976) – from which we reprint an essay on
Pinter – has as its first chapter a treatment of the two main strands:
Language and Money.

The post-1950 period, then, has been a lively one in theatre and
drama criticism. Some of the flavour of it can be found in *The 'Encore'
Reader*, an anthology of articles covering the years 1956–63. But the
difficulties of coping with the demands of drama and the exigencies of
the theatre remain. In *Free Shakespeare* (1971) we find John Russell
Brown arguing for a return to performance as opposed to production;
while in *The Shakespeare Revolution* (1977) by J. L. Styan, a chapter of
which is reproduced here, we can follow the vagaries of production and
criticism. Professor Styan begins with an axiom (or what, by now, has
the force of axiom): 'The first and last values of drama are revealed in
the response of an audience in a theatre, and all else must be secondary
and speculative' (p. 3). Styan also notes that, while in 1900, readers
turned to the scholar to elucidate plays, in 1970 scholarship seems
suspect and the stage seems to be more in touch with the spirit of the
plays.

The statement is contentious. The number of people who can or do
get to a theatre remains very small, and so we are faced with the
prospect of a majority of people out of touch with drama altogether.
Unless? Unless we accept that cinema and television have become the
normal dramatic media for most people. Martin Esslin, in his *Illustrated
Encyclopaedia of World Theatre* (1977), suggests that whereas the cinema
and television, in spite of their derivation from theatre, are mechanised,
industrial processes involving vast capital equipment and expenditure,
the theatre is still handicrafted. This may be so, but it could be argued
that the National Theatre is really television, not that large building on
the South Bank.

Presumably criticism in these fields will grow. It has not so far been
very encouraging, but it has been excluded from this anthology more on
the grounds of space than judgement. Yet this recognition, once more,
of the audience reminds us that drama is both an art and a trade.
Though subsidy from the public purse has confused the situation, the
claims for drama as an art must be balanced with the recognition that it
is also a commodity that has to be paid for.

The hybrid nature of drama – drama as text in apposition with drama as performance – results in hybrid criticism. The study of drama criticism will range from, say, Coleridge to, say, Bernard Levin. So the final part of this Casebook glances briefly at the practice of dramatic criticism. The last word goes, as it should, to a dramatist, John Arden. But before that we have three views of the function and writing of dramatic criticism. Leigh Hunt's 'Rules' may be facetious, but they have a deadly accuracy we can all appreciate. More gravely, we have the opinions of A. B. Walkley, drama critic of *The Times* from 1900 to 1926 (to whom Shaw dedicated *St Joan*), and George Jean Nathan, one of the most famous and influential critics of his day. According to Somerset Maugham in *The Summing Up* (1938; paperback reprint 1976, p. 92.), the critic is the worst judge of the play because he is there not to feel but to judge: 'He must hold aloof from the contagion that has captured the group and keep his self-possession. He must not allow his heart to carry him away; his head must remain well-screwed on his shoulders. He must not become part of the audience.' Such a critic asks for different things from a play, and Maugham sees no reason why he should get them. But for George Jean Nathan criticism is always personal. It can never be a science, and at its best will have about it the flavour of 'the unconscious, grotesque and unpremeditated'. It must, in short, balance interpretation (which is theatrical) with judgement (which is drama) – or, as Nathan expressed it in *The Critic and the Drama* (1922, p. 133):

Dramatic criticism, at its best, is the adventure of an intelligence among emotions. The chief end of drama is the enkindling of emotions; the chief end of dramatic criticism is to rush into the burning building and rescue the metaphysical weaklings who are wont to be overcome by the first faint whiffs of smoke.

PART ONE

Prologue

Aristotle (c. 330 BC)

A tragedy, then, is the imitation of an action that is serious and also, as having magnitude, complete in itself; in language with pleasurable accessories, each kind brought in separately in the parts of the work; in a dramatic, not in a narrative, form; with incidents arousing pity and fear, wherewith to accomplish its catharsis of such emotions.

Plots are either simple or complex, since the actions they represent are naturally of this twofold description. The action, proceeding in the way defined, as one continuous whole, I call simple, when the change in the hero's fortunes takes place without Peripety or Discovery; and complex, when it involves one or other, or both. These should each of them arise out of the structure of the Plot itself, so as to be the consequence, necessary or probable, of the antecedents. There is a great difference between a thing happening *propter hoc* and *post hoc*.

There remains, then, the intermediate kind of personage, a man not pre-eminently virtuous and just, whose misfortune, however, is brought upon him not by vice and depravity but by some error of judgement . . . . The perfect Plot, accordingly, must have a single, and not (as some tell us) a double, issue; the change in the hero's fortunes must not be from misery to happiness, but on the contrary from happiness to misery; and the cause of it must lie not in any depravity, but in some great error on his part; the man himself being either such as we have described, or better, not worse, than that.

SOURCE: extracts from chapters VI, X and XIII of *The Poetics*, translated by Ingram Bywater (Oxford, 1909).

Saint Augustine (c. 397)

Stage-plays also carried me away, full of images of my miseries, and of fuel to my fire. Why is it, that man desires to be made sad, beholding doleful and tragical things, which yet himself would by no means suffer? Yet he desires as a spectator to feel sorrow at them, and this very sorrow is his pleasure. What is this but a miserable madness? For a man is the more affected with these actions, the less free he is from such affections. Howsoever, when he suffers in his own person, it uses to be styled misery: when he compassionates others, then it is mercy. But what sort of compassion is this for feigned and scenical passions? For the auditor is not called on to relieve, but only to grieve: and he applauds the actor of these fictions the more, the more he grieves. And if the calamities of those persons (whether of old times, or mere fiction) be so acted, that the spectator is not moved to tears, he goes away disgusted and criticising; but if he be moved to passion, he stays intent, and weeps for joy.

SOURCE: extract from the *Confessions*, translated by E. B. Pusey; Everyman edition (London, 1907), p. 33.

William Shakespeare (1603)

HAMLET   Speak the speech, I pray you, as I pronounced it to you, trippingly on the tongue. But if you mouth it, as many of our players do, I had as lief the town crier spoke my lines. Nor do not saw the air too much with your hand, thus, but use all gently, for in the very torrent, tempest, and (as I may say) whirlwind of your passion, you must acquire and beget a temperance that may give it smoothness. O, it offends me to the very soul to hear a robustious periwig-pated fellow tear a passion to tatters, to very rags, to split the ears of the groundlings, who for the most part are capable of nothing but inexplicable dumb shows and noise. I would have such a fellow whipped for o'erdoing Termagant. It out-herods Herod. Pray you avoid it.

PLAYER   I warrant your honour.

HAMLET   Be not too tame neither, but let your own discretion be your tutor. Suit the action to the word, the word to the action, with this special observance, that you o'erstep not the modesty of nature. For anything so o'erdone is from the purpose of playing, whose end, both at the first and now, was and is, to hold, as 'twere, the mirror up to nature; to show virtue her own feature, scorn her own image, and the very age and body of the time his form and pressure. Now, this overdone, or come tardy off, though it make the unskilful laugh, cannot but make the judicious grieve; the censure of the which one must in your allowance o'erweigh a whole theatre of others. O, there be players that I have seen play, and heard others praise, and that highly (not to speak it profanely), that neither having th'accent of Christians, nor the gait of

Christian, pagan, nor man, have so strutted and bellowed that I have thought some of Nature's journeymen had made men, and not made them well, they imitated humanity so abominably.

PLAYER   I hope we have reformed that indifferently with us, sir.

HAMLET   O, reform it altogether! And let those that play your clowns speak no more than is set down for them, for there be of them that will themselves laugh, to set on some quantity of barren spectators to laugh too, though in the meantime some necessary question of the play be then to be considered. That's villainous and shows a most pitiful ambition in the fool that uses it. Go make you ready.

SOURCE: extract from *Hamlet*, Act III, Scene ii, ll. 1–47.

John Dryden   (1668)

. . . Shakespeare . . . was the man who of all modern, and perhaps ancient, poets had the largest and most comprehensive soul. All the images of nature were still present to him, and he drew them, not laboriously, but luckily; when he describes anything, you more than see it, you feel it too. Those who accuse him to have wanted learning, give him the greater commendation: he was naturally learned; he needed not the spectacles of books to read nature; he looked inwards, and found her there. I cannot say he is everywhere alike; were he so, I should do him injury to compare him with the greatest of mankind. He is many times flat, insipid; his comic wit degenerating into clenches, his serious swelling into bombast. But he is always great, when some great occasion is presented to him; no man can say he ever had a fit subject for his wit, and did not then raise himself as high above the rest of poets,

Quantum lenta solent inter viburna cupressi.[1]

The consideration of this made Mr Hales of Eaton say, that there was no subject of which any poet ever wrote but he would produce it much better done in Shakespeare; and however others are now generally preferred before him, yet the age wherein he lived, which had contemporaries with him Fletcher and Jonson, never equalled them to him in their esteem: and in the last king's court, when Ben's reputation was at highest, Sir John Suckling, and with him the greater part of the courtiers, set our Shakespeare far above him.

Beaumont and Fletcher, of whom I am next to speak, had, with the advantage of Shakespeare's wit, which was their precedent, great natural gifts, improved by study: Beaumont especially being so accurate a judge of plays that Ben Jonson, while he lived, submitted all his writings to his censure, and, 'tis thought, used his judgement in correcting, if not contriving, all his plots. What value he had for him, appears by the verses he writ to him; and therefore I need speak no farther of it. The first play that brought Fletcher and him in esteem was their *Philaster*: for before that, they had written two or three very unsuccessfully, as the like is reported of Ben Jonson, before he wrote *Every Man in his Humour*. Their plots were generally more regular than Shakespeare's, especially those which were made before Beaumont's death; and they understood and imitated the conversation of gentlemen much better; whose wild debaucheries, and quickness of wit in repartees, no poet before them could paint as they have done. Humour which Ben Jonson derived from particular persons they made it not their business to describe: they represented all the passions very lively, but above all, love. I am apt to believe the English language in them arrived to its highest perfection; what words have since been taken in, are rather superfluous than ornamental. Their plays are now the most pleasant and frequent entertainments of the stage; two of theirs being acted through the year for one of Shakespeare's or Jonson's: the reason is, because there is a certain gaiety in their comedies and pathos in their more serious plays which suits generally with all men's humours. Shakespeare's language is likewise a little obsolete, and Ben Jonson's wit comes short of theirs.

As for Jonson, to whose character I am now arrived, if we look upon him while he was himself (for his last plays were but his dotages), I think him the most learned and judicious writer which any theatre ever had. He was a most severe judge of himself, as well as of others. One cannot say that he wanted wit, but rather that he was frugal of it. In his works you find little to retrench or alter. Wit, and language, and humour also in some measure, we had before him; but something of art was wanting to the drama, till he came. He managed his strength to more advantage than any who preceded him. You seldom find him making love in any of his scenes, or endeavouring to move the passions; his genius was too sullen and saturnine to do it gracefully, especially when he knew he came after those who had performed both to such a height. Humour was his proper sphere; and in that he was delighted most to represent mechanic people. He was deeply conversant with the ancients, both Greek and Latin, and he borrowed boldly from them: there is scarce a poet or historian among the Roman authors of those times whom he has not translated in *Sejanus* and *Catiline*. But he has done his robberies so openly, that one may see he fears not to be taxed by any law. He invades authors like a monarch; and what would be theft in other poets is only victory in him. With the spoils of these writers he so represents old Rome to us, in its rites, ceremonies, and customs, and if one of their poets had written either of his tragedies, we had seen less of it than in him. If there was any fault in his language, 'twas that he weaved it too closely and laboriously, in his comedies especially: perhaps too, he did a little too much Romanise our tongue, leaving the words which he translated almost as much Latin as he found them: wherein, though he learnedly followed their language, he did not enough comply with the idiom of ours. If I would compare him with Shakespeare, I must acknowledge him the more correct poet, but Shakespeare the greater wit. Shakespeare was the Homer, or father of our dramatic poets; Jonson was the Virgil, the pattern of elaborate writing; I admire him, but I love Shakespeare. To conclude of him; as he has given us the most correct plays, so in the precepts which he has laid down in his *Discoveries*, we have as many and profitable rules for perfecting the stage, as any wherewith the French can furnish us. . . .

SOURCE: extract from Neander's discourse in Dryden's *Essay of Dramaticke Poesie* (1668).

NOTE

1. As cypresses often do among bending osiers: Virgil, *Eclogues*, 1, 25 [Ed.]

Anonymous (1740)

Betterton's *Hamlet*

. . . . I have lately been told by a Gentleman who has frequently seen Mr Betterton perform this part of *Hamlet*, that he has observ'd his Countenance (which was naturally ruddy and sanguin) in this Scene of the fourth Act[1] where his Father's Ghost appears, thro' the violent and sudden Emotions of Amazement and Horror, turn instantly on the Sight of his Father's Spirit, as pale as his Neckcloth, when every Article of his Body seem'd to be affected with a Tremor inexpressible; so that, had his Father's Ghost actually risen before him, he could not have been seized with more real Agonies; and this was felt so strongly by the Audience, that the Blood seem'd to shudder in their Veins likewise, and they in some Measure partook of the Astonishment and Horror, with which they saw this excellent Actor affected. . . .

SOURCE: extract from *The Laureat, or the Right Side of Colley Cibber, Esq.* (London, 1740); reprinted in A. M. Nagler, *A Source Book in Theatrical History* (New York, 1952), p.219.

NOTE

1. The Ghost does not appear in Act IV in modern texts of the play. The reference here is probably to the last scene of Act III. The anonymous 'Gentleman's' recollection may have been faulty but it is quite possible that, in the performance he saw, the Ghost did indeed appear early on in 'The fourth Act'. Cf. Samuel Johnson, on the division between III iv and IV i:

This play is printed in the old editions without any separation of the acts. The division is modern and arbitrary; and is here not very happy. For the pause is made at a time when there is more continuity of action than in almost any other of the scenes.
[Ed.]

Samuel Johnson   (1765)

. . . The necessity of observing the unities of time and place arises from the supposed necessity of making the drama credible. The criticks hold it impossible, that an action of months or years can be possibly believed to pass in three hours; or that the spectator can suppose himself to sit in the theatre, while ambassadors go and return between distant kings, while armies are levied and towns besieged, while an exile wanders and returns, or till he whom they saw courting his mistress, shall lament the untimely fall of his son. The mind revolts from evident falsehood, and fiction loses its force when it departs from the resemblance of reality.

From the narrow limitation of time necessarily arises the contraction of place. The spectator, who knows that he saw the first act at *Alexandria*, cannot suppose that he sees the next at *Rome*, at a distance to which not the dragons of *Medea* could, in so short a time, have transported him; he knows, with certainty, that he has not changed his place; and he knows that place cannot change itself; that what was a house cannot become a plain; that what was *Thebes* can never be *Persepolis*.

Such is the triumphant language with which a critick exults over the misery of an irregular poet, and exults commonly without resistance or reply. It is time therefore to tell him, by the authority of *Shakespeare*, that he assumes, as an unquestionable principle, a position, which, while his breath is forming it into words, his understanding pronounces to be false. It is false, that any representation is mistaken for reality; that any dramatick fable in its materiality was ever credible, or, for a single moment, was ever credited.

The objection arising from the impossibility of passing the first hour at *Alexandria*, and the next at *Rome*, supposes, that when the play opens the spectator really imagines himself at *Alexandria*, and believes that his walk to the theatre has been a voyage to *Egypt*, and that he lives in the days of *Antony* and *Cleopatra*. Surely he that imagines this may imagine more. He that can take the stage at one time for the palace of the *Ptolemies*, may take it in half an hour for the promontory of *Actium*. Delusion, if delusion be admitted, has no certain limitation; if the spectator can be once persuaded, that his old acquaintance are *Alexander* and *Cæsar*, that a room illuminated with candles is the plain of *Pharsalia*, or the bank of *Granicus*, he is in a state of elevation above the reach of reason, or of truth, and from the heights of empyrean poetry, may despise the circumscriptions of terrestrial nature. There is no reason why a mind thus wandering in extasy should count the clock, or why an hour should not be a century in that calenture of the brains that can make the stage a field.

The truth is, that the spectators are always in their senses, and know, from the first act to the last, that the stage is only a stage, and that the players are only players. They came to hear a certain number of lines recited with just gesture and elegant modulation. The lines relate to some action, and an action must be in some place; but the different actions that compleat a story may be in places very remote from each other; and where is the absurdity of allowing that space to represent first *Athens*, and then *Sicily*, which was always known to be neither *Sicily* nor *Athens*, but a modern theatre?

By supposition, as a place is introduced, time may be extended; the time required by the fable elapses for the most part between the acts; for, of so much of the action as is represented, the real and poetical duration is the same. If, in the first act, preparations for war against *Mithridates* are represented to be made in *Rome*, the event of the war may, without absurdity, be represented, in the catastrophe, as happening in *Pontus*; we know that there is neither war, nor preparation for war; we know that we are neither in *Rome* nor *Pontus*; that neither *Mithridates* nor *Lucullus* are before us. The drama exhibits successive imitations of successive actions, and why may not the second imitation represent an action that happened years after the first; if it be so connected with it, that nothing but time can be supposed to intervene. Time is, of all modes of existence, most obsequious to the imagination; a lapse of years is as easily conceived as a passage of hours. In contemplation we easily contract the time of real actions, and therefore willingly permit it to be contracted when we only see their imitation.

It will be asked, how the drama moves, if it is not credited. It is credited with all the credit due to a drama. It is credited, whenever it moves, as a just picture of a real original; as representing to the auditor what he would himself feel, if he were to do or suffer what is there feigned to be suffered or to be done. The reflection that strikes the heart is not, that the evils before us are real evils, but that they are evils to which we ourselves may be exposed. If there be any fallacy, it is not that we fancy the players, but that we fancy ourselves unhappy for a moment; but we rather lament the possibility than suppose the presence of misery, as a mother weeps over her babe, when she remembers that death may take it from her. The delight of tragedy proceeds from our consciousness of fiction; if we thought murders and treasons real, they would please no more.

Imitations produce pain or pleasure, not because they are mistaken for realities, but because they bring realities to mind. When the imagination is recreated by a painted landscape, the trees are not supposed capable to give us shade, or the fountains coolness; but we consider, how we should be pleased with such fountains playing beside us, and such woods waving over us. We are agitated in reading the history of *Henry* the Fifth, yet no man takes his book for the field of *Agencourt*. A dramatick exhibition is a book recited with concomitants that encrease or diminish its effect. Familiar comedy is often more powerful in the theatre, than on the page; imperial tragedy is always less. The humour of *Petruchio* may be heightened by grimace; but what voice or what gesture can hope to add dignity or force to the soliloquy of *Cato*.

A play read, affects the mind like a play acted. It is therefore evident, that the action is not supposed to be real, and it follows that between the acts a longer or shorter time may be allowed to pass, and that no more account of space or duration is to be taken by the auditor of a drama, than by the reader of a narrative, before whom may pass in an hour the life of a hero, or the revolutions of an empire.

Whether *Shakespeare* knew the unities, and rejected them by design, or deviated from them by happy ignorance, it is, I think, impossible to decide, and useless to enquire. We may reasonably suppose, that, when he rose to notice, he did not want the counsels and admonitions of scholars and criticks, and that he at last deliberately persisted in a practice, which he might have begun by chance. As nothing is essential to the fable, but unity of action, and as the unities of time and place arise evidently from false assumptions, and, by circumscribing the extent of the drama, lessen its variety, I cannot think it much to be lamented, that they were not known by him, or not observed: Nor, if such another poet could arise, should I very vehemently reproach him, that his first act passed at *Venice*, and his next in *Cyprus*. Such violations of rules merely positive, become the comprehensive genius of *Shakespeare*, and such censures are suitable to the minute and slender criticism of *Voltaire:*

> *Non usque adeo permiscuit imis*
> *Longus summa dies, ut non, si voce Metelli*
> *Serventur leges, malint a Cæsare tolli.*[1]

Yet when I speak thus slightly of dramatick rules, I cannot but recollect how much wit and learning may be produced against me; before such authorities I am afraid to stand, not that I think the present question one of those that are to be decided by mere authority, but because it is to be suspected, that these precepts have not been so easily received but for better reasons than I have yet been able to find. The result of my enquiries, in which it would be ludicrous to boast of impartiality, is, that the unities of time and place are not essential to a just drama, that though they may sometimes conduce to pleasure, they are always to be sacrificed to the nobler beauties of variety and instruction; and that a play, written with nice observation of critical rules, is to be contemplated as an elaborate curiosity, as the product of superfluous and ostentatious art, by which is shewn, rather what is possible, than what is necessary. . . .

SOURCE extract from the Preface to Johnson's edition of Shakespeare's Works (London, 1765); reprinted in D. Nichol Smith (ed.), *Shakespeare Criticism: A Selection, 1623–1840* (Oxford, 1916; reset 1946), pp. 93–7.

NOTE

1. Lucan, *Pharsalia*, III, 138–40:

> Nor time, nor chance breeds such confusion yet,
> Nor are the mean so rais'd, nor sunk the great;
> But laws themselves would rather chose to be
> Suppress'd by Caesar, than preserv'd by thee.

Nicholas Rowe's translation – which was praised by Johnson [Ed.].

Georg Christoph Lichtenberg (1774–75)

Macklin's Shylock

. . . Shylock is not one of those mean, plausible cheats who could expatiate for an hour on the virtues of a gold watch-chain of pinchbeck; he is heavy, and silent in his unfathomable cunning, and, when the law is on his side, just to the point of malice. Imagine a rather stout man with a coarse yellow face and a nose generously fashioned in all three dimensions, a long double chin, and a mouth so carved by nature that the knife appears to have slit him right up to the ears, on one side at least, I thought. He wears a long black gown, long wide trousers, and a red tricorne, after the fashion of Italian Jews, I suppose. The first words he utters, when he comes on to the stage, are slowly and impressively spoken: 'Three thousand ducats.' The double 'th' and the two sibilants, especially the second after the 't', which Macklin lisps as lickerishly as if he were savouring the ducats and all that they could buy, make so deep an impression in the man's favour that nothing can destroy it. Three such words uttered thus at the outset give the keynote of his whole character. In the scene where he first misses his daughter, he comes on hatless, with disordered hair, some locks a finger long standing on end, as if raised by a breath of wind from the gallows, so distracted was his demeanour. Both his hands are clenched, and his movements abrupt and convulsive. To see a deceiver, who is usually calm and resolute, in such a state of agitation, is terrible. . . .

SOURCE: extract from *Briefe aus England* (1776–78: record of Lichtenberg's visit in 1774–75); translated by Margaret L. Mare and W. H. Quarrell as *Lichtenberg's Visits to England as Described in his Letters and Diaries* (Oxford, 1938) p. 40. (On pp. 9–11 of the same volume there is a remarkable account of Garrick's interpretation of Hamlet in the Ghost scene in Act I.)

Samuel Taylor Coleridge (1813)

Greek Drama and Shakespeare's Drama

Having intimated that times and manners lend their form and pressure to genius, let me once more draw a slight parallel between the ancient modern stage, the stages of Greece and of England. The Greeks were polytheists; their religion was local; almost the only object of all their knowledge, art and taste, was their gods; and, accordingly, their productions were, if the expression may be allowed, statuesque, while those of the moderns are picturesque. The Greeks reared a structure, which in its parts, and as a whole, filled the mind with the calm and elevated impression of perfect beauty and symmetrical proportion. The moderns also produced a whole, a more striking whole; but it was by blending materials and fusing the parts together. And as the Pantheon is to York Minster or Westminster Abbey, so is Sophocles compared with Shakspeare; in the one a completeness, a satisfaction, an excellence, on which the mind rests with complacency; in the other a multitude of interlaced materials, great and little, magnificent and mean, accompanied, indeed, with the sense of a falling short of perfection, and yet, at the same time, so promising of our social and individual progression, that we would not, if we could, exchange it for that repose of mind which dwells on the forms of symmetry in the acquiescent admiration of grace. This general characteristic of the ancient and modern drama might be illustrated by a parallel of the ancient and modern music – the one consisting of melody arising from a succession only of pleasing sounds, the modern embracing harmony also, the result of combination and the effect of a whole.

I have said, and I say it again, that great as was the genius of Shakspeare, his judgement was at least equal to it. Of this any one will be convinced, who attentively considers those points in which the dramas of Greece and England differ, from the dissimilitude of circumstances by which each was modified and influenced. The Greek stage had its origin in the ceremonies of sacrifice, such as of the goats to Bacchus, whom we most erroneously regard as merely the jolly god of wine – for among the ancients he was venerable, as the symbol of that power which acts without our consciousness in the vital energies of nature – the *vinum mundi* – as Apollo was that of the conscious energy of our intellectual being. The heroes of old under the influences of this Bacchic enthusiasm performed more than human actions – hence tales of the favourite champions soon passed into dialogue. On the Greek stage the chorus was always before the audience; the curtain was never dropped, as we should say; and change of place being therefore, in general, impossible, the absurd notion of condemning it merely as improbable in itself was never entertained by any one. If we can believe ourselves at Thebes in one act, we may believe ourselves at Athens in the next. If a story lasts twenty-four hours or twenty-four years, it is equally improbable. There seems to be no just boundary but what the feelings prescribe. But on the Greek stage where the same persons were perpetually before the audience, great judgement was necessary in venturing on any such change. The poets, never, therefore, attempted to impose on the senses by bringing places to men, but they did bring men to places, as in the well known instance in *The Eumenides*, where during an evident retirement of the chorus from the orchestra, the scene is changed to Athens, and Orestes is first introduced in the temple of Minerva, and the chorus of Furies come in afterwards in pursuit of him.

In the Greek drama there were no formal divisions into scenes and acts; there were no means, therefore, of allowing for the necessary lapse of time between one part of the dialogue and another, and unity of time in a strict sense was, of course, impossible. To overcome that difficulty of accounting for time, which is effected on the modern stage by dropping a curtain, the judgement and great genius of the ancients supplied music and measured motion, and with the lyric ode filled up the vacuity. In the story of the Agamemnon of Æschylus, the capture of Troy is supposed to be announced by a fire lighted on the Asiatic shore, and the transmission of the signal by successive beacons to Mycenæ. The signal is first seen at the 21st line, and the herald from Troy itself enters at the 486th, and Agamemnon himself at the 783rd line. But the practical absurdity of this was not felt by the audience, who, in imagination stretched minutes into hours, while they listened to the lofty narrative odes of the chorus which almost entirely fill up the interspace. Another fact deserves attention here, namely, that regularly on the Greek stage a drama, or acted story, consisted in reality of three dramas, called together a trilogy, and performed consecutively in the course of one day. Now you may conceive a tragedy of Shakspeare's as a trilogy connected in one single representation. Divide *Lear* into three parts, and each would be a play with the ancients; or take the three Æschylean dramas of Agamemnon, and divide them into, or call them, as many acts and they together would be one play. The first act would comprise the usurpation of Ægisthus, and the murder of Agamemnon; the second, the revenge of Orestes, and the murder of his mother; and the third, the penance and absolution of Orestes; – occupying a period of twenty-two years.

The stage in Shakspeare's time was a naked room with a blanket for a curtain; but he made it a field for monarchs. The law of unity, which has its foundations, not in the factitious necessity of custom, but in nature itself, the unity of feeling, is every where and at all times observed by Shakspeare in his plays. Read *Romeo and Juliet*, – all is youth and spring; – youth with its follies, its virtues, its precipitancies; – spring with its odours, its flowers, and its transiency; it is one and the same feeling that commences, goes through, and ends the play. The old men, the Capulets and the Montagues, are not common old men; they have an eagerness, a heartiness, a vehemence, the effect of spring; with Romeo, his change of passion, his sudden marriage, and his rash death, are all the effects of youth; – whilst in Juliet love has all that is tender and melancholy in the nightingale, all that is voluptuous in the rose, with whatever is sweet in the freshness of spring; but it ends with a long deep sigh like the last breeze of the Italian evening. This unity of feeling and character pervades every drama of Shakspeare.

It seems to me that his plays are distinguished from those of all other dramatic poets by the following characteristics:

1. Expectation in preference to surprise. It is like the true reading of the passage; – 'God said, Let there be light, and there was *light;*' – not there *was* light. As the feeling with which we startle at a shooting star, compared with that of watching the sunrise at the preestablished moment, such and so low is surprise compared with expectation.

2. Signal adherence to the great law of nature, that all opposites tend to attract and temper each other. Passion in Shakspeare generally displays libertinism, but involves morality; and if there are exceptions to this, they are independently of their intrinsic value, all of them indicative of individual character and like the farewell admonitions of a parent, have an end beyond the parental relation. Thus the Countess's beautiful precepts to Bertram, by elevating her character, raise that of Helena her favourite, and soften down the point in her which Shakspeare does not mean us not to see, but to see and to forgive, and at length to justify. And so it is in Polonius, who is the personified memory of wisdom no longer actually possessed. This admirable character is always misrepresented on the stage. Shakspeare never intended to exhibit him as a buffoon; for although it was natural that Hamlet, – a young man of fire and genius, detesting formality, and disliking Polonius on political grounds, as imagining that he had assisted his uncle in his usurpation, – should express himself satirically, yet this must not be taken as exactly the poet's conception of him. In Polonius a certain induration of character had arisen from long habits of business; but take his advice to Laertes, and Ophelia's reverence for his memory,

and we shall see that he was meant to be represented as a statesman somewhat past his faculties, – his recollections of life all full of wisdom, and showing a knowledge of human nature, whilst what immediately takes place before him, and escapes from him, is indicative of weakness.

But as in Homer all the deities are in armour, even Venus; so in Shakspeare all the characters are strong. Hence real folly and dulness are made by him the vehicles of wisdom. There is no difficulty for one being a fool to imitate a fool; but to be, remain, and speak like a wise man and a great wit, and yet so as to give a vivid representation of a veritable fool, – *hic labor, hoc opus est.* A drunken constable is not uncommon, nor hard to draw; but see and examine what goes to make up a Dogberry.

3. Keeping at all times in the high road of life. Shakspeare has no innocent adulteries, no interesting incests, no virtuous vice; – he never renders that amiable which religion and reason alike teach us to detest, or clothes impurity in the garb of virtue, like Beaumont and Fletcher, the Kotzebues of the day. Shakspeare's fathers are roused by ingratitude, his husbands stung by unfaithfulness; in him, in short, the affections are wounded in those points in which all may, nay, must, feel. Let the morality of Shakspeare be contrasted with that of the writers of his own, or the succeeding, age, or of those of the present day, who boast their superiority in this respect. No one can dispute that the result of such a comparison is altogether in favour of Shakspeare; – even the letters of women of high rank in his age were often coarser than his writings. If he occasionally disgusts a keen sense of delicacy, he never injures the mind; he neither excites, nor flatters, passion, in order to degrade the subject of it; he does not use the faulty thing for a faulty purpose, nor carries on warfare against virtue, by causing wickedness to appear as no wickedness, through the medium of a morbid sympathy with the unfortunate. In Shakspeare vice never walks as in twilight; nothing is purposely out of its place; – he inverts not the order of nature and propriety, – does not make every magistrate a drunkard or glutton, nor every poor man weak, humane, and temperate; he has no benevolent butchers, nor any sentimental rat-catchers.

4. Independence of the dramatic interest on the plot. The interest in the plot is always in fact on account of the characters, not *vice versa*, as in almost all other writers; the plot is a mere canvass and no more. Hence arises the true justification of the same stratagem being used in regard to Benedict and Beatrice, – the vanity in each being alike. Take away from the *Much Ado About Nothing* all that which is not indispensable to the plot, either as having little to do with it, or, at best, like Dogberry and his comrades, forced into the service, when any other less ingeniously

absurd watchmen and night-constables would have answered the mere necessities of the action; – take away Benedict, Beatrice, Dogberry, and the reaction of the former on the character of Hero, – and what will remain? In other writers the main agent of the plot is always the prominent character; in Shakspeare it is so, or is not so, as the character is in itself calculated, or not calculated, to form the plot. Don John is the main-spring of the plot of this play; but he is merely shown and then withdrawn.

5. Independence of the interest on the story as the ground-work of the plot. Hence Shakspeare never took the trouble of inventing stories. It was enough for him to select from those that had been already invented or recorded such as had one or other, or both, of two recommendations, namely, suitableness to his particular purpose, and their being parts of popular tradition, – names of which we had often heard, and of their fortunes, and as to which all we wanted was, to see the man himself. So it is just the man himself, the Lear, the Shylock, the Richard, that Shakspeare makes us for the first time acquainted with. Omit the first scene in *Lear*, and yet every thing will remain; so the first and second scenes in the *Merchant of Venice*. Indeed it is universally true.

6. Interfusion of the lyrical – that which in its very essence is poetical – not only with the dramatic, as in the plays of Metastasio, where at the end of the scene comes the *aria* as the *exit* speech of the character, – but also in and through the dramatic. Songs in Shakspeare are introduced as songs only, just as songs are in real life, beautifully as some of them are characteristic of the person who has sung or called for them, as Desdemona's 'Willow,' and Ophelia's wild snatches, and the sweet carollings in *As You like It*. But the whole of the *Midsummer Night's Dream* is one continued specimen of the dramatised lyrical. And observe how exquisitely the dramatic of Hotspur; –

> Marry, and I'm glad on't with all my heart;
> I had rather be a kitten and cry – mew, &c

melts away into the lyric of Mortimer; –

> I understand thy looks: that pretty Welsh
> Which thou pourest down from these swelling heavens,
> I am too perfect in, &c.

Henry IV. part I. act III sc. i.

7. The characters of the *dramatis personæ*, like those in real life, are to be inferred by the reader;—they are not told to him. And it is well worth remarking that Shakspeare's characters, like those in real life, are very commonly misunderstood, and almost always understood by different persons in different ways. The causes are the same in either case. If you take only what the friends of the character say, you may be deceived, and still more so, if that which his enemies say; nay, even the character himself sees himself through the medium of his character, and not exactly as he is. Take all together, not omitting shrewd hint from the clown or the fool, and perhaps your impression will be right; and you may know whether you have in fact discovered the poet's own idea, by all the speeches receiving light from it, and attesting its reality by reflecting it.

Lastly, in Shakspeare the heterogeneous is united, as it is in nature. You must not suppose a pressure or passion always acting on or in the character; – passion in Shakspeare is that by which the individual is distinguished from others, not that which makes a different kind of him. Shakspeare followed the main march of the human affections. He entered into no analysis of the passions or faiths of men, but assured himself that such and such passions and faiths were grounded in our common nature and not in the mere accidents of ignorance of disease. This is an important consideration, and constitutes our Shakspeare the morning star, the guide and the pioneer, of true philosophy.

SOURCE: 'Recapitulation and Summary of the Characteristics of Shakspeare's Dramas', from one of Coleridge's Lectures (1813); reprinted in D. Nichol Smith (ed.), op. cit. (See previous extract), pp. 233–41.

William Hazlitt (1817)

On Actors and Acting

Players are 'the abstract and brief chronicles of the time'; the motley representatives of human nature. They are the only honest hypocrites. Their life is a voluntary dream; a studied madness. The height of their ambition is to be *beside themselves*. Today kings, tomorrow beggars, it is only when they are themselves that they are nothing. Made up of mimic laughter and tears, passing from the extremes of joy or woe at the prompter's call, they wear the livery of other men's fortunes; their very thoughts are not their own. They are, as it were, train-bearers in the pageant of life, and hold a glass up to humanity, frailer than itself. We

see ourselves at second-hand in them: they show us all that we are, all
that we wish to be, and all that we dread to be. The stage is an epitome,
a bettered likeness of the world, with the dull part left out: and, indeed,
with this omission, it is nearly big enough to hold all the rest. What
brings the resemblance nearer is that, as *they* imitate us, we, in our turn,
imitate them. How many fine gentlemen do we owe to the stage! How
many romantic lovers are mere Romeos in masquerade! How many soft
bosoms have heaved with Juliet's sighs! They teach us when to laugh
and when to weep, when to love and when to hate, upon principle and
with a good grace! Wherever there is a playhouse, the world will not go
on amiss. The stage not only refines the manners, but it is the best
teacher of morals, for it is the truest and most intelligible picture of life.
It stamps the image of virtue on the mind by first softening the rude
materials of which it is composed, by a sense of pleasure. It regulates the
passions, by giving a loose to the imagination. It points out the selfish
and depraved to our detestation; the amiable and generous to our
admiration; and if it clothes the more seductive vices with the borrowed
graces of wit and fancy, even those graces operate as a diversion to the
coarser poison of experience and bad example, and often prevent or
carry off the infection by inoculating the mind with a certain taste and
elegance. To show how little we agree with the common declamations
against the immoral tendency of the stage on this score, we will hazard a
conjecture that the acting of the *Beggar's Opera* a certain number of
nights every year since it was first brought out has done more towards
putting down the practice of highway robbery, than all the gibbets that
ever were erected. A person, after seeing this piece, is too deeply imbued
with a sense of humanity, is in too good humour with himself and the
rest of the world, to set about cutting throats or rifling pockets.
Whatever makes a jest of vice leaves it too much a matter of indifference
for any one in his senses to rush desperately on his ruin for its sake. We
suspect that just the contrary effect must be produced by the
representation of *George Barnwell*, which is too much in the style of the
Ordinary's sermon to meet with any better success. The mind in such
cases, instead of being deterred by the alarming consequences held out
to it, revolts against the denunciation of them as an insult offered to its
free-will, and, in a spirit of defiance, returns a practical answer to them,
by daring the worst that can happen. The most striking lesson ever read
to levity and licentiousness is in the last act of *The Inconstant*, where
young Mirabel is preserved by the fidelity of his mistress, Orinda, in the
disguise of a page, from the hands of assassins, into whose power he had
been allured by the temptations of vice and beauty. There never was a
rake who did not become in imagination a reformed man, during the

representation of the last trying scenes of this admirable comedy.

If the stage is useful as a school of instruction, it is no less so as a source of amusement. It is a source of the greatest enjoyment at the time, and a never-failing fund of agreeable reflection afterwards. The merits of a new play, or of a new actor, are always among the first topics of polite conversation. One way in which public exhibitions contribute to refine and humanise mankind, is by supplying them with ideas and subjects of conversation and interest in common. The progress of civilisation is in proportion to the number of commonplaces current in society. For instance, if we meet with a stranger at an inn or in a stage-coach, who knows nothing but his own affairs – his shop, his customers, his farm, his pigs, his poultry – we can carry on no conversation with him on these local and personal matters: the only way is to let him have all the talk to himself. But if he has fortunately ever seen Mr Liston act, this is an immediate topic of mutual conversation, and we agree together the rest of the evening in discussing the merits of that inimitable actor, with the same satisfaction as in talking over the affairs of the most intimate friend.

If the stage thus introduces us familiarly to our contemporaries, it also brings us acquainted with former times. It is an interesting revival of past ages, manners, opinions, dresses, persons and actions – whether it carries us back to the wars of York and Lancaster, or half-way back to the heroic times of Greece and Rome, in some translation from the French, or quite back to the age of Charles II in the scenes of Congreve and of Etherege (the gay Sir George!) – happy age, when kings and nobles led purely ornamental lives; when the utmost stretch of a morning's study went no farther than the choice of a sword-knot, or the adjustment of a side curl; when the soul spoke out in all the pleasing elegance of dress; and beaux and belles, enamoured of themselves in one another's follies, fluttered like gilded butterflies in giddy mazes through the walks of St James's Park!

A good company of comedians, a Theatre-Royal judiciously managed, is your true Herald's College; the only Antiquarian Society that is worth a rush. It is for this reason that there is such an air of romance about players, and that it is pleasanter to see them, even in their own persons, than any of the three learned professions. We feel more respect for John Kemble in a plain coat than for the Lord Chancellor on the woolsack. He is surrounded, to our eyes, with a greater number of imposing recollections: he is a more reverend piece of formality; a more complicated tissue of costume. We do not know whether to look upon this accomplished actor as Pierre, or King John, or Coriolanus, or Cato, or Leontes, or the Stranger. But we see in him a stately hieroglyphic of humanity; a living monument of departed greatness; a sombre comment on the rise and fall of kings. We look after him till he is out of sight, as we listen to a story of one of Ossian's heroes, to 'a tale of other times'!

The most pleasant feature in the profession of a player, and which, indeed, is peculiar to it, is that we not only admire the talents of those who adorn it, but we contract a personal intimacy with them. There is no class of society whom so many persons regard with affection as actors. We greet them on the stage; we like to meet them in the streets; they almost always recall to us pleasant associations; and we feel our gratitude excited, without the uneasiness of a sense of obligation. The very gaiety and popularity, however, which surround the life of a favourite performer, make the retiring from it a very serious business. It glances a mortifying reflection on the shortness of human life, and the vanity of human pleasures. Something reminds us that 'all the world's a stage, and all the men and women merely players'.

It has been considered as the misfortune of first-rate talents for the stage, that they leave no record behind them except that of vague rumour, and that the genius of a great actor perishes with him, 'leaving the world no copy'. This is a misfortune, or at least a mortifying reflection, to actors; but it is, perhaps, an advantage to the stage. It leaves an opening to originality. The *semper varium et mutabile* of the poet may be transferred to the stage, 'the inconstant stage', without losing the original felicity of the application: it has its necessary ebbs and flows, from its subjection to the influence of popular feeling, and the frailty of the materials of which it is composed, its own fleeting and shadowy essence, and cannot be expected to remain for any great length of time stationary at the same point, either of perfection or debasement. Acting, in particular, which is the chief organ by which it addresses itself to the mind – the eye, tongue, hand by which it dazzles, charms, and seizes on the public attention – is an art that seems to contain in itself the seeds of perpetual renovation and decay, following in this respect the order of nature rather than the analogy of the productions of human intellect; for whereas in the other arts of painting and poetry, the standard works of genius, being permanent and accumulating, for awhile provoke emulation, but, in the end, overlay future efforts, and transmit only their defects to those that come after; the exertions of the greatest actor die with him, leaving to his successors only the admiration of his name, and the aspiration after imaginary excellence; so that, in effect, no one generation of actors binds another; the art is always setting out afresh on the stock of genius and nature, and the success depends (generally speaking) on accident, opportunity, and encouragement. The harvest of excellence (whatever it may be) is removed from the ground, every twenty or thirty years, by Death's sickle; and there is room left for another to sprout up and tower to any equal height, and spread into equal luxuriance – to 'dally with the wind, and court the sun' – according to the health and vigour of the stem, and the favourableness of the season. But books, pictures, remain like fixtures in the public mind, beyond a certain point encumber the soil of living truth and nature, distort or stunt the growth of original genius. When an author dies, there is a void produced in society, a gap which requires to be filled up. The literary amateur may find employment for his time in reading old authors only, and exhaust his entire spleen in scouting new ones: but the lover of the stage cannot amuse himself, in his solitary fastidiousness, by sitting to witness a play got up by the departed ghosts of first-rate actors; or be contented with the perusal of a collection of old play-bills: he may extol Garrick, but he must go to see Kean; and, in his own defence, must admire, or at least tolerate, what he sees, or stay away against his will. If, indeed, by any spell or power of necromancy, all the celebrated actors, for the last hundred years, could be made to appear again on the boards of Covent Garden and Drury Lane, for the last time, in their most brilliant parts, what a rich threat to the town, what a feat for the critics, to go and see Betterton, and Booth, and Wilks, and Sandford, and Nokes, and Leigh, and Penkethman, and Bullock, and Estcourt, and Dogget, and Mrs Barry, and Mrs Montfort, and Mrs Oldfield, and Mrs Bracegirdle, and Mrs Cibber and Cibber himself, the prince of coxcombs, and Macklin, and Quin, and Rich, and Mrs Clive, and Mrs Pritchard, and Mrs Abington, and Weston, and Shuter, and Garrick, and all the rest of those who 'gladdened life', and whose death 'eclipsed the gaiety of nations'! We should certainly be there. We should buy a ticket for the season. We should enjoy *our hundred days* again. We should not miss a single night. We would not, for a great deal, be absent from Betterton's Hamlet or his Brutus, or from Booth's Cato, as it was first acted to the contending applause of Whigs and Tories. We should be in the first row when Mrs Barry (who was kept by Lord Rochester, and with whom Otway was in love) played Monimia or Belvidera; and we suppose we should go to see Mrs Bracegirdle (with whom all the world was in love) in all her parts. We should then know exactly whether Penkethman's manner of picking a chicken, and Bullock's mode of devouring asparagus, answered to the ingenious account of them in the *Tatler*; and whether Dogget was equal to Dowton – whether Mrs Montfort or Mrs Abington was the finest lady – whether Wilks or Cibber was the best Sir Harry Wildair – whether Macklin was really 'the Jew that Shakespeare drew', and whether Garrick was, upon the whole, so great an actor as the world would have him made out! Many people have a strong desire to pry into the secrets of futurity; for our own parts, we should be satisfied if we had the power to recall the dead, and live the past over again, as often as we pleased! Players, after all, have little reason to complain of their hard-earned, short-lived popularity. One thunder of applause from pit, boxes and gallery, is equal to a whole immortality of posthumous fame; and when we hear an actor (Liston), whose modesty is equal to his merit, declare that he would like to see a dog wag his tail in approbation, what must he feel when he sets the whole house in a roar! Besides, Fame, as if their reputation had been entrusted to her alone, has been particularly careful of the renown of her theatrical favourites: she forgets, one by one, and year by year, those who have been great lawyers, great statesmen, and great warriors in their day; but the name of Garrick still survives with the works of Reynolds and of Johnson.

Actors have been accused, as a profession, of being extravagant and dissipated. While they are said to be so, as a piece of common cant, they are likely to continue so. But there is a sentence in Shakespeare which should be stuck as a label in the mouths of our beadles and whippers-in of morality: 'The web of our life is of mingled yarn, good and ill together: our virtues would be proud if our faults whipped them not: and our crimes would despair if they were not cherished by our virtues.' With respect to the extravagance of actors, as a traditional character, it is not to be wondered at. They live from hand to mouth, they plunge from want into luxury; they have no means of making money *breed*, and all professions that do not live by turning money into money, or have not a certainty of accumulating it in the end by parsimony, spend it. Uncertain of the future they make sure of the present moment. This is not unwise. Chilled with poverty, steeped in contempt, they sometimes pass into the sunshine of fortune, and are lifted to the very pinnacle of public favour; yet even there they cannot calculate on the continuance of success, but are, 'like the giddy sailor on the mast, ready with every blast to topple down into the fatal bowels of the deep!' Besides, if the young enthusiast, who is smitten with the stage, and with the public as a mistress, were naturally a close *hunks*, he would become or remain a city clerk, instead of turning player. Again, with respect to the habit of convivial indulgence, an actor, to be a good one, must have a great spirit of enjoyment in himself – strong impulses, strong passions, and a strong sense of pleasure: for it is his business to imitate the passions, and to communicate pleasure to others.

A man of genius is not a machine. The neglected actor may be excused if he drinks oblivion of his disappointments; the successful one if he quaffs the applause of the world, and enjoys the friendship of those who are the friends of the favourites of fortune, in draughts of nectar. There is no path so steep as that of fame: no labour so hard as the pursuit of excellence. The intellectual excitement, inseparable from those professions which call forth all our sensibility to pleasure and pain, requires some corresponding physical excitement to support our failure, and not a little to allay the ferment of the spirits attendant on success. If there is any tendency to dissipation beyond this in the profession of a player, it is owing to the prejudices entertained against them – to that spirit of bigotry which in a neighbouring country would deny actors Christian burial after their death, and to that cant of criticism which, in our own, slurs over their characters, while living, with a half-witted jest. Players are only not so respectable as a profession as they might be, because their profession is not respected as it ought to be.

A London engagement is generally considered by actors as the *ne plus ultra* of their ambition, as 'a consummation devoutly to be wished', as the great prize in the lottery of their professional life. But this appears to us, who are not in the secret, to be rather the prose termination of their adventurous career: it is the provincial commencement that is the poetical and truly enviable part of it. After that, they have comparatively little hope or fear. 'The wine of life is drunk, and but the lees remain.' In London they become gentlemen, and the King's servants; but it is the romantic mixture of the hero and the vagabond that constitutes the essence of the player's life. It is the transition from their real to their assumed characters, from the contempt of the world to the applause of the multitude, that gives its zest to the latter, and raises them as much above common humanity at night as in the daytime they are depressed below it. 'Hurried from fierce extremes, by contrast made more fierce' – it is rags and a flock bed which give their splendour to a plume of feathers and a throne. We should suppose that if the most admired actor on the London stage were brought to confession on this point, he would acknowledge that all the applause he had received from 'brilliant and overflowing audiences' was nothing to the light-headed intoxication of unlooked-for success in a barn. In towns, actors are criticised: in country places, they are wondered at, or hooted at: it is of little consequence which, so that the interval is not too long between. For ourselves, we own that the description of the strolling player in *Gil Blas*, soaking his dry crusts in the well by the roadside, presents to us a perfect picture of human felicity.

SOURCE: essay 'On Actors and Acting', *The Examiner* (15 January 1817).

Henry Morley (1856)

Charles John Kean's *A Midsummer Night's Dream*

I do not think money ill-spent upon stage-furniture, and certainly can only admire the exquisite scenery of the play now being presented at the Princess's; but there may be a defect of taste that mars the effect of the richest ornament, as can best be shown by one or two examples.

Shakespeare's direction for the opening scene of the *Midsummer Night's Dream* is: 'Athens, A Room in the Palace of Theseus'. For this read at the Princess's Theatre: 'A Terrace adjoining the Palace of Theseus, overlooking the City of Athens'; and there is presented an elaborate and undoubtedly most beautiful bird's-eye view of Athens as it was in the time of Pericles. A great scenic effect is obtained, but it is, as far as it goes, damaging to the poem. Shakespeare took for his mortals people of heroic times, Duke Theseus and Hippolyta, and it suited his romance to call them Athenians; but the feeling of the play is marred when out of this suggestion of the antique mingled with the fairy world the scene-painter finds the opportunity to bring into hard and jarring contrast the Athens of Pericles and our own world of Robin Goodfellow and all the woodland elves. 'A Room in the House of Theseus' left that question of the where or when of the whole story to be touched as lightly as a poet might desire; the poetry was missed entirely by the painting of the scene, beautiful as it is, which illustrates the first act of the *Midsummer Night's Dream* at the Princess's.

In the second act there is a dream-like moving of the wood, beautifully managed, and spoilt in effect by a trifling mistake easily corrected. Oberon stands before the scene waving his wand, as if he were exhibitor of the diorama, or a fairy conjurer causing the rocks and trees to move. Nobody, I believe, ever attributed to fairies any power of that sort. Oberon should either be off the stage or on it still as death, and it should be left for the spectators to feel the dreamy influence of wood and water slipping by their eyes unhindered and undistracted. This change leads to the disclosure of a fairy ring, a beautiful scenic effect, and what is called in large letters upon the play-bills, 'Titania's Shadow Dance'. Of all things in the world, a shadow dance of fairies! If anything in the way of an effect of light was especially desirable, it would have been such an arrangement as would have made the fairies appear to be dancing in a light so managed that it cast no shadow, and give them the true spiritual attribute. Elaborately to produce and present, as an especial attraction, fairies of large size, casting shadows made as black and distinct as possible, and offering in dance to pick them up, as if even they also were solid, is as great a sacrifice of Shakespeare to the purposes of the ballet-master, as the view of Athens in its glory was a sacrifice of poetry to the scene-painter. Enough has been said to show the direction in which improvement is necessary to make the stage-ornament at the Princess's Theatre as perfect as it is beautiful. The Puck is a pretty little girl, belted and garlanded with flowers! From the third act we miss a portion of the poem most essential to its right effect – the quarrel between Hermia and Helena; but we get at the end, a ballet of fairies round a maypole that shoots up out of an aloe, after the way of a transformation in a pantomime, and rains down garlands. Fairies, not airy beings of the colour of the greenwood, or the sky or robed in misty white, but glittering in the most brilliant dresses, with a crust of bullion about their legs, cause the curtain to fall on a splendid ballet; and it is evidence enough of the depraved taste of the audience to say that the ballet is encored.

I make these comments in no censorious mood. It is a pleasure to see Shakespeare enjoyed by the large number of persons who are attracted to the Princess's Theatre by the splendours for which it is famous. I do not wish the splendour less, or its attraction less, but only ask for more heed to the securing of a perfect harmony between the conceptions of the decorator and those of the poet.

SOURCE: extract from the section on theatrical productions in 1856, in *Journal of a London Playgoer* (London, 1891); reprinted in A. M. Nagler, *A Source Book in Theatrical History* (New York, 1952), p. 485.

Henrik Ibsen (1883)

'Declamation is not a dramatic art'

Dear Mrs Wolf,[1]
At the beginning of this month, we had the unexpected pleasure of receiving a letter from you. The letter was addressed to my wife; but as it chiefly concerns me, I am taking the liberty of answering it.

You wish me to write a prologue for the festival to be given at the Christiania Theatre in June to celebrate the thirtieth anniversary of your debut on its stage.

I wish I could comply with your request. Nothing would please me more than to be able to do it. But I cannot; my convictions and my artistic philosophy forbid me. Prologues, epilogues, and everything of the kind ought to be banished from the stage. The stage is for dramatic art alone; and declamation is not a dramatic art.

The prologue would of course have to be in verse, since that is the established custom. But I will take no part in perpetuating this custom. Verse has been most injurious to the art of the drama. A true artist of the stage, whose repertoire is the contemporary drama, should not be willing to let a single verse cross her lips. It is improbable that verse will be employed to any extent worth mentioning in the drama of the immediate future since the aims of the dramatists of the future are almost certain to be incompatible with it. Consequently it is doomed. For art forms become extinct, just as the preposterous animal forms of prehistoric time became extinct when their day was over.

A tragedy in iambic pentameters is already as rare a phenomenon as the dodo, of which only a few specimens are still in existence on some African island.

During the last seven or eight years I have hardly written a single verse, devoting myself exclusively to the very much more difficult art of writing the straightforward, plain language spoken in real life. It is by means of this language that you have become the excellent artist you now are. You have never used smooth verses to delude anyone about your art.

But there is yet another argument, which I think is the chief one. In a prologue all kinds of agreeable things are said to the public. The public is thanked for its leniency and its instructive criticism, while the artist makes himself as insignificant as possible by crawling into the nooks and corners of rhymed verses. Is this honest? You know as well as I do that it is not. The exact opposite is the truth. It is not you who are in debt to the public; it is the public who are deeply in debt to you for your thirty years of faithful work.

In my opinion this is the point of view that an important artist has a duty to maintain out of respect for himself and his profession. And I am certain that you yourself will admit that, holding such opinions, I cannot very well undertake to compose a prologue for the occasion in question.

But though I am unable to serve you in this matter, I trust that you will, nevertheless, accept the tribute of thanks I herewith offer you, thanks for all you have meant and still mean to our stage, and my special thanks for the important share you have had in rendering so many of my own dramatic works.

Hoping and heartily wishing that there will be a long and bright artistic career still before you, I remain

Your attached old friend,
Henrik Ibsen

SOURCE: letter to Lucie Wolf, written from Rome, 25 May 1883; reprinted in Evert Sprinchorn (ed.). *Ibsen: Letters and Speeches* (New York and London, 1965), pp. 218–19.

NOTE

1. Lucie Wolf was a leading actress at the Christiania Theatre in Oslo (then called Christiania).

PART TWO

Plays and Players

1 . THE LATE-VICTORIAN SCENE

Henry James The London Theatres (1877)

... In speaking of what is actually going on at the London theatres I suppose the place of honour, beyond comparison, belongs to Mr Henry Irving. This gentleman enjoys an esteem and consideration which, I believe, has been the lot of no English actor since Macready left the stage, and he may at the present moment claim the dignity of being a bone of contention in London society second only in magnitude to the rights of the Turks and the wrongs of the Bulgarians. I am told that London is divided, on the subject of his merits, into two fiercely hostile camps; that he has sown dissention in families, and made old friends cease to 'speak.' His appearance in a new part is a great event; and if one has the courage of one's opinion, at dinner tables and elsewhere, a conversational godsend. Mr Irving has 'created,' as the French say, but four Shakespearean parts; his Richard III has just been given to the world. Before attempting Hamlet, which up to this moment has been his greatest success, he had attracted much attention as a picturesque actor of melodrama, which he rendered with a refinement of effect not common upon the English stage. Mr Irving's critics may, I suppose, be divided into three categories: those who justify him in whatever he attempts, and consider him an artist of unprecedented brilliancy; those who hold that he did very well in melodrama, but that he flies too high when he attempts Shakespeare; and those who, in vulgar parlance, can see nothing in him at all.

I shrink from ranging myself in either of these divisions, and indeed I am not qualified to speak of Mr Irving's acting in general. I have seen none of his melodramatic parts; I do not know him as a comedian – a capacity in which some people think him at his best; and in his Shakespearean repertory I have seen only his Macbeth and his Richard. But judging him on the evidence of these two parts, I fall hopelessly among the sceptics. Mr Henry Irving is a very convenient illustration. To a stranger desiring to know how the London stage stands, I should say, 'Go and see this gentleman; then tell me what you think of him.' And I should expect the stranger to come back and say, 'I see what you mean. The London stage has reached that pitch of mediocrity at which Mr Henry Irving overtops his fellows – Mr Henry

Irving figuring as a great man – *c'est tout dire*.' I hold that there is an
essential truth in the proverb that there is no smoke without fire. No
reputations are altogether hollow, and no valuable prizes have been
easily won. Of course Mr Irving has a good deal of intelligence and
cleverness; of course he has mastered a good many of the mysteries of his
art. But I must nevertheless declare that for myself I have not mastered
the mystery of his success. His defects seem to me in excess of his qualities
and the lessons he has not learned more striking than the lessons he has
learned.

That an actor so handicapped, as they say in London, by nature and
culture should have enjoyed such prosperity is a striking proof of the
absence of a standard, of the chaotic condition of taste. Mr Irving's
Macbeth, which I saw more than a year ago and view under the
mitigations of time, was not pronounced one of his great successes; but it
was acted, nevertheless, for many months, and it does not appear to
have injured his reputation. Passing through London, and curious to
make the acquaintance of the great English actor of the day, I went with
alacrity to see it; but my alacrity was more than equalled by the vivacity
of my disappointment. I sat through the performance in a sort of
melancholy amazement. There are barren failures and there are
interesting failures, and this performance seemed to me to deserve the
less complimentary of these classifications. It inspired me, however,
with no ill-will toward the artist, for it must be said of Mr Irving that his
aberrations are not of a vulgar quality, and that one likes him,
somehow, in spite of them. But one's liking takes the form of making one
wish that really he had selected some other profession than the
histrionic. Nature has done very little to make an actor of him. His face
is not dramatic; it is the face of a sedentary man, a clergyman, a lawyer,
an author, an amiable gentleman – of anything other than a possible
Hamlet or Othello. His figure is of the same cast, and his voice
completes the want of illusion. His voice is apparently wholly
unavailable for purposes of declamation. To say that he speaks badly is
to go too far; to my sense he simply does not speak at all – in any way
that, in an actor, can be called speaking. He does not pretend to declaim
or dream of declaiming. Shakespeare's finest lines pass from his lips
without his paying the scantiest tribute to their quality. Of what the
French. call *diction* – of the art of delivery – he has apparently not a
suspicion. This forms three-fourths of an actor's obligations, and in Mr
Irving's acting these three-fourths are simply cancelled. What is left to
him with the remaining fourth is to be 'picturesque'; and this even his
partisans admit he has made his specialty. This concession darkens Mr
Irving's prospects as a Shakespearean actor. You can play hop-scotch

on one foot, but you cannot cut with one blade of a pair of scissors, and you cannot play Shakespeare by being simply picturesque. Above all, before all, for this purpose you must have the art of utterance; you must be able to give value to the divine Shakespearean line – to make it charm our ears as it charms our mind. It is of course by his picturesqueness that Mr Irving has made his place; by small ingenuities of 'business' and subtleties of action; by doing as a painter does who 'goes in' for colour when he cannot depend upon his drawing. Mr Irving's colour is sometimes pretty enough; his ingenuities and subtleties are often felicitous; but his picturesqueness, on the whole, strikes me as dry and awkward, and, at the best, where certain essentials are so strikingly absent, these secondary devices lose much of their power.

Mr Fechter in Hamlet was preponderantly a 'picturesque' actor; but he had a certain sacred spark, a heat, a lightness and suppleness, which Mr Irving lacks; and though, with his incurable foreign accent, he could hardly be said to *declaim* Shakespeare in any worthy sense, yet on the whole he spoke his part with much more of the positively agreeable than can possibly belong to the utterance of Mr Irving. His speech, with all its fantastic Gallicisms of sound, was less foreign and more comprehensible than that strange tissue of arbitrary pronunciations which floats in the thankless medium of Mr Irving's harsh, monotonous voice. Richard III is of all Shakespeare's parts the one that can perhaps best dispense with declamation, and in which the clever inventions of manner and movement in which Mr Irving is proficient will carry the actor furthest. Accordingly, I doubt not, Mr Irving is seen to peculiar advantage in this play; it is certainly a much better fit for him than Macbeth. He has had the good taste to discard the vulgar adaptation of Cibber, by which the stage has so long been haunted, and which, I believe, is played in America to the complete exclusion of the original drama. I believe that some of the tenderest Shakespeareans refuse to admit the authenticity of *Richard III*; they declare that the play has, with all its energy, a sort of intellectual grossness, of which the author of *Hamlet* and *Othello* was incapable. This same intellectual grossness is certainly very striking; the scene of Richard's wooing of Lady Anne is a capital specimen of it. But here and there occur passages which, when one hears the play acted, have all the vast Shakespearean sense of effect.

> – To hear the piteous moans that Edward made
> When black-faced Clifford shook his sword at him.

It is hard to believe that Shakespeare did not write that. And when

Richard, after putting an end to Clarence, comes into Edward IV's presence, with the courtiers ranged about, and announces hypocritically that Providence has seen fit to remove him, the situation is marked by one or two speeches which are dramatic as Shakespeare alone is dramatic. The immediate exclamation of the Queen –

All-seeing heaven, what a world is this!

– followed by that of one of the gentlemen –

Look I so pale, Lord Dorset, as the rest?

– such touches as these, with their inspired vividness, seem to belong to the brushwork of the master. Mr Irving gives the note of his performance in his first speech – the famous soliloquy upon 'the winter of our discontent.' His delivery of these lines possesses little but hopeless staginess and mannerism. It seems indeed like staginess gone mad. The spectator rubs his eyes and asks himself whether he has not mistaken his theatre, and stumbled by accident upon some preposterous burlesque. It is fair to add that Mr Irving is here at his worst, the scene offering him his most sustained and exacting piece of declamation. But the way he renders it is the way he renders the whole part – slowly, draggingly, diffusively, with innumerable pauses and lapses, and without a hint of the rapidity, the intensity and *entrain* which are needful for carrying off the improbabilities of so explicit and confidential a villain and so melodramatic a hero.

Just now, when a stranger in London asks where the best acting is to be seen, he receives one of two answers. He is told either at the Prince of Wales's theatre or at the Court. Some people think that the last perfection is to be found at the former of these establishments, others at the latter. I went first to the Prince of Wales's, of which I had a very pleasant memory from former years, and I was not disappointed. The acting is very pretty indeed, and this little theatre doubtless deserves the praise which is claimed for it, of being the best conducted English stage in the world. It is, of course, not the Comédie Française; but, equally of course, it is absurd talking or thinking of the Comédie Française in London. The company at the Prince of Wales's play with a finish, a sense of detail, what the French call *ensemble*, and a general good grace, which deserve explicit recognition. The theatre is extremely small, elegant, and expensive, the company is very carefully composed, and the scenery and stage furniture lavishly complete. It is a point of honour with the Prince of Wales's to have nothing that is not 'real.' In the piece

now running at this establishment there is a representation of a boudoir
very delicately appointed, the ceiling of which is formed by festoons of
old lace suspended tent fashion or pavilion fashion. This lace, I am told,
has been ascertained, whether by strong opera glasses or other modes of
enquiry I know not, to be genuine, ancient, and costly. This is the very
pedantry of perfection, and makes the scenery somewhat better than the
actors. If the tendency is logically followed out, we shall soon be having
Romeo drink real poison and Medea murder a fresh pair of babes every
night.

The Prince of Wales's theatre, when it has once carefully mounted a
play, 'calculates,' I believe, to keep it on the stage a year. The play of the
present year is an adaptation of one of Victorien Sardou's cleverest
comedies – *Nos Intimes* – upon which the title of *Peril* has been conferred.
Of the piece itself there is nothing to be said; it is the usual hybrid drama
of the contemporary English stage – a firm, neat French skeleton,
around which the drapery of English conversation has been adjusted in
awkward and inharmonious folds. The usual feat has been attempted –
to extirpate 'impropriety' and at the same time to save interest. In the
extraordinary manipulation and readjustment of French immoralities
which goes on in the interest of Anglo-Saxon virtue, I have never known
this feat to succeed. Propriety may have been saved, in an awkward,
floundering, in-spite-of-herself fashion, which seems to do to something
in the mind a violence much greater than the violence it has been sought
to avert; but interest has certainly been lost. The only immorality I
know on the stage is the production of an ill-made play; and a play is
certainly ill made when the pointedness of the framework strikes the
spectator as a perpetual mockery upon the flatness of the 'developments.' M. Sardou's perfectly improper but thoroughly homogeneous
comedy has been flattened and vulgarised in the usual way; the pivot of
naughtiness on which the piece turns has been 'whittled' down to the
requisite tenuity; the wicked little Jack-in-the-Box has popped up his
head only just in time to pull it back again. The interest, from being
intense, has become light, and the play, from being a serious comedy,
with a flavour of the tragic, has become an elaborate farce, salted with a
few coarse grains of gravity. It is probable, however, that if *Peril* were
more serious, it would be much less adequately played.

The Prince of Wales's company contains in the person of Miss Madge
Robertson (or Mrs Kendal, as I believe she is nowadays called) the most
agreeable actress on the London stage. This lady is always pleasing, and
often charming; but she is more effective in gentle gaiety than in
melancholy or in passion. Another actor at the Prince of Wales's – Mr
Arthur Cecil – strikes me as an altogether superior comedian. He plays

in *Peril* (though I believe he is a young man) the part of a selfish, cantankerous, querulous, jaundiced old East Indian officer, who has come down to a country house to stay, under protest, accompanied by his only son, a stripling in roundabouts, whom he is bringing up in ignorance of the world's wickedness, and who, finding himself in a mansion well supplied with those books which no gentleman's library should be without, loses no time in taking down Boccaccio's *Decameron*. Mr Arthur Cecil represents this character to the life, with a completeness, an extreme comicality, and at the same time a sobriety and absence of violence which recalls the best French acting. Especially inimitable is the tone with which he tells his host, on his arrival, how he made up his mind to accept his invitation: 'So at last I said to Percy, "Well, Percy, my child, we'll go down and have done with it!"'

At the Court theatre, where they are playing, also apparently by the year, a 'revived' drama of Mr Tom Taylor – *New Men and Old Acres* – the acting, though very good indeed, struck me as less finished and, as a whole, less artistic. The company contains, however, two exceptionally good actors. One of them is Mr Hare, who leads it, and who, although nature has endowed him with an almost fatally meagre stage presence, has a considerable claim to be called an artist. Mr Hare's special line is the quiet natural, in high life, and I imagine he prides himself upon the propriety and good taste with which he acquits himself of those ordinary phrases and light modulations which the usual English actor finds it impossible to utter with any degree of verisimilitude. Mr Hare's companion is Miss Ellen Terry, who is usually spoken of by the 'refined' portion of the public as the most interesting actress in London. Miss Terry is picturesque; she looks like a preRaphaelitish drawing in a magazine – the portrait of the crop-haired heroine in the illustration to the serial novel. She is intelligent and vivacious, and she is indeed, in a certain measure, interesting. With great frankness and spontaneity, she is at the same time singularly delicate and lady-like, and it seems almost impertinent to criticise her harshly. But the favour which Miss Terry enjoys strikes me, like that under which Mr Henry Irving has expanded, as a sort of measure of the English critical sense in things theatrical. Miss Terry has all the pleasing qualities I have enumerated, but she has, with them, the defect that she is simply *not* an actress. One sees it sufficiently in her face – the face of a clever young Englishwoman, with a hundred merits, but not of a dramatic artist. These things are indefinable; I can only give my impression.

Broadly comic acting, in England, is businesslike, and high tragedy is businesslike; each of these extremes appears to constitute a trade – a *métier*, as the French say – which may be properly and adequately learned. But the acting which covers the middle ground, the acting of serious or sentimental comedy and of scenes that may take place in modern drawing-rooms – the acting that corresponds to the contemporary novel of manners – seems by an inexorable necessity given over to amateurishness. Most of the actors at the Prince of Wales's – the young lovers, the walking and talking gentlemen, the house-keeper and young ladies – struck me as essentially amateurish, and this is the impression produced by Miss Ellen Terry, as well as (in an even higher degree) by her pretty and sweet-voiced sister, who plays at the Haymarket. The art of these young ladies is awkward and experimental; their very speech lacks smoothness and firmness.

I am not sorry to be relieved, by having reached the limits of my space, from the necessity of expatiating upon one of the more recent theatrical events in London – the presentation, at the St James's theatre, of an English version of *Les Danicheff*. This extremely picturesque and effective play was the great Parisian success of last winter, and during the London season the company of the Odéon crossed the channel and presented it with an added brilliancy. But what the piece has been reduced to in its present form is a theme for the philosopher. Horribly translated and badly played, it retains hardly a ray of its original effectiveness. There can hardly have been a better example of the possible infelicities of 'adaptation.' Nor have I the opportunity of alluding to what is going on at the other London theatres, though to all of them I have made a conscientious pilgrimage. But I conclude my very desultory remarks without an oppressive sense of the injustice of omission. In thinking over the plays I have listened to, my memory arrests itself with more kindness, perhaps, than elsewhere, at the great, gorgeous pantomime given at Drury Lane, which I went religiously to see in Christmas week. They manage this matter of the pantomime very well in England, and I have always thought Harlequin and Columbine the prettiest invention in the world. (This is an 'adaptation' of an Italian original, but it is a case in which the process has been completely successful.) But the best of the entertainment at Drury Lane was seeing the line of rosy child faces in the boxes, all turned towards the stage in one round-eyed fascination. English children, however, and their round-eyed rosiness, would demand a chapter apart.

SOURCE: extract from 'The London Theatres' in *Galaxy* (May 1977); reprinted in Allan Wade (ed), *The Scenic Art* (London, 1948), pp. 102–11.

William Archer 'Ibsen and the English Theatre': *A Doll's House* (1889)

If we may measure fame by mileage of newspaper comment, Henrik Ibsen has for the past month been the most famous man in the English literary world. Since Robert Elsmere left the Church, no event in 'coëval fictive art' (to quote a modern stylist) has exercised men's, and women's, minds so much as Nora Helmer's departure from her Doll's House. Indeed the latter exit may be said to have awakened even more vibrant echoes than the former; for, while Robert made as little noise as possible, Nora slammed the door behind her. Nothing could be more trenchant than her action, unless it be her speech. Whatever its merits or defects, *A Doll's House* has certainly the property of stimulating discussion. We are at present bandying the very arguments which hurtled around it in Scandinavia and in Germany nine years ago. When the play was first produced in Copenhagen, some one wrote a charming little satire upon it in the shape of a debate as to its tendency between a party of little girls around a nursery tea-table. It ended in the hostess, aged ten, gravely declaring that had the case been hers, she would have done exactly as Nora did. I do not know whether the fame of *A Doll's House* has reached the British nursery, but I have certainly read some comments on it which might very well have emanated from that abode of innocence.

Puerilities and irrelevances apart, the adult and intelligent criticism of Ibsen as represented in *A Doll's House*, seems to run on three main lines. It is said, in the first place, that he is not an artist but a preacher; secondly, that his doctrine is neither new nor true; thirdly, that in order to enforce it, he oversteps the limits of artistic propriety. I propose to look into these three allegations. First, however, I must disclaim all right to be regarded as in any way a mouthpiece for the poet's own views. My personal intercourse with Henrik Ibsen, though to me very pleasant and memorable, has been but slight. I view his plays from the pit, not from the author's box. Very likely – nay, certainly – I often misread his meaning. My only right to take part in the discussion arises from a long and loving study of all his writings, and from the minute familiarity with *A Doll's House* in particular, acquired in the course of translating and staging it.

Is it true, then, that he is a dramatic preacher rather than a dramatic poet? or, in other words, that his art is vitiated by didacticism? Some writers have assumed that in calling him didactic they have said the last word, and dismissed him for ever from the ranks of the great artists. Of them I would fain enquire what really great art is not didactic? The true distinction is not between didactic art and 'art for art's sake', but between primarily didactic and ultimately didactic art. Art for art's sake, properly so called, is mere decoration; and even it, in the last analysis, has its gospel to preach. By primarily didactic art I mean that in which the moral bearing is obvious, and was clearly present to the artist's mind. By ultimately didactic art I mean that which essays to teach as life itself teaches, exhibiting the fact and leaving the observer to trace and formulate the underlying law. It is the fashion of the day to regard this unconsciously didactic art, if I may call it so – its unconsciousness is sometimes a very transparent pose – as essentially higher than the art which is primarily and consciously didactic, dynamic. Well, it is useless to dispute about higher and lower. From our point of view the Australians seem to be walking head-downwards, like flies on the ceiling; from their point of view we are in the same predicament; it all depends on the point of view. Ibsen certainly belongs, at any rate in his modern prose plays, to the consciously didactic artists whom you may, if you choose, relegate to a lower plane. But how glorious the company that will have to step down along with him! What were the Greek tragic poets if not consciously didactic? What is comedy, from time immemorial, but a deliberate lesson in life? Down Plautus; down Terence; down Molière and Holberg and Beaumarchais and Dumas! Calderon and Cervantes must be kind enough to follow; so must Schiller and Goethe. If German criticism is to be believed Shakespeare was the most hardened sermoniser of all literature; but in this respect I think German criticism is to be disbelieved. Shakespeare, then, may be left in possession of the pinnacle of Parnassus; but who shall keep him company? Flaubert, perhaps, and M. Guy de Maupassant?

The despisers of Ibsen, then, have not justified their position when they have merely proved, what no one disputes, that he is a didactic writer. They must further prove that his teaching kills his art. For my part, looking at his dramatic production all round, and excepting only two great dramas in verse, *Brand* and *Peer Gynt*, I am willing to admit that his teaching does now and then, in perfectly trifling details, affect his art for the worse. Not his direct teaching – that, as it seems to me, he always inspires with the breath of life – but his proclivity to what I may perhaps call symbolic side-issues. In the aforesaid dramas in verse this symbolism is eminently in place; not so, it seems to me, in the realistic plays. I once asked him how he justified this tendency in his art; he replied that life is one tissue of symbols. 'Certainly,' I might have answered; 'but when we have its symbolic side too persistently obtruded upon us, we lose the sense of reality, which, according to your own

theory, the modern dramatist should above all things aim at.' There
may be some excellent answer to this criticism; I give it for what it is
worth. Apart from these symbolic details, it seems to me that Ibsen is
singularly successful in vitalising his work; in reproducing the forms, the
phenomena of life, as well as its deeper meanings. Let us take the
example nearest at hand – *A Doll's House*. I venture to sa   'or this is a
matter of fact rather than of opinion – that in the minds of
thousands in Scandinavia and Germany, Nora Helmer lives with an
intense and palpitating life such as belongs to few fictitious characters.
Habitually and instinctively men pay Ibsen the compliment (so often
paid to Shakespeare) of discussing her as though she were a real woman,
living a life of her own, quite apart from the poet's creative intelligence.
The very critics who begin by railing at her as a puppet end by
denouncing her as a woman. She irritates, troubles, fascinates them as
no puppet ever could. Moreover, the triumph of the actress is the
dramatist's best defence. Miss Achurch might have the genius of Rachel
and Desclée in one, yet she could not transmute into flesh and blood the
doctrinary doll, stuffed with sawdust and sophistry, whom some people
declare Nora to be. Men do not shudder at the agony or weep over the
woes of an intellectual abstraction. As for Helmer, I am not aware that
any one has accused him of unreality. He is too real for most people – he
is commonplace, unpleasant, objectionable. The truth is, he touches us
too nearly; he is the typical husband of what may be called chattel
matrimony. If there are few Doll's -Houses in England, it is certainly for
lack of Noras, not for lack of Helmers. I admit that in my opinion Ibsen
has treated Helmer somewhat unfairly. He has not exactly disguised,
but has omitted to emphasise, the fact that if Helmer helped to make
Nora a doll, Nora helped to make Helmer a prig. By giving Nora all the
logic in the last scene (and she is not a scrupulous dialectician) he has
left the casual observer to conclude that he lays the whole responsibility
on Helmer. This conclusion is not just, but it is specious; and so far, and
so far only, I grant that the play has somewhat the air of a piece of
special pleading. I shall presently discuss the last scene in greater detail;
but even admitting for the moment that the polemist here gets the better
of the poet, can we call the poet, who has moved freely through two acts
and two-thirds, nothing but a doctrinary polemist?

Let me add that *A Doll's House* is, of all Ibsen's plays, the one in which
a definite thesis is most tangibly posited – the one, therefore, which is
most exposed to the reproach of being a mere sociological pamphlet.
His other plays may be said to scintillate with manifold ethical
meanings; here the light is focused upon one point in the social system. I
do not imply that *A Doll's House* is less thoroughly vitalised than *Ghosts*, or

Rosmersholm, or *The Lady from the Sea.* What I mean is, that the play may in some eyes acquire a false air of being merely didactic from the fortuitous circumstance that its moral can be easily formulated.

The second line of criticism is that which attacks the substance of Ibsen's so-called doctrines, on the ground that they are neither new nor true. To the former objection one is inclined to answer curtly but pertinently, 'Who said they were?' It is not the business of the creative artist to make the great generalisations which mark the stages of intellectual and social progress. Certainly Ibsen did not discover the theory of evolution or the doctrine of heredity, any more than he discovered gravitation. He was not the first to denounce the subjection of women; he was not the first to sneer at the 'compact liberal majority' of our pseudo-democracies. His function is to seize and throw into relief certain aspects of modern life. He shows us society as Kean was said to read Shakespeare – by flashes of lightning – luridly, but with intense vividness. He selects subjects which seem to him to illustrate such and such political, ethical, or sociological ideas; but he does not profess to have invented the ideas. They are common property; they are in the air. A grave injustice has been done him of late by those of his English admirers who have set him up as a social prophet, and have sometimes omitted to mention that he is a bit of a poet as well. It is so much easier to import an idea than the flesh and blood, the imagination, the passion, the style in which it is clothed. People have heard so much of the 'gospel according to Ibsen' that they have come to think of him as a mere hot-gospeller, the Boanerges of some strange social propaganda. As a matter of fact Ibsen has no gospel whatever, in the sense of a systematic body of doctrine. He is not a Schopenhauer, and still less a Comte. There never was a less systematic thinker. Truth is not, in his eyes, one and indivisible; it is many-sided, many-visaged, almost Protean. It belongs to the irony of fate that the least dogmatic of thinkers – the man who has said of himself, 'I only ask: my call is not to answer' – should figure in the imagination of so many English critics as a dour dogmatist, a vendor of social nostrums in pilule form. He is far more of a paradoxist than a dogmatist. A thinker he is most certainly, but not an inventor of brand new notions such as no one has ever before conceived. His originality lies in giving intense dramatic life to modern ideas, and often stamping them afresh, as regards mere verbal form, in the mint of his imaginative wit.

The second allegation, that his doctrines are not true, is half answered when we have insisted that they are not put forward (at any rate by Ibsen himself) as a body of inspired dogmas. No man rejects more consistently than he the idea of finality. He does not pretend to have said the last word on any subject. 'You needn't believe me unless you like,' says Dr Stockmann in *An Enemy of the People*, 'but truths are not the tough old Methuselahs people take them to be. A normally constituted truth lives, let us say, some seventeen or eighteen years; at most twenty.' The telling of absolute truths, to put it in another way, is scarcely Ibsen's aim. He is more concerned with destroying conventional lies, and exorcising the 'ghosts' of dead truths; and most of all concerned to make people think and see for themselves. Here again we recognise the essential injustice of regarding a dramatic poet as a sort of prophet-professor, who means all his characters say and makes them say all he means. I have been asked, for example, whether Ibsen intends us to understand by the last scene of *A Doll's House* that awakened wives ought to leave their husbands and children in order to cultivate their souls in solitude. Ibsen intends nothing of the sort. He draws a picture of a typical household; he creates a man and woman with certain characteristics; he places them in a series of situations which at once develop their characters and suggest large questions of conduct; and he makes the woman, in the end, adopt a course of action which he (rightly or wrongly) believes to be consistent with her individual nature and circumstances. It is true that this course of action is so devised as to throw the principles at stake into the strongest relief; but the object of that is to make people thoroughly realise the problem, not to force upon them the particular solution arrived at in this particular case. No two life-problems were ever precisely alike, and in stating and solving one, Ibsen does not pretend to supply a ready-made solution for all the rest. He illustrates, or, rather, illumines, a general principle by a conceivable case; that is all. To treat Nora's arguments in the last scene of *A Doll's House* as though they were the ordered propositions of an essay by John Stuart Mill is to give a striking example of the strange literalness of the English mind, its inability to distinguish between drama and dogma. To me that last scene is the most moving in the play, precisely because I hold it the most dramatic. It has been called a piece of pure logic – is it not rather logic conditioned by character and saturated with emotion? Some years ago I saw *Et Dukkehjem* acted in Christiania. It was an off season; only the second-rate members of the company were engaged; and throughout two acts and a half I sat vainly striving to recapture the emotions I had so often felt in reading the play. But the moment Nora and Helmer were seated face to face, at the words, 'No, that is just it; you do not understand me; and I have never understood you – till tonight' – at that moment, much to my own surprise, the thing suddenly gripped my heartstrings; to use an expressive Americanism, I 'sat up'; and every phrase of Nora's threnody over her dead dreams, her lost illusions, thrilled me to the very marrow. Night after night I went to see that scene; night after night I have watched it in the English version; it has never lost its power over me. And why? Not because Nora's sayings are particularly wise or particularly true, but because, in her own words, they are so true *for her*, because she feels them so deeply and utters them so exquisitely. Certainly she is unfair, certainly she is one-sided, certainly she is illogical; if she were not, Ibsen would be the pamphleteer he is supposed to be, not the poet he is. 'I have never been happy here – only merry. . . . You have never loved me – you have only found it amusing to be in love with me.' Have we not in these speeches the very mingling of truth and falsehood, of justice and injustice, necessary to humanise the character and the situation? After Nora has declared her intention of leaving her home, Helmer remarks, 'Then there is only one explanation possible – You no longer love me.' 'No,' she replies, 'that is just it.' 'Nora! can you say so?' cries Helmer, looking into her eyes. '*Oh, I'm so sorry, Torvald*,' she answers, '*for you've always been so kind to me*.' Is this pamphleteering? To me it seems like the subtlest human pathos. Again, when she says 'At that moment it became clear to me that I had been living here for eight years with a strange man and had borne him three children – Oh, I can't bear to think of it! I could tear myself to pieces' – who can possibly take this for anything but a purely dramatic utterance? It is true and touching in Nora's mouth, but it is obviously founded on a vague sentiment, that may or may not bear analysis. Nora postulates a certain transcendental community of spirit as the foundation and justification of marriage. The idea is very womanly and may also be very practical; but Ibsen would probably be the first to admit that before it can claim the validity of a social principle we must ascertain whether it be possible for any two human beings to be other than what Nora would call strangers. This further analysis the hearer must carry out for him, or her, self. The poet has stimulated thought; he has not tried to lay down a hard-and-fast rule of conduct. Again, when Helmer says, 'No man sacrifices his honour even for one he loves,' and Nora retorts, '*Millions of women have done that!*' we applaud the consummate claptrap, not on account of its abstract justice, but rather of its characteristic injustice. Logically, it is naught; dramatically, one feels it to be a masterstroke. Here, it is the right speech in the right place; in a sociological monograph it would be absurd. My position, in short, is that in Ibsen's plays, as in those of any other dramatist who keeps within the bounds of his form, we must look, not for the axioms and demonstrations of a scientific system, but simply for 'broken lights' of truth, refracted through character and circumstance. The playwright who sends on a Chorus or a lecturer, unconnected with the dramatic action, to moralise the spectacle and put all the dots on all the *is*, may fairly be taken to ask for the substance of his 'doctrines'. But that playwright is Dumas, not Ibsen.

Lastly, we come to the assertion that Ibsen is a 'coarse' writer, with a morbid love for using the theatre as a physiological lecture-room. Here again I can only cry out upon the chance which has led to so grotesque a misconception. He has written some twenty plays, of which all except two might be read aloud, with only the most trivial omissions, in any young ladies' boarding-school from Tobolsk to Tangiers. The two exceptions are *A Doll's House* and *Ghosts* – the very plays which happen to have come (more or less) within the ken of English critics. In *A Doll's House* he touches upon, in *Ghosts* he frankly faces, the problem of hereditary disease, which interests him, not in itself, but simply as the physical type and symbol of so many social and ethical phenomena. *Ghosts* I have not space to consider. If art is for ever debarred from entering upon certain domains of human experience, then *Ghosts* is an inartistic work. I can only say, after having read it, seen it on the stage, and translated it, that no other modern play seems to me to fulfil so entirely the Aristotelian ideal of purging the soul by means of terror and pity. In *A Doll's House*, again, there are two passages, one in the second and one in third act, which Mr Podsnap could not conveniently explain to the young lady in the dress-circle. Whether the young lady in the dress-circle would be any the worse for having them explained to her is a question I shall not discuss. As a matter of fact, far from being coarsely treated, they are so delicately touched that the young person suspects nothing and is in no way incommoded. It is Mr Podsnap himself that cries out – the virtuous Podsnap who, at the French theatre, writhes in his stall with laughter at speeches and situations *à faire rougir des singes*. I have more than once been reproached, by people who had seen *A Doll's House* at the Novelty, with having cut the speeches which the first-night critics pronounced objectionable. It has cost me some trouble to persuade them that not a word had been cut, and that the text they found so innocent contained every one of the enormities denounced by the critics. Mr Podsnap, I may add, has in this case shown his usual alacrity in putting the worst possible interpretation upon things. Dr Rank's declaration to Nora that Helmer is not the only man who would willingly lay down his life for her, has been represented as a hideous attempt on the part of a dying debauchee to seduce his friend's wife. Nothing is further from the mind of poor Rank, who, by the way, is not a debauchee at all. He knows himself to be at death's door; Nora, in her Doll's House, has given light and warmth to his lonely, lingering existence; he has silently adored her while standing with her, as with her husband, on terms of frank comradeship; is he to leave her for ever without saying, as he puts it, 'Thanks for the light'? Surely this is a piece either of inhuman austerity or of prurient prudery; surely Mrs Podsnap herself could not feel a suspicion of insult in such a declaration. True, it comes inaptly at that particular moment, rendering it impossible for Nora to make the request she contemplates. But essentially, and even from the most conventional point of view, I fail to see anything inadmissible in Rank's conduct to Nora. Nora's conduct to Rank, in the stocking scene, is another question; but that is merely a side-light on the relation between Nora and Helmer, preparatory, in a sense, to the scene before Rank's entrance in the last act.

In conclusion, what are the chances that Ibsen's modern plays will ever take a permanent place on the English stage? They are not great, it seems to me. The success of *A Doll's House* will naturally encourage Ibsen's admirers to further experiments in the same direction – interesting and instructive experiments I have no doubt. We shall see in course of time *The Young Men's League, The Pillars of Society, An Enemy of the People, Rosmersholm,* and *A Lady from the Sea* – I name them in chronological order. But none of these plays presents the double attraction that has made the success of *A Doll's House* – the distinct plea for female emancipation which appeals to the thinking public, and the overwhelming part for an actress of genius which attracts the ordinary playgoer. The other plays I cannot but foresee, will be in a measure antiquated before the great public is ripe for a thorough appreciation of them. I should like to see an attempt made to produce one of the poet's historical plays, but that would involve an outlay for costumes and mounting not to be lightly faced. On the other hand I have not the remotest doubt that Ibsen will bulk more and more largely as years go on in the consciousness of all students of literature in general, as opposed to the stage in particular. The creator of *Brand* and *Peer Gynt* is one of the great poets of the world.

Source: article on 'Ibsen and English Criticism', *The Fortnightly Review*, July 1889.

George Bernard Shaw   'Before and After Ibsen (1891)

. . . We have progressed so rapidly . . . under the impulse given to the drama by Ibsen that it seems strange now to contrast him favourably with Shakespear on the ground that he avoided the old catastrophes which left the stage strewn with the dead at the end of an Elizabethan tragedy. For perhaps the most plausible reproach levelled at Ibsen by modern critics of his own school is just that survival of the old school in him which makes the death rate so high in his last acts. Do Oswald Alving, Hedvig Ekdal, Rosmer and Rebecca, Hedda Gabler, Solness, Eyolf, Borkman, Rubeck and Irene die dramatically natural deaths, or are they slaughtered in the classic and Shakespearean manner, partly because the audience expects blood for its money, partly because it is difficult to make people attend seriously to anything except by startling them with some violent calamity? It is so easy to make out a case for either view that I shall not argue the point. The post-Ibsen playwrights apparently think that Ibsen's homicides and suicides were forced. In Tchekov's *Cherry Orchard*, for example, where the sentimental ideals of our amiable, cultured, Schumann playing propertied class are reduced to dust and ashes by a hand not less deadly than Ibsen's because it is so much more caressing, nothing more violent happens than that the family cannot afford to keep up its old house. In Granville-Barker's plays, the campaign against our society is carried on with all Ibsen's implacability; but the one suicide (in *Waste*) is unhistorical; for neither Parnell nor Dilke, who were the actual cases in point of the waste which was the subject of the play, killed himself. I myself have been reproached because the characters in my plays 'talk but do nothing', meaning that they do not commit felonies. As a matter of fact we have come to see that it is no true *dénouement* to cut the Gordian knot as Alexander did with a stroke of the sword. If people's souls are tied up by law and public opinion it is much more tragic to leave them to wither in these bonds than to end their misery and relieve the salutary compunction of the audience by outbreaks of violence. Judge Brack was, on the whole, right when he said that people dont do such things. If they did, the idealists would be brought to their senses very quickly indeed.

But in Ibsen's plays the catastrophe, even when it seems forced, and when the ending of the play would be more tragic without it, is never an accident; and the play never exists for its sake. His nearest to an accident is the death of little Eyolf, who falls off a pier and is drowned. But this instance only reminds us that there is one good dramatic use for an accident: it can awaken people. When England wept over the deaths of little Nell and Paul Dombey, the strong soul of Ruskin was moved to scorn: to novelists who were at a loss to make their books sell he offered the formula: When at a loss, kill a child. But Ibsen did not kill little Eyolf to manufacture pathos. The surest way to achieve a thoroughly bad performance of Little Eyolf is to conceive it as a sentimental tale of a drowned darling. Its drama lies in the awakening of Allmers and his wife to the despicable quality and detestable rancors of the life they have been idealizing as blissful and poetic. They are so sunk in their dream that the awakening can be effected only by a violent shock. And that is just the one dramatically useful thing an accident can do. It can shock. Hence the accident that befalls Eyolf.

As to the deaths in Ibsen's last acts, they are a sweeping up of the remains of dramátically finished people. Solness's fall from the tower is as obviously symbolic as Phaeton's fall from the chariot of the sun. Ibsen's dead bodies are those of the exhausted or destroyed: he does not kill Hilda, for instance, as Shakespear killed Juliet. He is ruthless enough with Hedvig and Eyolf because he wants to use their deaths to expose their parents; but if he had written Hamlet nobody would have been killed in the last act except perhaps Horatio, whose correct nullity might have provoked Fortinbras to let some of the moral sawdust out of him with his sword. For Shakespearean deaths in Ibsen you must go back to Lady Inger and the plays of his nonage, with which this book is not concerned.

The drama was born of old from the union of two desires: the desire to have a dance and the desire to hear a story. The dance became a rant: the story became a situation. When Ibsen began to make plays, the art of the dramatist had shrunk into the art of contriving a situation. And it was held that the stranger the situation, the better the play. Ibsen saw that, on the contrary, the more familiar the situation, the more interesting the play. Shakespear had put ourselves on the stage but not our situations. Our uncles seldom murder our fathers, and cannot legally marry our mothers; we do not meet witches; our kings are not as a rule stabbed and succeeded by their stabbers; and when we raise money by bills we do not promise to pay pounds of our flesh. Ibsen supplies the want left by Shakespear. He gives us not only ourselves, but ourselves in our own situations. The things that happen to his stage figures are things that happen to us. One consequence is that his plays are much more important to us than Shakespear's. Another is that they are capable both of hurting us cruelly and of filling us with excited hopes of escape from idealistic tyrannies, and with visions of intenser life in the future.

Changes in technique follow inevitably from these changes in the subject matter of the play. When a dramatic poet can give you hopes and visions, such old maxims as that stage-craft is the art of preparation become boyish, and may be left to those unfortunate playwrights who, being unable to make anything really interesting happen on the stage, have to acquire the art of continually persuading the audience that it is going to happen presently. When he can stab people to the heart by shewing them the meanness or cruelty of something they did yesterday and intend to do tomorrow, all the old tricks to catch and hold their attention become the silliest of superfluities. The play called *The Murder of Gonzago*, which Hamlet makes the players act before his uncle, is artlessly constructed; but it produces a greater effect on Claudius than the Œdipus of Sophocles, because it is about himself. The writer who practises the art of Ibsen therefore discards all the old tricks of preparation, catastrophe, *dénouement*, and so forth without thinking about it, just as a modern rifleman never dreams of providing himself with powder horns, percussion caps, and wads: indeed he does not know the use of them. Ibsen substituted a terrible art of sharpshooting at the audience, trapping them, fencing with them, aiming always at the sorest spot in their consciences. Never mislead an audience, was an old rule. But the new school will trick the spectator into forming a meanly false judgment, and then convict him of it in the next act, often to his grievous mortification. When you despise something you ought to take off your hat to, or admire and imitate something you ought to loathe, you cannot resist the dramatist who knows how to touch these morbid spots in you and make you see that they are morbid. The dramatist knows that as long as he is teaching and saving his audience, he is as sure of their strained attention as a dentist is, or the Angel of the Annunciation. And though he may use all the magic of art to make you forget the pain he causes you or to enhance the joy of the hope and courage he awakens, he is never occupied in the old work of manufacturing interest and expectation with materials that have neither novelty, significance, nor relevance to the experience or prospects of the spectators.

Hence a cry has arisen that the post-Ibsen play is not a play, and that its technique, not being the technique described by Aristotle, is not a technique at all. I will not enlarge on this: the fun poked at my friend Mr A. B. Walkley in the prologue of *Fanny's First Play* need not be repeated here. But I may remind him that the new technique is new only on the modern stage. It has been used by preachers and orators ever since speech was invented. It is the technique of playing upon the human conscience; and it has been practised by the playwright whenever the playwright has been capable of it. Rhetoric, irony, argument, paradox, epigram, parable, the rearrangement of haphazard facts into orderly and intelligent situations: these are both the oldest and the newest arts of the drama; and your plot construction and art of preparation are only the tricks of theatrical talent and the shifts of moral sterility, not the weapons of dramatic genius. In the theatre of Ibsen we are not flattered spectators killing an idle hour with an ingenious and amusing entertainment: we are 'guilty creatures sitting at a play'; and the technique of pastime is no more applicable than at a murder trial.

The technical novelties of the Ibsen and post-Ibsen plays are, then: first, the introduction of the discussion and its development until it so overspreads and interpenetrates the action that it finally assimilates it, making play and discussion practically identical; and, second, as a consequence of making the spectators themselves the persons of the drama, and the incidents of their own lives its incidents, the disuse of the old stage tricks by which audiences had to be induced to take an interest in unreal people and improbable circumstances, and the substitution of a forensic technique of recrimination, disillusion, and penetration through ideals to the truth, with a free use of all the rhetorical and lyrical arts of the orator, the preacher, the pleader, and the rhapsodist.

SOURCE: extract from *The Quintessence of Ibsenism* (1891), republished in *The Works of George Bernard Shaw* (London, 1931), vol. 19, pp. 152–7. [Shavian spelling usage is retained – Ed.]

2. SHAKESPEARE AND CLASSIC DRAMA: STUDIES AND REVIEWS, 1895–1977

George Bernard Shaw   Poor Shakespear! (1895)

The Two Gentlemen of Verona at Daly's Theatre

The piece founded by Augustin Daly on Shakespear's *Two Gentlemen of Verona*, to which I looked forward last week, is not exactly a comic opera, though there is plenty of music in it, and not exactly a serpentine dance, though it proceeds under a play of changing colored lights. It is something more old-fashioned than either: to wit, a vaudeville. And let me hasten to admit that it makes a very pleasant entertainment for those who know no better. Even I, who know a great deal better, as I shall presently demonstrate rather severely, enjoyed myself tolerably. I cannot feel harshly towards a gentleman who works so hard as Mr Daly does to make Shakespear presentable: one feels that he loves the bard, and lets him have his way as far as he thinks it good for him. His rearrangement of the scenes of the first two acts is just like him. Shakespear shews lucidly how Proteus lives with his father (Antonio) in Verona, and loves a lady of that city named Julia. Mr Daly, by taking the scene in Julia's house between Julia and her maid, and the scene in Antonio's house between Antonio and Proteus, and making them into one scene, convinces the unlettered audience that Proteus and Julia live in the same house with their father Antonio. Further, Shakespear shews us how Valentine, the other gentleman of Verona, travels from Verona to Milan, the journey being driven into our heads by a comic scene in Verona, in which Valentine's servant is overwhelmed with grief at leaving his parents, and with indignation at the insensibility of his dog to his sorrow, followed presently by another comic scene in Milan in which the same servant is welcomed to the strange city by a fellow servant. Mr Daly, however, is ready for Shakespear on this point too. He just represents the two scenes as occurring in the same place; and immediately the puzzle as to who is who is complicated by a puzzle as to where is where. Thus is the immortal William adapted to the requirements of a nineteenth-century audience.

In preparing the text of his version Mr Daly has proceeded on the usual principles, altering, transposing, omitting, improving, correcting, and transferring speeches from one character to another. Many of Shakespear's lines are mere poetry, not to the point, not getting the play along, evidently stuck in because the poet liked to spread himself in verse. On all such unbusinesslike superfluities Mr Daly is down with his blue pencil. For instance, he relieves us of such stuff as the following, which merely conveys that Valentine loves Silvia, a fact already sufficiently established by the previous dialogue:

> My thoughts do harbor with my Silvia nightly;
>> And slaves they are to me, that send them flying:
> Oh, could their master come and go as lightly,
>> Himself would lodge where senseless they are lying.
> My herald thoughts in thy pure bosom rest them,
>> While I, their king, that thither them importune,
> Do curse the grace that with such grace hath blessed them,
>> Because myself do want my servant's fortune.
> I curse myself, for they are sent by me,
>> That they should harbor where their lord would be.

Slaves indeed are these lines and their like to Mr Daly, who 'sends them flying' without remorse. But when he comes to passages that a stage manager can understand, his reverence for the bard knows no bounds. The following awkward lines, unnecessary as they are under modern stage conditions, are at any rate not poetic, and are in the nature of police news. Therefore they are piously retained:

> What halloing, and what stir, is this today?
> These are my mates, that make their wills their law,
> Have some unhappy passenger in chase.
> They love me well; yet I have much to do,
> To keep them from uncivil outrages.
> Withdraw thee, Valentine: whos this comes here?

The perfunctory metrical character of such lines only makes them more ridiculous than they would be in prose. I would cut them out without remorse to make room for all the lines that have nothing to justify their existence except their poetry, their humor, their touches of character –

in short, the lines for whose sake the play survives, just as it was for their sake it originally came into existence. Mr Daly, who prefers the lines which only exist for the sake of the play, will doubtless think me as great a fool as Shakespear; but I submit to him, without disputing his judgment, that he is, after all, only a man with a theory of dramatic composition, going with a blue pencil over the work of a great dramatist, and striking out everything that does not fit his theory. Now, as it happens, nobody cares about Mr Daly's theory; whilst everybody who pays to see what is, after all, advertised as a performance of Shakespear's play entitled *The Two Gentlemen of Verona*, and not as a demonstration of Mr Daly's theory, does care more or less about the art of Shakespear. Why not give them what they ask for, instead of going to great trouble and expense to give them something else?

In those matters in which Mr Daly has given the rein to his own taste and fancy: that is to say, in scenery, costumes, and music, he is for the most part disabled by a want of real knowledge of the arts concerned. I say for the most part, because his pretty fifteenth-century dresses, though probably inspired rather by Sir Frederic Leighton than by Benozzo Gozzoli, may pass. But the scenery is insufferable. First, for 'a street in Verona' we get a Bath bun colored operatic front cloth with about as much light in it as there is in a studio in Fitzjohn's Avenue in the middle of October. I respectfully invite Mr Daly to spend his next holiday looking at a real street in Verona, asking his conscience meanwhile whether a manager with eyes in his head and the electric light at his disposal could not advance a step on the Telbin (senior) style. Telbin was an admirable scene painter; but he was limited by the mechanical conditions of gas illumination; and he learnt his technique before the great advance made during the Impressionist movement in the painting of open-air effects, especially of brilliant sunlight. Of that advance Mr Daly has apparently no conception. The days of Macready and Clarkson Stanfield still exist for him; he would probably prefer a watercolor drawing of a foreign street by Samuel Prout to one of Mr T. M. Rooke; and I daresay every relic of the original tallow candlelight that still clings to the art of scene-painting is as dear to him as it is to most old playgoers, including, unhappily, many of the critics.

As to the elaborate set in which Julia makes her first entrance, a glance at it shews how far Mr Daly prefers the Marble Arch to the loggia of Orcagna. All over the scene we have Renaissance work, in its genteelest stages of decay, held up as the perfection of romantic elegance and beauty. The school that produced the classicism of the First Empire, designed the terraces of Regent's Park and the façades of Fitzroy Square, and conceived the Boboli Gardens and Versailles as places for human beings to be happy in, ramps all over the scenery, and offers as much of its pet colonnades and statues as can be crammed into a single scene, by way of a compendium of everything that is lovely in the city of San Zeno and the tombs of the Scaligers. As to the natural objects depicted, I ask whether any man living has ever seen a pale green cypress in Verona or anywhere else out of a toy Noah's Ark. A man who, having once seen cypresses and felt their presence in a north Italian landscape, paints them lettuce color, must be suffering either from madness, malice, or a theory of how nature should have colored trees, cognate with Mr Daly's theory of how Shakespear should have written plays.

Of the music let me speak compassionately. After all, it is only very lately that Mr Arnold Dolmetsch, by playing fifteenth-century music on fifteenth-century instruments, has shewn us that the age of beauty was true to itself in music as in pictures and armor and costumes. But what should Mr Daly know of this, educated as he no doubt was to believe that the court of Denmark should always enter in the first act of *Hamlet* to the march from Judas Maccabæus? Schubert's setting of Who is Silvia? he knew, but had rashly used up in *Twelfth Night* as Who's Olivia. He has therefore had to fall back on another modern setting, almost supernaturally devoid of any particular merit. Besides this, all through the drama the most horribly common music repeatedly breaks out on the slightest pretext or on no pretext at all. One dance, set to a crude old English popular tune, sundry eighteenth and nineteenth century musical banalities, and a titivated plantation melody in the first act which produces an indescribably atrocious effect by coming in behind the scenes as a sort of coda to Julia's curtain speech, all turn the play, as I have said, into a vaudeville. Needless to add, the accompaniments are not played on lutes and viols, but by the orchestra and a guitar or two. In the forest scene the outlaws begin the act by a chorus. After their encounter with Valentine they go off the stage singing the refrain exactly in the style of *La Fille de Madame Angot*. The wanton absurdity of introducing this comic opera convention is presently eclipsed by a thunderstorm, immediately after which Valentine enters and delivers his speech sitting down on a bank of moss, as an outlaw in tights naturally would after a terrific shower. Such is the effect of many years of theatrical management on the human brain.

Perhaps the oddest remark I have to make about the performance is that, with all its glaring defects and blunders, it is rather a handsome and elaborate one as such things go. It is many years now since Mr Ruskin first took the Academicians of his day aback by the obvious remark that Carpaccio and Giovanni Bellini were better painters than

Domenichino and Salvator Rosa. Nobody dreams now of assuming that Pope was a greater poet than Chaucer, that Mozart's Twelfth Mass is superior to the masterpieces of Orlandus Lassus and Palestrina, or that our 'ecclesiastical Gothic' architecture is more enlightened than Norman axe work. But the theatre is still wallowing in such follies; and until Mr Comyns Carr and Sir Edward Burne-Jones, Baronet, put King Arthur on the stage more or less in the manner natural to men who know these things, Mr Daly might have pleaded the unbroken conservatism of the playhouse against me. But after the Lyceum scenery and architecture I decline to accept a relapse without protest. There is no reason why cheap photographs of Italian architecture (sixpence apiece in infinite variety at the bookstall in the South Kensington Museum) should not rescue us from Regent's Park Renaissance colonnades on the stage just as the electric light can rescue us from Telbin's dun-colored sunlight. The opera is the last place in the world where any wise man would look for adequate stage illusion; but the fact is that Mr Daly, with all his colored lights, has not produced a single Italian scene comparable in illusion to that provided by Sir Augustus Harris at Covent Garden for *Cavalleria Rusticana*.

Of the acting I have not much to say. Miss Reham provided a strong argument in favor of rational dress by looking much better in her page's costume than in that of her own sex; and in the serenade scene, and that of the wooing of Silvia for Proteus, she stirred some feeling into the part, and reminded us of what she was in *Twelfth Night*, where the same situations are fully worked out. For the rest, she moved and spoke with imposing rhythmic grace. That is as much notice as so cheap a part as Julia is worth from an artist who, being absolute mistress of the situation at Daly's Theatre, might and should have played Imogen for us instead. The two gentlemen were impersonated by Mr Worthing and Mr Craig. Mr Worthing charged himself with feeling without any particular reference to his lines; and Mr Craig struck a balance by attending to the meaning of his speeches without taking them at all to heart. Mr Clarke, as the Duke, was emphatic, and worked up every long speech to a climax in the useful old style; but his tone is harsh, his touch on his consonants coarse, and his accent ugly, all fatal disqualifications for the delivery of Shakespearean verse. The scenes between Launce and his dog brought out the latent silliness and childishness of the audience as Shakespear's clowning scenes always do: I laugh at them like a yokel myself. Mr Lewis hardly made the most of them. His style has been formed in modern comedies, where the locutions are so familiar that their meaning is in no danger of being lost by the rapidity of his quaint utterance; but Launce's phraseology is another matter: a few of the funniest lines missed fire because the audience did not catch them. And with all possible allowance for Mr Daly's blue pencil, I cannot help suspecting that Mr Lewis's memory was responsible for one or two of his omissions. Still, Mr Lewis has always his comic force, whether he makes the most or the least of it; so that he cannot fail in such a part as Launce. Miss Maxine Elliot's Silvia was the most considerable performance after Miss Rehan's Julia. The whole company will gain by the substitution on Tuesday next of a much better play, *A Midsummer Night's Dream*, as a basis for Mr Daly's operations. No doubt he is at this moment, like Mrs Todgers, 'a dodgin' among the tender bits with a fork, and an eatin' of 'em'; but there is sure to be enough of the original left here and there to repay a visit. . . .

SOURCE: review article of 6 July 1895, collected in *Our Theatres in the Nineties*, vol. 1, republished in *The Works of George Bernard Shaw* (London, 1931), vol. 24, pp. 178–85. [Shavian spelling usage is retained – Ed.]

E. Gordon Craig   'Hypnotic Moments': Macbeth (1910)

. . . Consider, for instance . . . the play of *Macbeth*, in which 'the overwhelming pressure of preternatural agency urges on the tide of human passion with redoubled force'. [Hazlitt] The whole success of its representation depends upon the power of the stage-manager to suggest this preternatural agency and on the capacity of the actor to submit to the tide of the play, to that mysterious mesmerism which masters Macbeth and his 'troop of friends'.

I seem to see him in the first four acts of the play as a man who is hypnotised, seldom moving, but, when he does so, moving as a sleep-walker. Later on in the play the places are changed, and Lady Macbeth's sleep-walking is like the grim, ironical echo of Macbeth's whole life, a sharp, shrill echo quickly growing fainter, fainter, and gone.

In the last act Macbeth awakes. It almost seems to be a new rôle. Instead of a sleep-walker dragging his feet heavily he becomes an ordinary man startled from a dream to find the dream true. He is not the man some actors show him to be, the trapped, cowardly villain; nor yet is he to my mind the bold, courageous villain as other actors play him.

He is as a doomed man who has been suddenly awakened on the morning of his execution, and, in the sharpness and abruptness of that awakening, understands nothing but the facts before him, and even of these understands the external meaning only. He sees the army in front of him; he will fight, and he prepares to do so, puzzling all the time about the meaning of his dream. Occasionally he relapses into his state of somnambulism. While his wife lived he was not conscious of his state, he acted the part of her medium perfectly, and she in her turn acted as medium to the spirits whose duty it ever is to test the strength of men by playing with their force upon the weakness of women.

Nietzsche, writing of Macbeth, sees only the mad ambition of the man, this human passion of ambition; and he tells us that this sight, instead of irresistibly detracting from the evil ambition in us, rather augments it. Perhaps this is so; but it seems to me that behind all this there is much more than evil ambition and the idea of the hero and the villain.

Behind it all I seem to perceive the unseen forces already spoken of; those spirits that Shakespeare was always so fond of hinting stood behind all things of this earth, moved them, and moved them apparently to these great deeds for good or evil.

In *Macbeth* they are called by the old grandmother's title of the Three Witches, that elastic name which the public in the theatre may either laugh at or be serious about as it wishes.

Now when I speak of this hypnotic influence of these spirits as though I were mentioning something quite new, I am speaking entirely in relation to the interpretation of Shakespeare on the stage and not merely as his student. I know that the students have written about these spirits, comparing them to certain figures in the Greek tragedy and writing of them far more profoundly than I can do. But their writings are for those who read Shakespeare, or who see him acted, not for those who take part in the presentation of his plays. Whether the plays were ever intended to be acted or no, whether or not they gain by being acted, does not concern me here. But if I were asked to present this play of *Macbeth* upon the stage, I should need to bring to it an understanding different entirely from that which the student brings when he has only himself to consider as he sits reading it in private. You may feel the presence of these witches as you read the play, but which of you has ever felt their presence when you saw the play acted? And therein lies the failure of the producer and the actor.

In *Macbeth* it is, to my mind, during the hypnotic moments that we should feel the overpowering force of these unseen agencies; and how to make this felt, how to make it clear and yet not actual, is the problem of the stage-manager. To me it seems that the play has never yet been properly performed because we have never yet felt these spirits working through the woman at the man, and to achieve this would be one of the most difficult tasks which could be set the stage-manager, though not because of the difficulty of purchasing gauze which should be sufficiently transparent, not because of the difficulty of finding machinery capable of raising the ghosts, or any other such reason. The chief difficulty lies with the two performers of the rôles of Lady Macbeth and Macbeth, for if it is admitted that this spiritual element which Shakespeare called the Witches and Ghosts is in any way connected with the pain of these two beings, Macbeth and his Lady, then these two characters must show this to the audience.

But, while it rests with the actors of these two parts, it also rests with the actors of the witches, and above all with the stage-manager, to bring these spirits and their mediums into effective harmony.

On the stage the spirits are never seen during the scenes of Lady Macbeth, neither are we conscious of their influence; yet as we read the play we are not only conscious of the influence of these 'sightless substances'; we are somehow conscious of their presence. We feel it as the presence of the French Abbé was felt in Shorthouse's romance of *The Countess Eve*.

Are there not moments in the play when one of these three spirits seems to have clapped its skinny hand upon Lady Macbeth's mouth and answered in her stead? And who was it, if not one of them, who drew her by the wrist as she passed into the room of the old king with the two daggers in her hand? Who was it pushed her by the elbow as she smeared the faces of the grooms? Again, what is this dagger that Macbeth sees in the air? by what thread of hair does it hang? who dangles it? and whose is the voice heard as he returns from the chamber of the murdered king?

> MACB. I've done the deed. Didst thou not hear a noise?
> LADY M. I heard the owl scream and the crickets cry.
>   Did not you speak?
> MACB.   When?
> LADY M.   Now.
> MACB.   As I descended?

Who is this that was heard to speak as he descended?

And who are these mysterious three who dance gaily without making any sound around this miserable pair as they talk together in the dark after the dark deed? We know quite well as we read; we forget altogether when we see the play presented upon the stage. There we see only the weak man being egged on by the ambitious woman who is assuming the manners of what is called the 'Tragedy Queen'; and in other scenes we see the same man, having found that the same ambitious lady does not assist him, calling upon some bogies and having an interview with them in a cavern.

What we *should* see is a man in that hypnotic state which can be both terrible and beautiful to witness. We should realise that this hypnotism is transmitted to him through the medium of his wife, and we should recognise the witches as spirits, more terrible because more beautiful than we can conceive except by making them terrible. We should see them, not as Hazlitt imagined them, as 'hags of mischief, obscene panderers to iniquity, malicious from their impotence of enjoyment, enamoured of destruction, because they are themselves unreal, abortive, half-existences, who become sublime from their exemption from all human sympathies and contempt for all human affairs,' but rather picture them to ourselves as we picture the militant Christ scourging the moneylenders, the fools who denied Him. Here we have the idea of the supreme God, the supreme Love, and it is that which has to be brought into *Macbeth* on the stage. We see in this instance the God of Force as exemplified in these witches, placing these two pieces of mortality upon the anvil and crushing them because they were not hard enough to resist; consuming them because they could not stand the fire: offering the woman a crown for her husband, flattering her beyond measure, whispering to her of her superior force, of her superior intellect; whispering to him of his bravery.

See how persuasively the spirits can work upon the man or the woman when separated and alone! listen to the flow of their language; they are drunk with the force of these spirits though unaware of their presence.

But note the moment when these two come together. In each other's faces they see, as it were, something so strange that they seem to be surprised by a reminiscence. 'Where have I seen that before or felt that which I now see?' Each becomes furtive, alert, fearful, on the defensive, and so there is no outpouring of speech here, but their meeting is like the cautious approach of two animals.

What is it they see? – the spirit which clings round the feet or hangs upon the neck, or, as in the old Dürer picture, is whispering in the ear? Yet why, one wonders, should these spirits appear so horrible when a moment ago we were speaking of them as beings so divine as to resemble the militant Christ? and the answer seems obvious. Is it not possible that the spirit may take as many forms as the body, as many forms as thought? These spirits are the many souls of nature, inexorable to the weak, yet obedient to those who obey.

But now let us come to the appearance of Banquo at the feast.

The whole play leads up to, and down from, this point. It is here that are pronounced the most terrible words heard during the play, here that is offered the most amazing impression for the eye. And in order to reach this moment decently, intelligently, that is to say, artistically, the figures must not walk about on the ground for the first two acts and suddenly appear on stilts in the third act or line, for then a great truth will appear as a great lie, Banquo's ghost as nothing.

We must open this play high up in an atmosphere loftier than that in which we generally grope, and which is a matter-of-fact, put-on-your-boots atmosphere; for this is a matter of fancy, a matter of that strangely despised thing, the imagination; that which we call the spiritual.

We should be conscious of the desire of the spirit to see the woman utterly annihilated herself rather than submit to the influence which this spirit brings upon the flesh as a test. We should see the horror of the spirit on perceiving the triumph of this influence.

Instead, we see of all this nothing on the stage. We do not know why the witches are worrying these two people; we feel that it is rather unpleasant. But that is not the feeling which should be created in us. We see bogies and imps of the cauldron, and pitchforks, and the little mosquito-like beings of the pantomimes, but we never see the God, the Spirit, which we ought to see; that is to say, the beautiful spirit, that patient, stern being who demands of a hero at least the heroic.

Shakespeare's characters are so often but weak beings; Lady Macbeth is perhaps the weakest of them all, and if that is the beauty – and unmistakably it is a great beauty – it is the beauty of disease and not the supreme beauty.

Having read of these characters, we are left to ourselves and our own contemplation, and each will add that thought which Shakespeare left to be added by each. There is great freedom permitted to the reader, for much has been left unsaid, but so much has also been said that nearly all is indicated, and to the imaginative brain these spirits are clearly implied and the fruits of the imagination are always welcomed by the unimaginative, who devour them as Eve must have devoured the forbidden fruit. . . .

SOURCE: extract from *On the Art of the Theatre* (1910); reprinted edition (New York, 1956), pp. 269–77. Paperback edition (London, 1968).

T. S. Eliot 'Jonson's Tragedies and Comedies' (1919)

The reputation of Jonson has been of the most deadly kind that can be compelled upon the memory of a great poet. To be universally accepted; to be damned by the praise that quenches all desire to read the book; to be afflicted by the imputation of the virtues which excite the least pleasure; and to be read only by historians and antiquaries – this is the most perfect conspiracy of approval. For some generations the reputation of Jonson has been carried rather as a liability than as an asset in the balance-sheet of English literature. No critic has succeeded in making him appear pleasurable or even interesting. Swinburne's book on Jonson satisfies no curiosity and stimulates no thought. For the critical study in the 'Men of Letters Series' by Mr Gregory Smith there is a place; it satisfies curiosity, it supplies many just observations, it provides valuable matter on the neglected masques; it only fails to remodel the image of Jonson which is settled in our minds. Probably the fault lies with several generations of our poets. It is not that the value of poetry is only its value to living poets for their own work; but appreciation is akin to creation, and true enjoyment of poetry is related to the stirring of suggestion, the stimulus that a poet feels in his enjoyment of other poetry. Jonson has provided no creative stimulus for a very long time; consequently we must look back as far as Dryden – precisely, a poetic practitioner who learned from Jonson – before we find a living criticism of Jonson's work.

Yet there are possibilities for Jonson even now. We have no difficulty in seeing what brought him to this pass; how, in contrast, not with Shakespeare, but with Marlowe, Webster, Donne, Beaumont and Fletcher, he has been paid out with reputation instead of enjoyment. He is no less a poet than these men, but his poetry is of the surface. Poetry of the surface cannot be understood without study; for to deal with the surface of life, as Jonson dealt with it, is to deal so deliberately that we too must be deliberate, in order to understand. Shakespeare, and smaller men also, are in the end more difficult, but they offer something at the start to encourage the student or to satisfy those who want nothing more; they are suggestive, evocative, a phrase, a voice; they offer poetry in detail as well as in design. So does Dante offer something, a phrase everywhere (*tu se' ombra ed ombra vedi*) even to readers who have no Italian; and Dante and Shakespeare have poetry of design as well as of detail. But the polished veneer of Jonson only reflects the lazy reader's fatuity; unconscious does not respond to unconscious; no swarms of inarticulate feelings are aroused. The immediate appeal of Jonson is to the mind; his emotional tone is not in the single verse, but in the design of the whole. But not many people are capable of discovering for themselves the beauty which is only found after labour; and Jonson's industrious readers have been those whose interest was historical and curious, and those who have thought that in discovering the historical and curious interest they had discovered the artistic value as well. When we say that Jonson requires study, we do not mean study of his classical scholarship or of seventeenth-century manners. We mean intelligent saturation in his work as a whole; we mean that, in order to enjoy him at all, we must get to the centre of his work and his temperament, and that we must see him unbiased by time, as a contemporary. And to see him as a contemporary does not so much require the power of putting ourselves into seventeenth-century London as it requires the power of setting Jonson in our London.

It is generally conceded that Jonson failed as a tragic dramatist; and it is usually agreed that he failed because his genius was for satiric comedy and because of the weight of pedantic learning with which he burdened his two tragic failures. The second point marks an obvious error of detail; the first is too crude a statement to be accepted; to say that he failed because his genius was unsuited to tragedy is to tell us nothing at all. Jonson did not write a good tragedy, but we can see no reason why he should not have written one. If two plays so different as *The Tempest* and *The Silent Woman* are both comedies, surely the category of tragedy could be made wide enough to include something possible for Jonson to have done. But the classification of tragedy and comedy, while it may be sufficient to mark the distinction in a dramatic literature of more rigid form and treatment – it may distinguish Aristophanes from Euripides – is not adequate to a drama of such variations as the Elizabethans. Tragedy is a crude classification for plays so different in their tone as *Macbeth*, *The Jew of Malta*, and *The Witch of Edmonton*; and it does not help us much to say that *The Merchant of Venice* and *The Alchemist* are comedies. Jonson had his own scale, his own instrument. The merit which *Catiline* possesses is the same merit that is exhibited more triumphantly in *Volpone*; *Catiline* fails, not because it is too laboured and conscious, but because it is not conscious enough; because Jonson in this play was not alert to his own idiom, not clear in his mind as to what his temperament wanted him to do. In *Catiline* Jonson conforms, or attempts to conform, to conventions; not to the conventions of antiquity, which he had exquisitely under control, but to the conventions of tragico-historical drama of his time. It is not the Latin erudition that sinks *Catiline*, but the application of that erudition to a form which was not the proper vehicle for the mind which had amassed the erudition.

If you look at *Catiline* – that dreary Pyrrhic victory of tragedy – you find two passages to be successful: Act II Sc. i, the dialogue of the political ladies, and the Prologue of Sylla's ghost. These two passages are genial. The soliloquy of the ghost is a characteristic Jonson success in content and in versification–

> Dost thou not feel me, Rome? not yet! is night
> So heavy on thee, and my weight so light?
> Can Sylla's ghost arise within thy walls,
> Less threatening than an earthquake, the quick falls
> Of thee and thine? Shake not the frighted heads
> Of thy steep towers, or shrink to their first beds?
> Or as their ruin the large Tyber fills,
> Make that swell up, and drown thy seven proud hills? . . .

This is the learned, but also the creative, Jonson. Without concerning himself with the character of Sulla, and in lines of invective, Jonson makes Sylla's ghost, while the words are spoken, a living and terrible force. The words fall with as determined beat as if they were the will of the morose Dictator himself. You may say: merely invective; but mere invective, even if as superior to the clumsy fisticuffs of Marston and Hall as Jonson's verse is superior to theirs, would not create a living figure as Jonson has done in this long tirade. And you may say: rhetoric; but if we are to call it 'rhetoric' we must subject that term to a closer dissection than any to which it is accustomed. What Jonson has done here is not merely a fine speech. It is the careful, precise filling in of a strong and simple outline, and at no point does it overflow the outline; it is far more careful and precise in its obedience to this outline than are many of the speeches in *Tamburlaine*. The outline is not Sulla, for Sulla has nothing to do with it, but 'Sylla's ghost'. The words may not be suitable to an historical Sulla, or to anybody in history, but they are a perfect expression for 'Sylla's ghost'. You cannot say they are rhetorical 'because people do not talk like that', you cannot call them 'verbiage'; they do not exhibit prolixity or redundancy or the other vices in the rhetoric books; there is a definite artistic emotion which demands expression at that length. The words themselves are mostly simple words, the syntax is natural, the language austere rather than adorned. Turning then to the induction of *The Poetaster*, we find another success of the same kind –

> Light, I salute thee, but with wounded nerves . . .

Men may not talk in that way, but the Spirit of Envy does, and in the words of Jonson Envy is a real and living person. It is not human life that informs Envy and Sylla's ghost, but it is energy of which human life is only another variety.

Returning to *Catiline*, we find that the best scene in the body of the play is one which cannot be squeezed into a tragic frame, and which appears to belong to satiric comedy. The scene between Fulvia and Galla and Sempronia is a living scene in a wilderness of oratory. And as it recalls other scenes – there is a suggestion of the college of ladies in *The Silent Woman* – it looks like a comedy scene. And it appears to be satire.

> They shall all give and pay well, that come here,
> If they will have it; and that, jewels, pearl,
> Plate, or round sums to buy these. I'm not taken
> With a cob-swan or a high-mounting bull,
> As foolish Leda and Europa were;
> But the bright gold, with Danaë. For such price
> I would endure a rough, harsh Jupiter,
> Or ten such thundering gamesters, and refrain
> To laugh at'em, till they are gone, with my much suffering.

This scene is no more comedy than it is tragedy, and the 'satire' is merely a medium for the essential emotion. Jonson's drama is only incidentally satire, because it is only incidentally a criticism upon the actual world. It is not satire in the way in which the work of Swift or the work of Molière may be called satire: that is, it does not find its source in any precise emotional attitude or precise intellectual criticism of the actual world. It is satire perhaps as the work of Rabelais is satire; certainly not more so. The important thing is that if fiction can be divided into creative fiction and critical fiction, Jonson's is creative. That he was a great critic, our first great critic, does not affect this assertion. Every creator is also a critic; Jonson was a conscious critic, but he was also conscious in his creations. Certainly, one sense in which the term 'critical' may be applied to fiction is a sense in which the term might be used of a method antithetical to Jonson's. It is the method of *Education Sentimentale*. The characters of Jonson, of Shakespeare, perhaps of all the greatest drama, are drawn in positive and simple outlines. They may be filled in, and by Shakespeare they are filled in, by much detail or many shifting aspects; but a clear and sharp and simple form remains through these – though it would be hard to say in what the clarity and sharpness and simplicity of Hamlet consists. But Frédéric Moreau is not made in that way. He is constructed partly by negative definition, built up by a great number of observations. We cannot isolate him from the environment in which we find him; it may be an environment which is or can be universalized; nevertheless it, and the figure in it, consist of very many observed particular facts, the actual world. Without this world the figure dissolves. The ruling faculty is a critical perception, a commentary upon experienced feeling and sensation. If this is true of Flaubert, it is true in a higher degree of Molière than of Jonson. The broad farcical lines of Molière may seem to be the same drawing as Jonson's. But Molière—say in Alceste or Monsieur Jourdain—is criticizing the actual; the reference to the actual world is more direct. And having a more tenuous reference, the work of Jonson is much less directly satirical.

This leads us to the question of Humours. Largely on the evidence of the two Humour plays, it is sometimes assumed that Jonson is occupied with types; typical exaggerations, or exaggerations of type. The Humour definition, the expressed intention of Jonson, may be satisfactory for these two plays. *Every Man in his Humour*; is the first mature work of Jonson, and the student of Jonson must study it; but it is not the play in which Jonson found his genius: it is the last of his plays to read first. If one reads *Volpone*, and after that re-reads the *Jew of Malta*; then returns to Jonson and reads *Bartholomew Fair*, *The Alchemist*, *Epicœne* and *The Devil is an Ass*, and finally *Catiline*, it is possible to arrive at a fair opinion of the poet and the dramatist.

The Humour, even at the beginning, is not a type, as in Marston's satire, but a simplified and somewhat distorted individual with a typical mania. In the later work, the Humour definition quite fails to account for the total effect produced. The characters of Shakespeare are such as might exist in different circumstances than those in which Shakespeare sets them. The latter appear to be those which extract from the characters the most intense and interesting realization; but that realization has not exhausted their possibilities. Volpone's life, on the other hand, is bounded by the scene in which it is played; in fact, the life is the life of the scene and is derivatively the life of Volpone; the life of the character is inseparable from the life of the drama. This is not dependence upon a background, or upon a substratum of fact. The emotional effect is single and simple. Whereas in Shakespeare the effect is due to the way in which the characters *act upon* one another, in Jonson it is given by the way in which the characters *fit in* with each other. The artistic result of *Volpone* is not due to any effect of Volpone, Mosca, Corvino, Corbaccio, Voltore have upon each other, but simply to their combination into a whole. And these figures are not personifications of passions; separately, they have not even that reality, they are constituents. It is a similar indication of Jonson's method that you can hardly pick out a line of Jonson's and say confidently that it is great poetry; but there are many extended passages to which you cannot deny that honour.

> I will have all my beds blown up, not stuft;
> Down is too hard; and then, mine oval room
> Fill'd with such pictures as Tiberius took
> From Elephantis, and dull Aretine
> But coldly imitated. Then, my glasses
> Cut in more subtle angles, to disperse
> And multiply the figures, as I walk. . . .

Jonson is the legitimate heir of Marlowe. The man who wrote, in *Volpone*:

> for thy love,
> In varying figures, I would have contended
> With the blue Proteus, or the hornèd flood. . . .

and

> See, a carbuncle
> May put out both the eyes of our Saint Mark;
> A diamond would have bought Lollia Paulina,
> When she came in like star-light, hid with jewels. . . .

is related to Marlowe as a poet; and if Marlowe is a poet, Jonson is also. And, if Jonson's comedy is a comedy of humours, then Marlowe's tragedy, a large part of it, is a tragedy of humours. But Jonson has too exclusively been considered as the typical representative of a point of view toward comedy. He has suffered from his great reputation as a critic and theorist, from the effects of his intelligence. We have been taught to think of him as the man, the dictator (confusedly in our mind with his later namesake), as the literary politician impressing his views upon a generation; we are offended by the constant reminder of his scholarship. We forget the comedy in the humours, and the serious artist in the scholar. Jonson has suffered in public opinion, as anyone must suffer who is forced to talk about his art.

If you examine the first hundred lines or more of *Volpone* the verse appears to be in the manner of Marlowe, more deliberate, more mature, but without Marlowe's inspiration. It looks like mere 'rhetoric', certainly not 'deeds and language such as men do use'. It appears to us, in fact, forced and flagitious bombast. That it is not 'rhetoric', or at least not vicious rhetoric, we do not know until we are able to review the whole play. For the consistent maintenance of this manner conveys in the end an effect not of verbosity, but of bold, even shocking and terrifying directness. We have difficulty in saying exactly what produces this simple and single effect. It is not in any ordinary way due to management of intrigue. Jonson employs immense dramatic constructive skill: it is not so much skill in plot as skill in doing without a plot. He never manipulates as complicated a plot as that of *The Merchant of Venice*; he has in his best plays nothing like the intrigue of Restoration comedy. In *Bartholomew Fair* it is hardly a plot at all; the marvel of the play is the bewildering rapid chaotic action of the fair; it is the fair itself, not anything that happens in the fair. In *Volpone*, or *The Alchemist*, or *The Silent Woman*, the plot is enough to keep the players in motion; it is rather an 'action' than a plot. The plot does not hold the play together; what holds the play together is a unity of inspiration that radiates into plot and personages alike.

We have attempted to make more precise the sense in which it was said that Jonson's work is 'of the surface'; carefully avoiding the word 'superficial'. For there is work contemporary with Jonson's which is superficial in a pejorative sense in which the word cannot be applied to Jonson – the work of Beaumont and Fletcher. If we look at the work of Jonson's great contemporaries, Shakespeare, and also Donne and Webster and Tourneur (and sometimes Middleton), have a depth, a third dimension, as Mr Gregory Smith rightly calls it, which Jonson's work has not. Their words have often a network of tentacular roots reaching down to the deepest terrors and desires. Jonson's most certainly have not; but in Beaumont and Fletcher we may think that at times we find it. Looking closer, we discover that the blossoms of Beaumont and Fletcher's imagination draw no sustenance from the soil, but are cut and slightly withered flowers stuck into sand.

> Wilt thou, hereafter, when they talk of me,
> As thou shalt hear nothing but infamy,
> Remember some of these things? . . .
> I pray thee, do; for thou shalt never see me so again.

> Hair woven in many a curious warp,
> Able in endless error to enfold
> The wandering soul; . . .

Detached from its context, this looks like the verse of the greater poets; just as lines of Jonson, detached from their context, look like inflated or empty fustian. But the evocative quality of the verse of Beaumont and Fletcher depends upon a clever appeal to emotions and associations which they have not themselves grasped; it is hollow. It is superficial with a vacuum behind it; the superficies of Jonson is solid. It is what it is; it does not pretend to be another thing. But it is so very conscious and deliberate that we must look with eyes alert to the whole before we apprehend the significance of any part. We cannot call a man's work superficial when it is the creation of a world; a man cannot be accused of dealing superficially with the world which he himself has created; the superficies *is* the world. Jonson's characters conform to the logic of the emotions of their world. They are not fancy, because they have a logic of their own; and this logic illuminates the actual world, because it gives us a new point of view from which to inspect it.

A writer of power and intelligence, Jonson endeavoured to promulgate as a formula and programme of reform, what he chose to do himself; and he not unnaturally laid down in abstract theory what is in reality a personal point of view. And it is in the end of no value to discuss Jonson's theory and practice unless we recognize and seize this point of view, which escapes the formulæ, and which is what makes his plays worth reading. Jonson behaved as the great creative mind that he was: he created his own world, a world from which his followers, as well as the dramatists who were trying to do something wholly different, are excluded. Remembering this, we turn to Mr Gregory Smith's objection – that Jonson's characters lack the third dimension, have no life out of the theatrical existence in which they appear – and demand an inquest. The objection implies that the characters are purely the work of intellect, or the result of superficial observation of a world which is faded or mildewed. It implies that the characters are lifeless. But if we dig beneath the theory, beneath the observation, beneath the deliberate drawing and the theatrical and dramatic elaboration, there is discovered a kind of power, animating Volpone, Busy, Fitzdottrel, the literary ladies of *Epicœne*, even Bobadil, which comes from below the intellect, and for which no theory of humours will account. And it is the same kind of power which vivifies Trimalchio, and Panurge, and some but not all of the 'comic' characters of Dickens. The fictive life of this kind is not to be circumscribed by a reference to 'comedy' or to 'farce'; it is not exactly the kind of life which informs the characters of Molière or that which informs those of Marivaux – two writers who were, besides, doing something quite different the one from the other. But it is something which distinguishes Barabas from Shylock, Epicure Mammon from Falstaff, Faustus from – if you will – Macbeth; Marlowe and Jonson from Shakespeare and the Shakespearians, Webster, and Tourneur. It is not merely Humours: for neither Volpone nor Mosca is a humour. No theory of humours could account for Jonson's best plays or the best characters in them. We want to know at what point the comedy of humours passes into a work of art, and why Jonson is not Brome.

The creation of a work of art, we will say the creation of a character in a drama, consists in the process of transfusion of the personality, or, in a deeper sense, the life, of the author into the character. This is a very different matter from the orthodox creation in one's own image. The ways in which the passions and desires of the creator may be satisfied in the work of art are complex and devious. In a painter they may take the form of a predilection for certain colours, tones, or lightings; in a writer the original impulse may be even more strangely transmuted. Now, we may say with Mr Gregory Smith that Falstaff or a score of Shakespeare's characters have a 'third dimension' that Jonson's have not. This will mean, not that Shakespeare's spring from the feelings or imagination and Jonson's from the intellect or invention; they have equally an emotional source; but that Shakespeare's represent a more complex tissue of feelings and desires, as well as a more supple, a more susceptible temperament. Falstaff is not only the roast Manningtree ox with the pudding in his belly; he also 'grows old', and, finally, his nose is as sharp as a pen. He was perhaps the *satisfaction* of more, and of more complicated feelings; and perhaps he was, as the great tragic characters must have been, the offspring of deeper, less apprehensible feelings: deeper, but not necessarily stronger or more intense, than those of Jonson. It is obvious that the spring of the difference is not the difference between feeling and thought, or superior insight, superior perception, on the part of Shakespeare, but his susceptibility to a greater range of emotion, and emotion deeper and more obscure. But his characters are no more 'alive' than are the characters of Jonson.

The world they live in is a larger one. But small worlds – the worlds which artists create – do not differ only in magnitude; if they are complete worlds, drawn to scale in every part, they differ in kind also. And Jonson's world has this scale. His type of personality found its relief in something falling under the category of burlesque or farce – though when you are dealing with a *unique* world, like his, these terms fail to appease the desire for definition. It is not, at all events, the farce of Molière: the latter is more analytic, more an intellectual redistribution. It is not defined by the word 'satire'. Jonson poses as a satirist. But satire like Jonson's is great in the end not by hitting off its object, but by creating it; the satire is merely the means which leads to the æsthetic result, the impulse which projects a new world into a new orbit. In *Every Man in his Humour* there is a neat, a very neat, comedy of humours. In discovering and proclaiming in this play the new genre Jonson was simply recognizing, unconsciously, the route which opened out in the proper direction for his instincts. His characters are and remain, like Marlowe's, simplified characters; but the simplification does not consist in the dominance of a particular humour or monomania. That is a very superficial account of it. The simplification consists largely in reduction of detail, in the seizing of aspects relevant to the relief of an emotional impulse which remains the same for that character, in making the character conform to a particular setting. This stripping is essential to the art, to which is also essential a flat distortion in the drawing; it is an art of caricature, of great caricature, like Marlowe's. It is a great caricature, which is beautiful; and a great humour, which is serious. The 'world' of Jonson is sufficiently large; it is a world of poetic imagination; it is sombre. He did not get the third dimension, but he was not trying to get it.

If we approach Jonson with less frozen awe of his learning, with a clearer understanding of his 'rhetoric' and its applications, if we grasp the fact that the knowledge required of the reader is not archæology but knowledge of Jonson, we can derive not only instruction in two-dimensional life – but enjoyment. We can even apply him, be aware of him as a part of our literary inheritance craving further expression. Of all the dramatists of his time, Jonson is probably the one whom the present age would find the most sympathetic, if it knew him. There is a brutality, a lack of sentiment, a polished surface, a handling of large bold designs in brilliant colours, which ought to attract about three thousand people in London and elsewhere. At least, if we had a contemporary Shakespeare and a contemporary Jonson, it might be the Jonson who would arouse the enthusiasm of the intelligentsia. Though he is saturated in literature, he never sacrifices the theatrical qualities – theatrical in the most favourable sense – to literature or to the study of character. His work is a titanic show. Jonson's masques, an important part of his work, are neglected; our flaccid culture lets shows and literature fade, but prefers faded literature to faded shows. There are hundreds of people who have read *Comus* to ten who have read the *Masque of Blackness*. *Comus* contains fine poetry, and poetry exemplifying some merits to which Jonson's masque poetry cannot pretend. Nevertheless, *Comus* is the death of the masque; it is the transition of a form of art – even of a form which existed for but a short generation – into 'literature,' literature cast in a form which has lost its application. Even though *Comus* was a masque at Ludlow Castle, Jonson had, what Milton came perhaps too late to have, a sense for the living art; his art was applied. The masques can still be read, and with pleasure, by anyone who will take the trouble – a trouble which in this part of Jonson is, indeed, a study of antiquities – to imagine them in action, displayed with the music, costumes, dances, and the scenery of Inigo Jones. They are additional evidence that Jonson had a fine sense of form, of the purpose for which a particular form is intended; evidence that he was a literary artist even more than he was a man of letters.

SOURCE: 'Ben Jonson' (1919); reprinted in T. S. Eliot, *Selected Essays* (London, 1932; 3rd edition 1951), pp. 147–60.

Harley Granville–Barker 'Producer's Problems': *Love's Labour's Lost* (1930)

Here is a fashionable play; now, by three hundred years, out of fashion. Nor did it ever, one supposes, make a very wide appeal. It abounds in jokes for the elect. Were you not numbered among them you laughed, for safety, in the likeliest places. A year or two later the elect themselves might be hard put to it to remember what the joke was.

Were this all one could say of *Love's Labour Lost*, the question of its staging today – with which we are first and last concerned – would be quickly answered, and Lose No Labour here would be the soundest advice. For spontaneous enjoyment is the life of the theatre. If a performance must be accompanied by a lecture – (if, for example, when Holofernes is at the point of 'Bone, bone for benè; Priscian a little scratched. 'Twill serve',—we need his modern exemplar in cap and gown, standing on one side of the proscenium, to interrupt with 'One moment, please! The allusion here, if you wish to appreciate its humour, is to . . .'; or if he must warn us, 'In the next scene, ladies and gentlemen, you will notice a reference to the charge-house on the top of the mountain. This is thought by the best authorities to denote . . .'), not much fun will survive. For a glossary in the programme something might be said, even for a preliminary lecture. No; this last, one fears, would leave the actors with too hard a task turning classroom back to theatre. Half-digested information lies a little heavily on one's sense of humour.

It is true that with no play three hundred years old can we press our

'spontaneous' too hard. For the full appreciation of anything in
Shakespeare some knowledge is asked of its why and wherefore. Hamlet
and Falstaff, however, Rosalind and Imogen, are compact of qualities
which fashion cannot change; the barriers of dramatic convention,
strange habits, tricks of speech are of small enough account with them.
But what is back of these word-gymnastics of Rosaline and Berowne,
Holofernes' jargon, Armado's antics? The play is a satire, a comedy of
affectations. The gymnastics, the jargon and the antics are the fun. Yet
a play hardly lives by such brilliancies alone. While the humour of them
is fresh and holds our attention, actors may lend it a semblance of life;
for there at least *they* are, alive in their kind! No play, certainly, can
count on survival if it strikes no deeper root nor bears more perennial
flowers. If its topical brilliance were all, Shakespeare's name tagged to
this one would keep it a place on the scholar's dissecting table; in the
theatre *Love's Labour's Lost* would be dead, past all question. But there is
life in it. The satire beside, Shakespeare the poet had his fling. It
abounds in beauties of fancy and phrase, as beautiful today as ever. We
find in it Shakespeare the dramatist learning his art. To students the
most interesting thing about the play is the evidence of this; of the trial
and error, his discovery of fruitful soil and fruitless. The producer,
pledged to present an audience with a complete something, cannot, of
course, be content with promise and experiment. Measuring this early
Shakespeare by the later, we may as well own there is not much more.
But the root of the matter is already in him; he is the dramatist born, and
all, or nearly all, is at least instinct with dramatic life. It is oftenest his
calculations and his cleverness that betray him.

   For satire and no more is too apt to prove dramatically fruitless. A
play's values are human values, and a playwright's first task is to give his
creatures being. Imaginative love for them may help him to; even hate
may; but a mocking detachment cannot. If he is to shoot at their follies
he must yet build up the target first; and if it is not a convincing one
there will be little credit in the shooting. He cannot, of course, in a play,
take direct aim himself, unless he use the method of the Moralities or its
like. There is the less direct method of twisting a set of familiar heroic
figures awry. Shakespeare made this experiment, not too successfully, in
Troilus and Cressida. But his obvious plan will be to turn one or more of
his creatures satirists themselves, and under their cover plant his own
shafts. Even so, he must give the victims their chance, or the play will be
lopsided and come tumbling down.

   The Shakespeare who sets out to write *Love's Labour's Lost* is a very
clever young man, a wit, a sonneteer. He is 'in the movement'. He
flatters his admirers by excelling in the things they admire; he will flatter

his rivals hardly less by this attention he means to pay them. But your clever young man is usually more than a little impressed by the things he mocks at; he mocks at them in self-defence, it may be, lest they impress him too much. Mockery is apt, indeed, to capitulate to the thing mocked, to be absorbed by it. And these academic follies of Navarre, the fantastic folly of Armado, the pedantic folly of schoolmaster and parson – sometimes the satire is so fine that the folly seems the clever young man's own. Yet this weakness of the would-be satirist is the budding dramatist's strength. Shakespeare cannot resist his creatures; he never quite learned to. He cannot make mere targets of them. He cannot resist his own genius, poetic or dramatic; all through the play we find the leaven of it working.

He has not written ten lines before the poet in him breaks bounds. Is this the voice of the frigid wiseacre Navarre; does this suggest the 'little academe'?

> Therefore, brave conquerors – for so you are,
> That war against your own affections
> And the huge army of the world's desires.

But the clever young man recollects himself; and here, soon enough, is the sort of thing he has set out to write.

KING	How well he's read, to reason against reading!
DUMAIN	Proceeded well, to stop all good proceeding!
LONGAVILLE	He weeds the corn, and still lets grow the weeding.
BEROWNE	The spring is near, when green geese are a-breeding.
DUMAIN	How follows that?
BEROWNE	Fit in his place and time.
DUMAIN	In reason nothing.
BEROWNE	Something then in rhyme.

Pretty tricksy stuff! Well enough done to show that he quite enjoyed doing it, but the sort of thing that almost anyone could learn to do. No signpost on the road to *Hamlet*, certainly.

But mark the dramatist in his provision at the outset of the conflict and balance that every play needs, in the setting of Berowne against his companions, one man's common sense against the crowding affectations (a sporting conflict), an ounce of reality for counterweight to a ton of shams (an instructive balance). Here also, for the moralist-critic, is the play's moral issue defined at the outset; but let us not suppose Shakespeare to have been oppressed by this. Despite his present-day idolaters he was probably not high-purposed from his cradle; moreover, he is likely to have gained most of his knowledge of life by writing plays about it. That is not a provocative paradox, but a key to the mind and method of the artist. Time and again Shakespeare tells us that he sees the world as a stage. He would not think that a belittling comparison; he takes his art too seriously. Not portentously, but as simply seriously as any man will take his purpose in life when he is lucky enough to be sure of it. We all need some centre of experience to argue from, if the world beyond our experience is to have any meaning for us. The artist transforms and multiplies experience by imagination, and may even come to think that what is true of his art will be true of the world it mirrors. This sounds absurd. But life does seem to be governed by surprisingly simple laws; and human beings, wherever and whatever they may be, do not greatly differ in essentials. That is the working hypothesis upon which art and religion, with imaginative genius to vitalise them, proceed. And let it be said of the theatre that a very short time in it will teach one how little fine clothes and fine manners may amount to. The theatre was for Shakespeare a laboratory where he worked – if but in a mimic sense – with human material. His method, his means to enlightenment, was to take a story and put the worth of it, its truth to nature, to the test of personal expression. The story might suffer; if it was not true to nature, it generally would. But Shakespeare was, on the whole, a most unconscientious story-teller, except when history bound him. Sometimes he would make a sacrifice to symmetry, as when, in *Measure for Measure*, he marries Isabella to the Duke; but he may have felt this to be poetic justice upon such a morally consistent lady. The story may be burked, neglected or finished off anyhow, as in *Much Ado About Nothing, Twelfth Night* and *As You Like It*. It may hang at the heels of the chief character, as in *Hamlet*. What men are, in fact, comes to conern him far more than what they do. Already in this pretty play of *Love's Labour's Lost* it instinctively concerns him, though not even doing but mere clever talk is his ostensible concern. And when he passes to the giant theme of *King Lear*, to the sweep of historic vision that is in *Antony and Cleopatra*, stretching his medium of expression till it seems to crack and break, he concerns himself, even then, with little which cannot be rendered into human passion, human pity – which cannot, in fact, be put to this laboratory test. He – literally – has no use for theories and abstract ideas. He is neither philosopher nor moralist, except as he must seem to be making his creatures one or the other. He is a playwright; he projects character in action, and with the truth of the one to the other his power and responsibility end. If this is the playwright's limitation, it is also his strength; for to this test of human response – not mimic, truly, but real; yet the mimic but reflects the real – all philosophy and morality must finally be put.

In this earliest essay, then, we may divine the dramatist to be; and we find dramatist putting wit and poet to the proof, Shakespeare will have set out to do his best by his creatures one and all; but while Berowne grows under his hand into a figure, finally, of some dramatic stature, while the Princess, simple, straightforward, shrewd, is made flesh and blood, in the speaking of seven lines, Navarre, though a natural focus of attention and discussing himself unsparingly, remains a bundle of phrases, and Dumain and Longaville have about the substance of echoes. Of the humbler folk; Costard for three-quarters of the play is the stage Fool, but suddenly, when he comes to the acting of his Worthy, we have:

COSTARD   I Pompey am, Pompey surnam'd the Big –
DUMAIN   The Great.
COSTARD   It is 'Great', Sir; Pompey surnam'd the Great;
           That oft in field, with targe and shield, did make my foe to sweat;
           And travelling along this coast, I here am come by chance,
           And lay my arms before the legs of this sweet lass of France.
           If your ladyship would say, 'Thanks, Pompey,' I had done.
PRINCESS   Great thanks, great Pompey.
COSTARD   'Tis not so much worth; but I hope I was perfect: I made a little
           fault in 'Great'.

And these two last lines have, mysteriously and unexpectedly, given us the man beneath the jester. Then, with another thirty words or so, Costard (and Costard's creator) settles Sir Nathaniel the Curate, till now little but a figure of fun, snugly in our affections.

There, an't shall please you; a foolish mild man; an honest man, look you, and soon dashed! He is a marvellous good neighbour, in sooth; and a very good bowler: but, for Alisander, – alas, you see how 'tis; – a little o'erparted.

And settles himself there yet more snugly in the doing it! Throughout the play, but especially towards the end, we find such outcroppings of pure dramatic gold.

Drama, as Shakespeare will come to write it, is, first and last, the projection of character in action; and devices for doing this, simple and complex, must make up three-quarters of its artistry. We can watch his early discovery that dialogue is waste matter unless it works to this end; that wit, epigram, sentiment are like paper and sticks in a fireplace, the flaring and crackling counting for nothing if the fire itself won't light, if these creatures in whose mouths the wit is sounded won't 'come alive'. To the last he kept his youthful delight in a pun; and he would write an occasional passage of word-music with a minimum of meaning to it (but of maximum emotional value, it will be found, to the character that has to speak it). His development of verse to dramatic use is a study in itself. He never ceased to develop it, but for a while the dramatist had a hard time with the lyric poet. The early plays abound, besides, in elaborate embroidery of language done for its own sake. This was a fashionable literary exercise and Shakespeare was an adept at it. To many young poets of the time their language was a new-found wonder; its very handling gave them pleasure. The amazing things it could be made to do! He had to discover that they were not much to his purpose; but it is not easy to stop doing what you do so well. Yet even in this play we may note the difference between the Berowne of

> Light seeking light doth light of light beguile;
> So ere you find where light in darkness lies
> Your light grows dark by losing of your eyes!

and of the soliloquy beginning

> And I forsooth in love . . .[1]

Turn also from one of the many sets of wit to Katharine's haunting answer when Rosaline twits her with rebellion against Cupid:

ROSALINE You'll ne'er be friends with him: he kill'd your sister.
KATHERINE He made her melancholy, sad, and heavy;
> And so she died: had she been light, like you,
> Of such a merry, nimble, stirring spirit,
> She might have been a grandam ere she died;
> And so may you, for a light heart lives long.

Compare it with the set of wit that follows:

ROSALINE What's your dark meaning, mouse, of this light word?
KATHERINE A light condition in a beauty dark.
ROSALINE We need more light to find your meaning out.

> KATHERINE   You'll mar the light, by taking it in snuff;
> Therefore I'll darkly end the argument.

But Rosaline won't let her, and they manage to get five more rather spicer exchanges. It is all very charming; the mere sound is charming, and a 'set of wit' describes it well. Get a knowledge of the game and it may be as attractive to watch for a little as are a few sets of tennis. But pages on pages of such smart repartee will not tell us as much of the speakers as those few simple lines of Katharine's tell us – of herself and her love of her sister, and of Rosaline too.

The play sets out, as we said, to be a flattering satire upon such humours, and the playwright must set up before he pulls down, break before he satirises; and the two processes do, doubtless, get mixed. Can we detect a Shakespeare impatient, for a moment, with his pleasant task? He has punned and joked his best.

> BEROWNE   White-handed mistress, one sweet word with thee.
> PRINCESS   Honey, and milk and sugar; there is three.
> BEROWNE   Nay then, two treys, and if you grow so nice,
> Metheglin, wort and malmsey: – well run, dice!

Nor will he neglect the ever-satisfying humours of cuckoldry.

> KATHERINE   Veal, quoth the Dutchman: – is not veal a calf?
> LONGAVILLE   A calf, fair lady?
> KATHERINE   No, a fair lord calf.
> LONGAVILLE   Let's part the word.
> KATHERINE   No, I'll not be your half;
> Take all and wean it; it may prove an ox.
> LONGAVILLE   Look, how you butt yourself in these sharp mocks!
> Will you give horns, chaste lady? do not so.
> KATHERINE   Then die a calf, before your horns do grow.

It amused him, no doubt, as it amused his audience; it is just too well done to have been done mechanically. But when, of a sudden, the Princess breaks out with

> Are these the breed of wits so wondered at?

may we not hear for the moment his voice sounding through hers? For it is a barren business finally, and his fecund spirit could not long be subdued to it. With but little violence we could twist the play into a parable of his own dramatic progress. Even as Berowne at its end forswears

> Taffeta phrases, silken terms precise,
> Three-piled hyperboles, spruce affectation,
> Figures pedantical . . .

so might Shakespeare be swearing to pass from them himself on towards the prose of *As You Like It* and the strong verse of *Julius Caesar*. A notion not to be taken too seriously, perhaps. But a few years hence he is to let Hamlet record a taste for plays set down with as much modesty as cunning, with

> no sallets in the lines to make the matter savoury, nor no matter in the phrase that might indict the author of affectation; but . . . an honest method, as wholesome as a sweet and by very much more handsome than fine.

And certainly there are signs that, whether he knew it or not, the leaven was already working beneath this bright wit, this delight in words and their rhythm and melody, that was soon to turn a pretty speechifying Mercutio into the stark man of

> A plague of both your houses! They have made worms' meat of me: I have it,
> And soundly too. . . .

and the word-spinning Romeo into that doomed figure of

> It is even so? Then I defy you, stars!

The dramatist was in the making who was to fashion a Falstaff out of the old pickpurse of Gadshill, who was to pitch on the preposterous tale of *The Merchant of Venice*, and charge it (triumphantly, yet all but disastrously) with the passion of Shylock.[2]

But the producer must consider carefully just what the carrying-power of this embryonic drama is, and how he can effectively interpret to a modern audience the larger rest of the play. What life can his actors give to this fribble of talk and nice fantasy of behaviour? As satire it means nothing to us now. Where, then, are the prototypes of these cavaliers and ladies – of Armado and Holofernes, Moth and Nathaniel the Curate? We can at best cultivate an historical sense of them. There remains the verse, and the pretty moving picture of the action. Our spontaneous enjoyment will hang upon pleasant sounds and sights alone, sense and purpose apart. Really, it almost amounts to this! Better

face the difficulty at its worst. Is there any surmounting it? . . . [This
final question – a rhetorical one – gets its answer in the next section,
'The Method of the Acting', of the original essay – Ed.]

SOURCE: extract from the Preface for *Love's Labour's Lost* in *Prefaces to
Shakespeare*, second series (London, 1930), pp. 1–10.

NOTES

1. This soliloquy, says Dr Dover Wilson, belongs to the play's revising. But
this does not invalidate my point; rather the contrary.
2. He pitched, we may say, upon two preposterous tales, and redeemed the
second by the romantic beauty of Portia.

M. C. Bradbrook 'Characterisation in Shakespeare' (1932)

. . . Shakespeare's characters are not only the personal friends of
nineteenth-century critics; they offer them dramatic scope. Coleridge
made Hamlet in his own image and most of the lesser criticism involved
no more than mental productions of the play, the critic outdoing even
the Elizabethan actor by doubling all the parts. This shows how far
removed from the stage the plays had become, when each person's
private acting version was offered as a serious commentary.

It was only a step farther to put Shakespeare behind his puppets, and
to arrive at the Frank Harris method of interpretation. This has a
certain limiting effect, since Shakespeare's dramatic capabilities are
confined to the rôle of the hero. (Though I do not see why he should not
play a very effective Desdemona. Her adjective 'gentle' is notoriously
his: the Moor would be an easy avatar for the Dark Lady and Iago
would probably be a separate dramatisation of her baser self, ruining
her own better nature (Othello) and Mr W. H. (Cassio), the fair man
who had 'goneawooing' for his friend. W. H.'s relations with Desdemona (Shakespeare) are blackened, and his early platonic relationship with herself is likewise shattered.)

The personal interpretation has never been taken very seriously; but
the treatment of the characters as living beings died hard. Bradley's
Shakespearean Tragedy, with its appendices on Lady Macbeth's children

and similar subjects, was the brilliant *reductio ad absurdum* of the system; but such was its influence that for some years it prevented the percolation of the researches on stage conditions into appreciative criticism. Even studies of the dramatist, such as that of Brander Matthews, are thinly disguised gossip about the private lives of the dramatis personae; Helen of Narbon is still reproved for her conversation on virginity, 'impossible to a modest minded girl'.[1] The individual studies of *Hamlet* and *Othello* by Stoll, and Schücking's *Die Charakterprobleme bei Shakespeare*, were the first serious attacks upon orthodoxy.

Shakespeare was found to fall short in two respects of realistic treatment of his characters. He made them behave inconsistently, and motivated them inadequately. Sometimes he merely neglected to supply a motive; the critics were ready enough to do this for him, but they could not always fit it to the text. Coleridge, for instance, would have inserted a clause in the Oracle's message in *The Winter's Tale*, which, by obliging Hermione to live concealed until Perdita was found, would have relieved her from a possible charge of hard-heartedness.

But Shakespeare also neglected motivation when it was already supplied in his sources. King Leir had a perfectly watertight reason for his demand for a public declaration of affection. Isabella's original had a reason for begging the life of the wicked deputy. As it is there is not a single play of Shakespeare's where the motivation of every character is quite sufficient, except in those comedies where he assumes arbitrary conventions of love at first sight, sudden repentance, and miraculous coincidence. The most glaring example of his indifference to motivation is Coriolanus, whose change of party in the middle of the play (the event upon which the catastrophe directly depends) is absolutely unprepared and unexplained. Antonio, in *The Merchant of Venice*, is a less intractable person, but only to be explained by 'sentiments not avowed'.

Inadequate motivation may pass over into inconsistency. Leontes might be described by either label. The simplest cases of inconsistency occur when a character makes a speech 'out of character', such as Prince Hal's opening soliloquy – 'I know you all'. A single speech may be 'out of character' in a different way, however, by its manner as well as its matter. Mercutio on Queen Mab or Polonius' advice to Laertes are the usual examples of this. They are irrelevant and unsuitable, but not unnatural; they have the detachable quality of an operatic aria.

There are two parallel types of inconsistency in action. The behaviour of Isabella in *Measure for Measure*, of Claudio in *Much Ado*, simply contradicts their professions and their friends' views of them, as Hal's speech does. Henry v is turned into a country bumpkin in the final scene of the play, to give his wooing the right note of heartiness and democratic sentimentality, though hitherto he had been an adroit and polished diplomat. But the behaviour of Posthumus or Othello is contradictory in a different way. The Othello of the first act is no more than a magnificent study in poise, judgement and *savoir faire*. 'Put up your bright swords, for the dew will rust them!' It is impossible logically that he should ever become horn-mad: neither predisposition to jealousy, racial differences, nor the 'devilish' skill of Iago is adequate to explain his taking the word of a subordinate against his wife and his best friend.[2] He is as unjustified as Posthumus, for whom 'weakling' is the usual epithet, or as Imogen (who is deceived more easily than either of them, but who is always justified: it is amusing to see Granville-Barker gobbling up all the bait of excuses and evasions which Shakespeare has laid down about this passage).

Also, there are certain characters who seem altogether inconsistent: Hamlet, Falstaff, Cleopatra. Like the sacred griffin in the *Purgatorio* they seem to have two natures, and we can see them reflected in Shakespeare 'or con uni, or con altri reggimenti'. This 'inconsistency' is precisely the cause of their greatness; but it has puzzled the critics, and, unwilling to bear the ills they have, they have flown to others. . . .

Source: extract from the chapter 'The Question of Characterisation' in *Elizabethan Stage Conditions* (London, 1932), pp. 82–7.

NOTES

1. Brander Matthews, *Shakespeare the Dramatist.*
2. Stoll has treated this question at great length.

G. Wilson Knight   'The Ideal Production' – *The Merchant of Venice* (1936)

. . . For any extrinsic aids and decorations we invent, there is one essential condition: they must point and be pointed by the significant action of the drama itself and must lend themselves to human and naturalistic touches in the acting. The setting must be *interwoven* with the performance: it is not enough . . . to devise an elaborate artistic background, however suitable, running all the time a parallel and rival appeal to the eye. All additions must interlock with both the poetry and the action. I now outline some rough suggestions for the ideal production of *The Merchant of Venice*. . . .

The meaning of *The Merchant of Venice* is never sufficiently brought out. We must take the play seriously. Its deeper significances do not correspond at every point with a surface realism as they do in *Macbeth*, but for this very reason we must take care to bring the inherent meaning out as harmoniously and as naturally, yet powerfully, as we can.

The play, as I have shown in *The Shakespearian Tempest*, presents two contrasted worlds: Venice and Belmont. The one is a world of business competition, usury, melancholy, and tragic sea-disaster; the other, a spelled land of riches, music and romance. Many of our Venetian scenes are comparatively jovial; but Gratiano is scarcely a pleasant man. Venice has romantic associations, but here they are darkly toned. The supposedly pleasant people are not all that they might be. Antonio is cruel to Shylock, Bassanio a spendthrift, Gratiano vulgar, and honesty certainly not the strongest point of Lorenzo and Jessica. Shylock towers over the rest, grand but scarcely amiable. The tragedy depends on sea-wreck, tempests and such like, Shakespeare's usual tragedy associations. At Belmont all is changed. The people become noble as soon as they arrive there: Bassanio is the loyal friend, Lorenzo the perfect lover, Gratiano comparatively subdued. The name 'Belmont' suggests a height overlooking the water-logged world of Venetian rivalry and pettiness. At Belmont we have music: at Venice, none. The projected Masque does not, so far as our persons are concerned, come off after all (II vi 64), but it serves for Shylock's line about the 'vile squealing of the wry-neck'd fife' (II v 30), which might be compared with his even less pretty 'bagpipe' reference later. Certainly, Venice is not here a place of romantic music. Belmont is. The Belmont world is dominated by Portia, expressly Christian as against Shylock, her only rival in dramatic importance, and of infinite wealth as against the penurious Bassanio and thieving Lorenzo. Everyone in Venice is in money difficulties of some sort, even the rich ones. Antonio's fortune is all at sea. Shylock has to borrow from Tubal, loses a great part of his wealth with his daughter, and bemoans his lost ducats in the street. But Portia is infinitely rich. Her riches hold dramatically a spiritual quality.

Our permanent set must help to mark out these contrasted worlds. I suggest dividing the stage into two levels, the rise making a straight diagonal from up L to down R. The higher level is thus mainly on stage right. Half-way along this diagonal steps can be used to lead from one level to the other. Venetian scenes will concentrate on the lower,

Belmont on the higher, level. I do not mean that no Venetian in Venice should ascend the higher: merely that the Venetian action should focus on the lower with a force proportional to the particular significance. Certainly in the Belmont scenes the lower space must never be quite empty, which would tend to rob the figures above of any dignity their raised position gives them. We can arrange a background that gives a wide and variable range of tones according to the lights. For the casket scenes the suitors enter down R or down L and ascend the steps ceremoniously. Nothing must seem too rigid. Portia, standing aside during Bassanio's meditations, would probably come down L on the lower level and afterwards meet him as he descends the steps, an action that suits the submissive femininity of her speech and his victorious choice.

The three caskets will be large and solid-looking, and must be allowed to dominate. They are symbolically central. At the heart of this play is the idea of riches, of false and true wealth. Jesus's parables are suggested. Venice is lost in the varied complexities of the false; Portia possesses the true. Love and beauty are regularly in Shakespeare compared to riches; Portia is vitally associated with Christianity; and she is an heiress with an infinite bank-balance. In this play of greed her serene disregard of exact sums is supernal:

> PORTIA   What sum owes he the Jew?
> BASSANIO For me, three thousand ducats.
> PORTIA   What, no more?
>   Pay him six thousand, and deface the bond;
>   Double six thousand, and then treble that . . .

He shall have gold 'to pay the petty debt twenty times over'.

Portia's office in the play is to demonstrate the futility of business and legal exactitudes. The action drives home the truth that money is only an aspect of life, and that life itself must come before money and the laws of money.[1] The contrast is pointed by a man giving a pound of flesh as security. Everyone wants to save his life, but there seems no loophole. His life is now subject to laws made only for money. Observe how Portia deals with the absurd situation. She dispels the clouding precisions and intellectualities of the law court by a serene common-sense, not unlike the common-sense of Jesus. Her 'mercy' speech exactly reflects His teaching. The white beam of her intuition shows, as genius has a way of showing, as Jesus' teaching so often shows, that the academic intelligence is vulnerable to its own weapons. Shylock's worst danger is to be allowed the rights he fights for:

> The words expressly are 'a pound of flesh':
> Then take thy bond; take thou thy pound of flesh;
> But, in the cutting it, if thou dost shed
> One drop of Christian blood . . .

This is what comes of not distinguishing between the counters of finance and the bread and wine, the silver flesh and golden blood, of life itself. The serene wisdom of life works by refusing validity to false abstractions. We may cut money into bits, but not life; there any piece involves the whole. Such are the lines of Portia's poetic and holistic reasoning. As soon as we begin to think in such poetic and holistic terms there are certain supposed exactitudes that lose all meaning: so next Portia supports her first argument by insisting that Shylock shall take exactly a pound of flesh, neither less nor more. His whole position crumbles.

At Belmont Portia's caskets of gold, silver and lead, containing respectively death, folly, and infinite love and wealth, must be solid and dominating.

Venice and Belmont alternate. The play works up to the climax of the Trial scene, where the protagonists of the two worlds, Portia and Shylock, meet for the first time. Portia descends from Belmont almost as a divine being: her office is that of a *dea ex machina*. Morocco has compared her to a 'shrine' and called her a 'mortal-breathing saint' (II vii 40), and her wooers will have faced her as she stands above them on the steps, as pilgrims before a sanctuary. For the Trial I would have the court sitting on the high level R, some using the level itself for a seat. The Duke's chair will be half-way along. Bassanio and Antonio are down R; Shylock moves between up L, L, and C. Some spectators can edge in down L and Gratiano stand L between them and Shylock, coming forward for his big speeches.

Portia enters down R, circles up-stage to the steps, and ascends the higher level, standing beside the Duke. Her doctor's gown is better neither black nor red. Her doctorate is one of Christian wisdom and feminine intuition. Let her therefore wear a correctly cut doctor-of-laws gown of spotless white, making a blend of realism and symbolic meaning suiting the nature of Shakespearian drama. She stands high and central dominating the whole court. The light should be intensified on her gown and golden hair just showing under her cap as she speaks her Mercy speech. As the situation ripens, she descends, the movement using our levels to capture the essence of her arrival in Venice to render assistance, her *descent* from the happier world of her home. She comes nearly, but not quite, down at: 'I pray you, let me look upon the bond'. Shylock gives it her. She warns him: 'Shylock, there's thrice thy money offer'd thee'. She is kind, is meeting these people on their own terms, descending to their level. But Shylock will have none of it. She tries again. He returns to his corner, talking to Tubal, adamant. Portia, on the steps, begins to prepare judgement. She asks for balances and a surgeon, and addresses Antonio. Antonio says his farewell. Now, swaying slightly, she pronounces judgement, the speed gathers as the whirl of her repetition gains force, the whirl of a lasso:

> The court awards it and the law doth give it,

and

> The law allows it and the court awards it.

Shylock in ecstasy of hatred cries 'A sentence! Come, prepare!' Unleashed, he springs down-stage. Bassanio shields Antonio. The Duke stands. The crowds murmur. But at this instant Portia takes the last step down to the lower level and cuts off Shylock's attack with a raised hand. 'Tarry a little.' There is silence. In a quiet voice she continues:

> . . . there is something else.
> This bond doth give thee here no jot of blood . . .

The terrifying judgement of a fathomless simplicity and a divine common-sense.

It is an amazing scene, its impact deriving from the clash of the two dominating forces in the play, Shylock and Portia, and all that they stand for. Our set of two levels and Portia's descent will assist; so will her white gown and her barring of Shylock's attack at the crucial moment, which must be given expressive action. We must work from the profound issues implicit in the dramatic thrill if it is to have full power. Portia's standing on the same steps where previously we have seen her meet her suitors, with the caskets behind, priestess of the knowledge of true and false wealth, helps this scene. We are aware of her bringing her own world and all that it symbolises into the new context.

For the rest of the scene we need not be afraid of an anti-climax. Portia must be firm and not too pitiful. Shylock's exit, c to down l through the crowd, can be as pathetic as you will, but not too long delayed. The play shows a Christian, romantic and expressly feminine Portia against a down-trodden, vengeful, racially grand, usurious Jew. I do not claim that all the difficulties inherent in this opposition are finally settled, but I would claim that this dramatic opposition is a profound one. We must not suppose that since Portia has all our sympathy Shylock can have none: poetic drama can be paradoxical. Portia stands serene in white purity, symbol of Christian romance. Shylock, saying he is ill, picks up his cloak and goes out robed in purple: the purple of tragedy. Two vast imaginative issues conflict: the romantic dream and tragic realism. Later on Shakespeare is to reconcile them. Here the opposition must be stark: neither must be watered down.

The last scene at Belmont acts itself easily, but I object to so unfortunate a back-cloth as one with *waves* painted on it. Our set here might for the first time dispose of the change in level. The action's dualism may not have been perfectly unified, but we are not supposed now to be worrying about it. Or again, we might keep it, and get significant comedy out of the lovers chasing each other, as they usually do, from one level to the other. On second thoughts, I think this best. It would have meaning. Lorenzo and Jessica would be comfortably placed on the steps at the beginning.

SOURCE: extracts from *Shakespearean Production* (London, 1964; new edition 1968), pp. 126–31. (*Shakespearean Production* incorporates the author's *Principles of Shakespearean Production*, published in 1936).

NOTE

1. I acknowledge a debt in my thinking around this point to Max Plowman's illuminating note, 'Money and the Merchant', *The Adelphi*, New Series, II, vi (Sept. 1931).

James Agate 'Olivier's *Macbeth*' (1937)

We have each our private ideal of Macbeth, Hamlet, Othello, Lear; we have all of us read of, if we have not seen, great performances of these parts; so that every actor who undertakes them has to pass through a triple ordeal, encountering, first, our imagination, kindled by Shakespeare; second, our idealised memory of performances which used to please our, perhaps unripe, judgement; third, our conceptions of the great actors of the past, gathered from the often extravagant panegyrics of contemporaries. –

WILLIAM ARCHER

Perhaps this is the place to say – and if it isn't I shall still say it! – that I have been more 'got at' over Mr Olivier's performance than by any other in my recollection. Chelsea semaphored, 'Unable conceive Macbeth as gigolo.' Bloomsbury signalled, 'No use for Macbeth as mountebank.' A young gentleman in corduroy trousers and a velvet smoking-jacket opined to my face that Macbeth should not be like a retired Army colonel. Reflecting that what the young gentleman stood in need of was an active drill-sergeant, I proceeded to turn a deaf, but not altogether deaf, ear to another of the mincing brigade, who suggested that the new Macbeth shouted too loudly.

I say 'not altogether deaf' because even the austerest critic is none the worse for knowing what is being said by the mob! I am persuaded that those monuments to incorruptibility, our judges, take a good keek at anonymous letters before they consign them to the wastepaper-basket. Now my mentors, though self-appointed, were not anonymous, and it so happens that I have the greatest respect for their opinions in the domains of art and music as well as drama. Nor did I get the impression that the plushy young gentleman was altogether a fool. Why, then, should a performance which interested me throughout and at times excited me greatly fail so completely with these others? Can it be that they were judging Mr Olivier's performance by some preconceived standard to which this actor's physical means, even if he were Garrick and Kean rolled into one would still not let him conform? Can it be that they were like a man going to the circus expecting to see lions and who, confronted with a cage of tigers, says: 'These lions are poor!' Or can it be that I was wrong?

Anyhow, I was sufficiently intrigued, as they say, to pay a second visit and sit the play out a second time. And sufficiently conscientious to consider whether one's rules for measuring performances in classic parts stand in need of revision. I look at it in this way. Every critic has his ideal Macbeth, Hamlet, Othello, Lear. But the attitude he must adopt is not that of a schoolmaster correcting schoolboy answers. A critic has not finished with Mr Jones's Hamlet by allotting it, say, 65 marks out of a possible 100. If I am not being too nice in this matter, let me suggest that this arithmetical judgement may be the only practicable method of assessing a newcomer about whom the critic knows nothing more than the immediate impersonation. Hazlitt, writing about Kean on his first appearance as Shylock, was in a very different position from Hazlitt years later considering Kean's Lear, when the actor's virtues and limitations, mental as well as physical, had become well known to him. This is why when it comes to allotting marks for a performance the critic must take into account not only how much that performance falls short of the ideal, but by how much it exceeds, or fails to exceed, that which the critic could reasonably expect from previous performances by the same actor.

Of course Mr Olivier's Macbeth, now presented for the first time, is inadequate, ideally considered. And perhaps we may first glance at what has been said of the adequacy or inadequacy on the part of actors greater than Mr Olivier pretends to be. First there is Garrick, about whom Francis Gentleman winds up a fulsome panegyric with the request to know 'who has heard Macbeth's speech, after receiving his death wound, uttered with the utmost agony of body and mind, but almost pities the expiring wretch though stained with crimes of the deepest dye?' One reflects that this speech, not to be found in Shakespeare, must have been uttered not only with the utmost of Garrick's bodily and mental pain, but at considerable cost of the great actor's invention as well! Quin 'could not be expected to exhibit the acute sensations of the character.' Barry 'made a lukewarm affair of Macbeth.' Powell 'dwindled into boyish whimpering.' So much for Francis Gentleman.

According to Hazlitt, Kean, being deficient in the poetry of the character, 'did not look like a man who had encountered the Weird Sisters.' This critic greatly preferred Kemble's Macbeth, although 'his tones had occasionally a learned quaintness, like the colouring of Poussin.' Of Macready, Lewes said that 'though unsurpassable in some aspects, he wanted the heroic thew and sinew to represent the character as a whole,' and that his Macbeth 'stole into the sleeping chamber of Duncan like a man going to purloin a purse, not like a warrior going to snatch a crown.' Henry Morley was so greatly overcome by, and wrote at such length of, Helen Faucit's Lady Macbeth that he dismissed Phelp's performance of her great partner as a 'rude, impulsive soldier,' while a lesser critic of the [1840s] complained that in the banquet scene 'dignity and kingly courtesy were wanting.' Irving, according to Ellen Terry, thought that his Macbeth, though universally discredited, was his finest performance, and of his last act she writes: 'He looked like a great famished wolf.' Of Bourchier's over-acting in the part Allan Monkhouse once said, if he did not write, that one left the theatre wondering whether murder was as serious as all that came to!

Since from the foregoing it would seem that a great Macbeth has never been in the calendar, it is reasonable to expect that the new one should be lacking in perfect adequacy. It is a part demanding great natural and physical gifts, to which Mr Olivier at present can only oppose natural and physical shortcomings. He does not, for example, look like coping with Russian bears, Hyrcan tigers, and rhinoceroses, whether armed or unarmed. His voice, which in the 'To-morrow and to-morrow' and the 'Sere and yellow leaf' speeches should vibrate like a 'cello, is of a pitch rather higher than the average. In other words, he is not a natural bass and has some difficulty in getting down to baritone. All the same, he brings off some magnificent vocal effects, and his verse-speaking has improved throughout. Ideally, Macbeth might be likened to some oak, magnificent in outer shell but lacking roots, and presently to be riven by the lightning of conscience. But Nature has not so endowed Mr Olivier, who is forced to play the whole part nervously among the high-tossed branches.

The whole performance, then, is a study in nerves, and, so far as I am concerned, this actor, largely by force of highly expressive play of feature, makes a notable conquest over what might so easily be monotony. He begins in a low key. We realise that Macbeth is rapt, as Banquo says, in something more than contemplation of the Witches' promises; his mind harks back to the earlier occasion when to his wife he tentatively broke the murderous enterprise. He hesitated then, and is not ready now, and this reading gives a chance upon which any great Lady Macbeth would eagerly seize. But, alas, Miss Judith Anderson throws it away by suggesting that 'He that's coming must be provided for' is no more than an allusion to clean sheets! As the murder draws near this Macbeth's passion increases. Many actors play the 'dagger' speech with the aplomb of a concert-singer reeling off 'Hybreas the Cretan'; the speech as it is now rendered is shot with apprehension. The ascent and descent of the staircase are done superbly, the voice falling at the duetted 'Amen' and rising to a magnificent resonance with the 'Sleep no more' speech, which has a Nordic, barbaric, and what I may call a Sibelius-like ring of doom. I pass over the nicely calculated scene with the murderers to welcome the beautiful and intensely Shakespearean delivery of

> Light thickens; and the crow
> Makes wing to the rooky wood.

The banquet scene a little disappoints in the same way that Phelps disappointed. Macbeth, who has put on kingship, should be more royal, and I am inclined to think that jumping on to the table is too much in Hamlet's vein after the play scene. This brings us to the last act, which is the best of any of the Macbeths that I have seen. It is played at white heat of both imagination and energy, so that it becomes a molten whole. Here the actor gathers up all his forces and all his knowledge of what ought to be done. It is the reverse of 'all over bar the shouting.' Mr

Olivier, who has made enough noise, and some people think too much, now gives the part the finest edge of his brain. 'Liar and slave!' is uttered with a cold, Irvingesque malignity. If the voice, expressing Macbeth's melancholy, still cannot accomplish the 'cello, it achieves a noble viola. The fight at the end is grandly done, and when sword and dagger are gone Macbeth's final gesture, in which he would fight Macduff with his bare shield, shows that not even the poetry in which he has been enwrapped, nor all the metaphysical stuff which has embroidered his wife's death, has robbed this soldier of his first valour.

To sum up, this may not be the whole of Macbeth. Ideally considered, the performance lacks grandeur, and the actor should look to his gait, which smacks too much of the modern prize-ring. But the mental grasp is here, and so too is enough to the character to take one spectator out of the Waterloo Road and set him down on that dubious heath. Further, is it not a point that whereas a stripling can fly at Hamlet, Macbeth is a weighty business which requires the momentum of age? Mr Olivier will probably play this part twice as well when he has twice his present years. Meanwhile he registers another step in a career of considerable achievement and increasing promise. Alas that he is insufficiently helped by his Lady Macbeth, about whom I shall echo what an earlier critic said about an earlier actress: 'Miss Laura Addison has a good conception of the part, draws a just outline of it, but is incapable of filling it up. She is a clever actress, with a very laudable intelligence of the character, but with natural powers inadequate to its just exhibition.' Where Mr Olivier is admirably aided is by the production of M. Michel Saint-Denis, by Motley's scenery, of dried-blood hue and consistency, and by the incidental music of M. Darius Milhaud. The perkiness of M. Milhaud's themes and the irrelevance of their toylike colouring suggest by audacity of contrast the time's form and pressure.

SOURCE: review (5 December 1937) of the Old Vic production of *Macbeth*; reprinted in Agate's *The Amazing Theatre* (London, 1939), pp. 62–7.

Kenneth Tynan 'Scofield's *Hamlet*' (1948)

Hamlet, as it is printed and played to-day, is an *uncomeatable* text. Its sinews are perplexed and self-involved, like strands of weed in a furious river: as Landor said of *Paradise Regained*, here and there a prominent muscle swells out from the vast mass of the collapsed. It is too long, and its length is spun out of frayed and trailing nerve-ends, growing wispier, as time passes, and less relevant: they cloud our vision at curtain-fall, ill-digested nothings, unresolved and unregarded. Our *Hamlet*, a judicious blend of the 2nd Quarto and 1st Folio, compares, dramatically and psychologically, very ill with the brief and unpolished First Quarto. It is confused where the First Quarto is clear, legato where the First Quarto is staccato; but its very complications tempt us to act it and make physical sense of its contrariness. The customary latter-day Hamlet has tended to be the kind of man Cyril Connolly was indicating when he wrote of Chamfort: 'His predicament is one with which we are all familiar . . . that of the revolutionary whose manners and ways of life are attached to the old régime, whose ideals and loyalties belong to the new, and who, by a kind of *courageous exhibitionism* is compelled to tell the truth about both.' It is a good compromise, more grateful to the eye than the egomaniac savage which Salvador de Madariaga has recently commended to us: but it fails to make the play a unity. Only the beholder-critic can do that, as only a beholder can discern in the random hoofprints of a horse the pattern of an exquisite tesselation. *Hamlet* remains a mangled, racked body of a play. Reflect, for example, upon the placing of the two central soliloquies. In our text the incisive plotting of 'The play's the thing Wherein I'll catch the conscience of the king' (an end to indecision and a signpost to action at the end of Act II) is inexplicably followed up, sixty lines later, with 'To be or not to be'. The core lies here of the arguments adduced to prove the mercurial, delaying quality of Hamlet's distraction; a subtlety which the First Quarto sensibly circumvents by putting the suicidal soliloquy into his mouth on his first entrance in Act II, when the last words we have heard from him have been: 'The time is out of joint; O cursed spite That *ever I was born* to set it right.' 'O what a rogue' (here changed to 'O what a dunghill idiot slave') does not occur until long after 'To be or not to be': their relative positions are *reversed*, thus making what is, to my mind, a much more likely progression.

But given the jumbled psychology of the received text, and given the jumbled psychology of our times, it is right that our young actors should continue to make their guesses at the part. The kind of modern Hamlet we had all been waiting for is beautifully defined by C. S. Lewis:

> I am trying to recall attention from the things an intellectual adult notices to the things a child or a peasant notices – night, ghosts, a castle, a lobby where a man can walk four hours together, a willow-fringed brook and a sad lady drowned, a graveyard and a terrible cliff above the sea – and amidst all these, a pale man in black clothes . . . with his stockings coming down, a dishevelled

man whose words make us at once think of loneliness and doubt and dread, of waste and dust and emptiness, and from whose hands, as from our own, we feel the richness of heaven and earth and the comfort of human affection slipping away.

What I am going to contend is that Paul Scofield, the Hamlet of Michael Benthall's production at Stratford [1948] is, for this generation, that pale man. A pale man; not even embryonically a pale hero; for Hamlet is perhaps the only Elizabethan protagonist with nothing heroic about him. 'He was likely, had he been put on, To have proved most royally' – he was *likely*, but he was never put on: the frustrations of fear and conscience intervened.

Mr Scofield underplays his Hamlet in a manner of which verbal analysis can never explain the success. Its very outlines are sketchy: the actor does not aim at any specific emotion at any given time. He does not aim at youth (he is a man, not a *young* man); he is not eager, he is not pathetic, not scornful, nor brutal. He is nothing definite, nothing capable of imprisonment in a few labels: he shares with Olivier this strange technique of not *insisting*. (And with Alec Guinness's Abel Drugger, his Clown in *The Winter's Tale* shares an ability to make goodness funny without deriding it.) I think even Lamb, who could not bear to see play acted, would have applauded this Hamlet: Lamb, who said:

. . . such is the actor's necessity of giving strong blows to the audience, that I have never seen a player in this character who did not exaggerate and strain to the utmost these ambiguous features, these temporary deformities in the character. They make him express a vulgar scorn at Polonius which utterly degrades his gentility . . . they make him show contempt, and curl up the nose at Ophelia's father – contempt in its very grossest and most hateful form: but they get applause by it: it is natural, people say: that is, the words are scornful and the actor expresses scorn, and that they can judge of: but why so much scorn, and of that sort, they never think of asking.

(What a clear picture is here of the nineteenth-century Hamlet! in the court scenes, behaving like Gulliver in Lilliput; in awful soliloquy, like Gulliver in Brobdingnag.)

Lamb is here getting at a very important point: he represents the decay in the spectator of that instinctive response to stock, stylised gestures and vocal tones; and the beginning of that embarrassment in the face of intensified stage emotion which finally produced the naturalistic style. Mr Scofield's gift, like that of many great modern actors, is that he never aims his whole being at any one bull's-eye of emotion. That is too easy: the art is in missing by inches, and thus creating for us a human being incidentally expressing anger, instead of an embodiment of anger who is only incidentally a human being. The lines serve to illuminate a man, not a passion: only the very greatest actors can fuse the two inalienably, and the rest are better advised not to try. Of the rest, Mr Scofield is among the finest.

Lamb's ideal Hamlet is (like himself) 'shy, negligent, and retiring'. Negligent and retiring we may concede, but Scofield is never shy, for that supposes a self-consciousness of which he knows nothing. Helplessness he has: to a nearly comic degree he needs strength and comfort; and the wan, stricken fullness of his face cries out to be soothed. Unconvinced and tentative, he pads about the wide solitary stage, his turned-out feet going two ways in two minds, his tired hands flickering, his lips pursed and worried, inly hopeless of ever grasping joy. The matronly spectator may meditate adopting him as a pet, lean and shaggy in his hunger for solace. No sound he utters, no step he takes is fixed or purposed: there are no roots, he is a wandering plant, in sapless perambulation. Sometimes he will seem to make stern his lips with terrible earnestness; he will prowl around, inclined stiffnecked forwards, surveying the ground with the bead-eyed intentness of a schoolmistress rolling up her sleeves to investigate an evil smell in the changing-room; but always the frailly shrugging hands contradict his designs. Again the plaintive voice breaks, and the unsought squalor of being tightly involved in murders and adulteries bursts afresh on his intelligent soul. Nothing he does is confidently predictable. Even the simplest move over the stage may be dammed and diverted by some new roaming of his vague, merciful eyes. He commands all the silent agonies of childhood; in him the gravity of extreme youth and the puckishness of old age commingle. To have these qualities, and yet resolutely repel any hint of pathos, is one negative mark of great acting. Two things await this Hamlet; of these alone, as we watch him, we can prophesy. He will be trapped, and die. What time he will not weep.

Mr Benthall has dressed him in the black frock-coat and flyaway tie of the 1860s, thus putting one constantly in mind of Matthew Arnold; except that Mr Scofield's vagrant beauty is nothing like Arnold, but closer to his Scholar Gipsy:

> . . . that Oxford scholar poor,
> Of pregnant parts and quick inventive brain,
> Who, tired of knocking at preferment's door,
>   One summer morn forsook
> His friends. . . .

The poem is full of lines which call up Mr Scofield's raptness in repose:

> . . . thy figure spare,
> Thy dark vague eyes, and soft abstracted air. . . .

– or best of all:

> seen by rare glimpses,pensive and tongue-tied

– for it is the crown of this Hamlet that, in one of the longest parts ever written, he never seems verbose or even anxious to speak at all. He must 'unpack his heart with words', but he does so with a reluctance, a dour and humble delicacy, which makes the privilege of listening to him seem all too sparingly granted.

This is the best Hamlet I have seen. I have admired the supple hysterics of Mr Gielgud's and stared aghast at the giant technical prowess of Mr Wolfit's; more nearly I have cherished the courtier of Mr Clunes and the agile puppet, sodden in tears, which Jean-Louis Barrault made of the part. Mr Scofield has ousted them all from my memory, and I know that there is now in England a young actor who is bond-slave to greatness, and can stand beside the other exciting young men (Mr Benthall, Mr Ustinov, Mr Quayle) who are going to make our theatre in the coming decade a thing of great pride and fruition. I think, in fine, that we can now speak of Paul Scofield as 'Scofield', and know whom we mean.

Something now of the pace and passion of Mr Benthall's production. By setting and costuming the play in a nineteenth-century Ruritania, hung with vast crimson curtains and gilt tassels, he has sidestepped any comparison with previous *Hamlets*: everything is new; there is no point of contact: we are seeing a new play. The soldiers are Life Guards; Polonius (played very tactfully by John Kidd) is a dwarf elder statesman, prim and monocled; Claudius becomes a nasty and boorish Prince Consort. Mr Benthall's mastery of the unexpected inflexion, the striking vocal novelty, is nearly as complete as Mr Brook's. Witness the first appearance of the Ghost to Hamlet: he does not even look at it as the others recoil, but stares fixedly away, deliberately crosses himself, and, with perfect steadiness, *murmurs*: 'Angels and ministers of grace, defend us.' Look, too, at the handling of Ophelia's madness: one cannot quickly forget the rising poignancy of 'If – thou – hadst – not – come – to – MY – BED!'; and her subsequent collapse, writhing and whimpering. Better still is Mr Benthall's quite original treatment of the scenes after the death of Polonius between Hamlet, Rosencrantz and Guildenstern.

These are usually played up to the comic hilt, but Mr Benthall makes them prickly with menace. The two spies, immaculate in evening dress, advance on Hamlet with swords lazily at guard; he hysterically jests with them, edging towards escape between the pillars; only to discover, by a gleam of helmet and another and yet another advancing figure, that the whole palace soldiery is joining in the man-hunt. The sense of trappedness is complete. Almost my only quibble with the production is Mr Benthall's resort to the traditional hairtriggered cannon when Fortinbras bids the soldiers shoot: this was an obvious cue for a volley of muskets, and the producer missed it.

After grateful praise to Anthony Quayle (Claudius), Claire Bloom (Ophelia), and Diana Wynyard (Gertrude), I must open the full throat of acclamation for Esmond Knight's Ghost. This overwhelming performance sent terror and alarm into one's very stomach: consternation rippled across the whole audience as is listened to Mr Knight's ghastly care in reaching after breath, an agonised inhaling as if he were scouring up the deepest fumes of hell to bear the noxious pain of his message to Hamlet's ears.

> If ever thou didst thy dear father love
> (*intake of breath*)
> Revenge his foul and most unnatural MURDER
> (*the voice rising to a shriek*)
> HAMLET: MURDER? (*A horrified yell*)
> GHOST: MURDER – most foul, as in the best it is. . . .

Those three full-volume 'Murders' and their endless echoing down corridors and along galleries of pillars, set the scene swimming up to a climax of banging horror. I was out of my seat for fright.

(I ought to add that Robert Helpmann alternated the leading part with Scofield, and gave a very clean-cut and passionless performance – not indeed of Hamlet, but Hamlet's moral tutor at Wittenberg University.)

SOURCE: review of the 1948 production of *Hamlet* at Stratford-on-Avon; reprinted in *He That Plays the King* (London, 1950), pp. 108–13.

Eric Bentley 'The *Place*, the *Actor* and the Psychology of *We*' (1957)

To begin with, the theatre is a place. This place, in all known forms, sets up such a vibration in those who frequent it that certain properties roughly suggested by the term magic are invariably attributed to the building itself. In our epoch, for example, how many journalists, and even college freshmen, have mentioned the expectant lull when the lights dim, and the thrill when the curtain rises! This, you say, may be partly a matter of audience psychology. It remains true that the paraphernalia of the theatre has of itself remarkable suggestive power. Even when no audience is present, even when the stage is bare of scenery and the brick wall at the rear is exposed, the curious machine retains an insidious attraction. No more than a human being does a theatre necessarily lose its fascination by taking its clothes off. Pirandello obviously had been struck by that fact before he wrote *Six Characters in Search of an Author*; and also by the fact that the procedures of theatre carry a similar 'magic.' Rationally speaking, the rehearsal doings of actors and stage staff alike are either so sensible as to be rather dull or so foolish and anachronistic as to be contemptible. To know how the dullness and contemptibility are avoided and transcended would be to have solved the mystery of the theatre as a place.

If there is something about the place, there is something, too, about its inhabitants, the actors. I have not spoken of the merits of one building as against another, nor do I have in mind the merits of one actor as against another. There is something about the actor as such, about the mere fact of impersonation: there is a 'magic' to this too. Various accounts have been given of the origin of such activity; various theories have been advanced to explain its continued and universal appeal. The fact itself is unequivocal. A child loves to dress up in grandmother's bonnet and feathers. Grownups go to carnivals and fancy dress balls. To give the greatest possible effect to his story, the raconteur adds mimicry to narrative. Some primitive people believe that they can appease the gods by dressing up in certain ways; some non-primitive people believe they can cure neuroses by a form of charade or group impersonation which they have christened psychodrama. A famous young actor was recently quoted by *The New York Times* as saying: 'To me acting is the most logical way for people's neuroses to manifest themselves.' I see no reason to believe him and several reasons for disbelieving him, yet I'm sure his heart was in the right place. He wanted to say something definitive when all he really sensed was that there's something about an actor.

There is something about an audience – that is, about a group of people in close physical proximity, with their faces all pointing one way, and their attention – their eyes, ears, hearts, and minds – focused upon a single object. There is something about ceasing to be merely an *I* and becoming, under such circumstances, in this *place*, before that *actor*, a part of a *we*. There is something about the cosiness and sociability of the whole physical setup.[1] And possibly – though one hesitates to believe it – there is something about its uncosiness, unsociability, and positive discomfort. The lack of knee room, the pest of people pushing past, and, in New York, the ban on smoking, the absence of bars, the shortage of lobby space – such things lend weight to the occasion. Again, whatever the explanation, the fact is familiar: an experience is changed by being shared in such company in such a manner.

The extreme and notorious cases of audience psychology are cases of hysterics and swooning and the premature delivery of babies. But if we judge theatre merely by the *degree* of effect, then the best theatrical entertainment is a revivalist meeting or a political rally. In dramatic art proper, we are more concerned with moderate responses – with the fact, for example, that the joke *I* imperceptibly smile at alone in my study, *we* perceptibly grin at, we perhaps all 'roar' at, in the theatre.

What's the matter, are we drunk? Boastful – wishing to show off our sociability? Polite – as one would laugh more loudly at a joke made by the president of the board? The less respectable motives no doubt enter in, as we are so directly under the noses of our fellow men, so mercilessly exposed and therefore bound to be on our 'best' behavior; but is it not chiefly the atmosphere of a full theatre, the psychology of *we*, that has put us at our ease, and caused a great deal of good feeling to pour out of us that normally we would suppress? That is, if we felt it in the first place; for much of the good feeling is created by the occasion, by the psychology of *we*. Or perhaps, more accurately still, while initiated by the *actor* and the *place*, such feeling is constantly *increased* by the occasion, by the psychology of *we*. One speaks of 'infectious enthusiasm,' and the enjoyment of an audience is a positive contagion. The Puritans were wrong to call the theatre a scarlet woman; they would have been less wrong had they called theatregoing a scarlet fever. We acknowledge freely enough, I believe, that men go to football matches to share the orgiastic experience of communal waving, shoving, cheering, and yelling. The orgiastic character of theatregoing is no longer overt, but surely it is one of the first things to take into account if we try to explain why anyone would pass up all the alternatives – especially TV at home and the movies on the corner – and go through hail and snow to an expensive but uncomfortable seat in an inconvenient building called a legitimate theatre. 'Fine word, legitimate!' To think of the little thrillers they put on there, that would yield in the movies a non-stop feature of at most ninety minutes, and on TV at most an hour program with interspersed commercials! In what one is tempted to call this bastard of a legitimate theatre such items are stretched out for over two hours by the surely illegitimate device of lengthy intermissions during which there is no bar or restaurant to go to and only a grossly overcrowded lobby to smoke in.

What assets has the theatre got, to offset its appalling liabilities? Clearly, the *place*, the *actor*, and the psychology of *we*. 'But the movies have all three,' counters someone, 'for how could you have a film without a place to show it in, actors to play in it, and a crowd to see it?' Ah yes, but there is a 'short' in that electrical system. No current flows from celluloid to audience – or, at any rate, no current flows from audience to celluloid. In the movie theatre, we can watch a story and we can admire many things that actors do, but we cannot be caught up in a flow of living feeling that passes from actor to audience and from the audience back again to the actor. In the movies, Shirley Booth may smile, and you may smile back at her; but she can scarcely catch your returning smile and toss it back again or change it and give it back in the form of a sob or a catch in the throat. Yet such are the dynamics of theatre. And, rightly or wrongly, there are people who undertake the trip to the Broadway theatre, through the worst bottleneck of traffic in the world, just to exchange smiles or tears with Miss Booth. Personally, I demand a little more. But if we want to know what theatre is we should know what is 'the least of it' – the minimum condition under which it can be said to exist.

What, by contrast, is the most that theatre could ever hope to offer? Or, at any rate, what is the most it ever *has* offered? To keep this chapter within bounds I shall forget about dance, pantomime, and song, and concentrate on the art which can advance the best claim to be the principal theatre art: the drama.

Histories of the drama customarily trace a development from what are called primitive beginnings to the great periods of flowering. But there is something misleading in the procedure, because, in the so-called primitive phases, art frequently shows what is called sophistication and, occasionally, far from remaining content with minimum demands, reaches out towards the maximum satisfaction. An instance is the art of tragedy at the moment of its very inception, as conjecturally established by Jane Harrison:

. . . we are apt to forget that from the *epos*, the narrative to the *drama*, the
enactment, is a momentous step, one, so far as we know, not taken in Greece till
after centuries of epic achievement, and then taken suddenly, almost in the
dark, and irrevocably. All we really know of this momentous step is that it was
taken some time in the sixth century B. C. and taken in connection with the
worship of Dionysos. Surely it is at least possible that the real impulse to the
drama lay not wholly in 'goat songs' and 'circular dancing places' but also in the
cardinal, the essentially dramatic, conviction of the religion of Dionysos, that
the worshipper can not only worship, but can become, can *be*, his god.[2]

Perhaps this passage suggests too much. If some historians write of the
later drama as if it were all but a falling away from Greek tragedy, Miss
Harrison likes to hint that even Greek tragedy might be a falling away
from that first sublime instant when the worshipper of Dionysos became
god. To me, the value of her idea is that it sets a standard: after this, for
example, we know what to expect of a tragic hero. Aristotle's dry,
accurate statement that a hero must be above life size takes on larger
significance. Our eyes are opened both to the god-seeking and the
blasphemy in tragic heroes from Oedipus to Halvard Solness. And we
sense how painful has been the loss when playwrights eschew this god-
seeking and blasphemy because neither they nor their culture believe in
heroes.

The origins of comedy also call to mind the highest claims that the
drama can make for itself. For, though the exact circumstances are even
less certain than those of the origins of tragedy, there is some agreement
that comedy derives from sheer celebration of fertility – of what
Bernard Shaw called the Life Force, and what modern culture in
general blithely nails down in that most outrageous of its simplifications,
the word Sex. If in tragedy we feel that we can be god, in comedy our
identification is with the spring, the seeds, the crops to come. A feeling of
oneness with nature is at the bottom of it, a profound and dedicated
acceptance of life, and of sexuality as central to life – an acceptance just
as sadly lacking in modern culture as genuine hero worship. No wonder
our wiser men, from Carlyle to D. H. Lawrence, plead with us to try and
recapture the ancient wisdom, the ancient ecstatic attachments!

Yet, though the very origins suggest what the maximum achievement
of the drama might be, it remains (*pace* Miss Harrison) for history and
culture and individual genius to furnish the proof: in the fullness of time
comes such a tragedy as *Hamlet*, such a comedy as *Le Misanthrope*. What
has been added to the moment of ecstatic identification with the god,
the hour of the celebration of sexual energy? In a word, that which
separates man from the beasts, and that which it was the glory of Greece
to display to the world in all its dignity and power: intellect, mind,

reason. *Le Misanthrope* is chiefly words. The old comic rhythms are at work but are given no direct corporeal expression. Comedy has been elevated into the realm of the spirit. And *Hamlet* is surely the first protagonist in world drama whom one would call an 'intellectual.' These are extreme cases. Yet the point is equally well illustrated by, say, *The Birds* and the *Oresteia*. Though Aristophanes's play wears its masquerade origin on its sleeve – for it was traditional to use animal disguises – just as surely as the plays of Molière and Shakespeare it represents the transformation of the drama by intellect. Doubtless there is no gain without some loss, and it is a pity that Aristophanes's birds and beasts retain no magic from any primeval past; the gain is that the art of drama is now something that the master spirits of the age can devote themselves to. And, though there are still people who see Aeschylus as barely emerging from the murk of superstition, the *Oresteia*, no less than the philosophy of Aristotle or Plato, is the very symbol of Hellas and its victories of mind over matter, law over lawlessness, civilisation over barbarism.

Pericles referred to Greek recreations as 'provision for the spirit,' and it is worth stressing the spiritual and intellectual side, because in our time the other side is so grossly overstressed, most of all by writers on theatre. But I am far from wishing simply to swing to the other extreme from those who represent the drama to be primitive. The achievement of all great drama is precisely the spanning of *both* sides of man's nature, the spiritual and the physical, the intellectual and the emotional.

However high in the air of the spirit the branches of the drama may rise, the tree still has its primitive roots, even if, as I said at the outset, our view of the primitive is a little arbitrary. The latest and most erudite study of *Twelfth Night* – by Leslie Hotson – shows that play to be a none too distant relative of fertility ritual. Deeply steeped in Christianity as he is, Shakespeare delights to celebrate in his comedies something that pagans as well as Christians have always delighted to celebrate: fruitful marriage. *As You Like It* culminates in a 'wedlock hymn':

> Wedding is great Juno's crown
> Oh, blessed bond of board and bed!
> 'Tis Hymen peoples every town,
> High wedlock then be honourèd.

A Midsummer Night's Dream ends with Oberon's promise that the wedding night of all three couples will have results:

> To the best bridebed will we
> Which by us shall blessèd be
> And the issue there create
> Ever shall be fortunate!

And *The Tempest* has a little wedding masque at its very center:

> Honour, riches, marriage blessing
> Long continuance and increasing,
> Hourly joys be still upon you!
> Juno sings her blessings on you.
> Earth's increase, foison plenty,
> Barns and garners never empty,
> Vines with clustering bunches growing,
> Plants with goodly burden bowing,
> Spring come to you at the farthest
> In the very end of harvest!

One of Shakespeare's first comedies, *Love's Labours Lost*, is about the futility of attempting to thwart nature by a life of celibacy, and it ends with two of the loveliest invocations of seasonal myth in literature, the winter and spring songs. In one of the last comedies, *A Winter's Tale*, seasonal myth is not merely invoked at the end, it is pervasive. Starting from the modest but clear hint of the title, the play says everything there is to say about winter and spring, taken both literally and figuratively; and the fourth act is Shakespeare's paean to spring time, to the fact of coming into this world, and hence to the process by which we come into it. Reaching for a hyperbole to indicate that he will not break faith, Florizel says that, if he does,

> Let Nature crush the sides o'the earth together
> And mar the seeds within!

In other words, the destruction of the seeds of life, the creation of infertility, is the ultimate horror.

If the comedies were written in celebration of fertility, the tragedies were written out of a sense of the horror of infertility or rather, one might say, but for the present-day associations of the word, of contraception. The extent of Lady Macbeth's villainy is measured by the statement that – if worst comes to worst – she would be prepared to murder the baby at her breast (i vii 54–9); and the farthest reach of her husband's wickedness is not the murder of king or friend but of

Macduff's little children. Commentators have been puzzled by Macduff's first remark after the terrible news has sunk in: 'he has no children.' Some have not wanted to take the 'he' as Macbeth at all; others have wished to limit the sense to 'he has no children for me to take revenge on.' But surely the speech is one of those supremely dramatic utterances that leap out of a situation, illogical yet prompted by some higher logic, spreading meaning in several directions. The childlessness of Macbeth – with all its associations: sterility, futility, unnaturalness, lack of posterity – that is the main idea.

Like Florizel, Macbeth uses the figure of the killing of the seeds to express the idea of ultimate horror. Even if all Nature is in disorder, he asks the witches (IV i), answer me – and the series of hyperboles in which he asks them culminates in:

> though the treasure
> Of nature's germens tumble all together
> Even till destruction sicken (58–60).

The same image appears at the very climax of *King Lear*:

> And thou, all-shaking thunder,
> Smite flat the thick rotundity o' the world!
> Crack nature's moulds, all germens spill at once
> That make ungrateful man! (III ii 6–9)

King Lear is about 'unnaturalness between the child and the parent.' The relation between Lear and Goneril is the precise opposite of that between Prospero and Miranda. And so when the old man casts about in his battered brain for the most terrible thing he can say, it is this:

> Hear, Nature, hear, dear goddess, hear!
> Suspend thy purpose if thou didst intend
> To make this creature fruitful.
> Into her womb convey sterility.
> Dry up in her the organs of increase,
> And from her derogate body never spring
> A babe to honour her! (I iv 297–303)

I dwell now on the primitive elements partly because scholars have indeed done justice to the non-primitive elements and partly to show that 'primitive' elements may be subtle and profound. Those who present Shakespeare as the practical man of the theatre who wanted to make money by providing a few evenings of soft emotion and broad fun will get as little comfort from the primitive part of *King Lear* as from its sophisticated, theological, and Christian part. This, *en passant*: the main point is that *King Lear* is both primitive and sophisticated, and that the power in Shakespeare that most compels our admiration is the synthetic power, the ability to span two such worlds as these. Of this man, our supreme playwright, we may say: he encountered no gap which he could not bridge.

Modern scholars have performed a service when they have demonstrated how, in *King Lear*, Shakespeare miraculously managed to present the whole 'Elizabethan world culture,' the universe around, human society on earth, and individual man, center and model of the other two. It is a pity that after reading these modern accounts we sometimes have to wonder if Shakespeare also had a mind of his own. One may legitimately appeal back from purely scholarly interpretation to the judgement of the great humanistic critics, many of whom were not primarily scholars. It is the poet Dryden who reminds us that Shakespeare is not only to be commended for summing up the thought of his time: none was ever in livelier direct touch than he with life. 'All the images of Nature,' Dryden says, 'were still present to him.' And, just as he brought together the primitive and the sophisticated, he lived in the happy possession, not only of the world without, but of the world within. 'He was the man who of all Modern, and perhaps Ancient Poets, had the largest and most comprehensive soul.' . . . .

SOURCE: extract from *What is Theatre? A Point of View* (1957); reprinted along with *The Dramatic Art* (London, 1969), pp. 240–51.

NOTES

1. . ' . . the New York theatre-goer . . . can step into almost any theatre lobby with that sense of virtuous expectation, of responsibility and enlightenment, that the drama peculiarly awakes, and that makes the theatre for New York what the café is for Paris, a pleasure and also a pride, a habit and a ritual, a diversion and a duty. To the extent that America has any communal life at all, it is centred in the New York theatre; here is the last refuge of sociability and humanism. . . . ' – Mary McCarthy, in *Sights and Spectacles*.

2. Jane Harrison, *Prologomena to the Study of Greek Religion*.

Peter Brook The Rough Theatre (1968)

Shakespeare is a model of a theatre that contains Brecht and Beckett, but goes beyond both. Our need in the post-Brecht theatre is to find a way forwards, back to Shakespeare. In Shakespeare the introspection and the metaphysics soften nothing. Quite the reverse. It is through the unreconciled opposition of Rough and Holy, through an atonal screech of absolutely unsympathetic keys that we get the disturbing and the unforgettable impressions of his plays. It is because the contradictions are so strong that they burn on us so deeply.

Obviously, we can't whistle up a second Shakespeare. But the more clearly we see in what the power of Shakespearian theatre lies, the more we prepare the way. For example, we have at last become aware that the absence of scenery in the Elizabethan theatre was one of its greatest freedoms. In England at least, all productions for quite some time have been influenced by the discovery that Shakespeare's plays were written to be performed continuously, that their cinematic structure of alternating short scenes, plot intercut with subplot, were all part of a total shape. This shape is only revealed dynamically, that is, in the uninterrupted sequence of these scenes, and without this their effect and power are lessened as much as would be a film that was projected with breaks and musical interludes between each reel. The Elizabethan stage was like the attic . . . in Hamburg [I have earlier described], it was a neutral open platform – just a place with some doors – and so it enabled the dramatist effortlessly to whip the spectator through an unlimited succession of illusions, covering, if he chose, the entire physical world. It has also been pointed out that the nature of the permanent structure of the Elizabethan playhouse, with its flat open arena and its large balcony and its second smaller gallery, was a diagram of the universe as seen by the sixteenth-century audience and playwright – the gods, the court and the people – three levels, separate and yet often intermingling – a stage that was a perfect philosopher's machine.

What has not been appreciated sufficiently is that the freedom of movement of the Elizabethan theatre was not only a matter of scenery. It is too easy to think that so long as a modern production moves fast from scene to scene, it has learnt the essential lesson from the old playhouse. The primary fact is that this theatre not only allowed the playwright to roam the world, it also allowed him free passage from the world of action to the world of inner impressions. I think it is here that we find what is most important to us today. In Shakespeare's time, the voyage of discovery in the real world, the adventure of the traveller setting out into the unknown, had an excitement that we cannot hope to recapture in an age when our planet has no secrets and when the prospect of interplanetary travel seems a pretty considerable bore. However, Shakespeare was not satisfied with the mysteries of the unknown continents: through his imagery – pictures drawn from the world of fabulous discoveries – he penetrates a psychic e~·⁻⁺⁻nce whose geography and movements remain just as vital for us to understand today.

In an ideal relation with a true actor on a bare stage we would continually be passing from long shot to close, tracking or jumping in and out and the planes often overlap. Compared with the cinema's mobility, the theatre once seemed ponderous and creaky, but the closer we move towards the true nakedness of theatre, the closer we approach a stage that has a lightness and range far beyond film or television. The power of Shakespeare's plays is that they present man simultaneously in all his aspects: touch for touch, we can identify and withdraw. A primitive situation disturbs us in our subconscious; our intelligence watches, comments, philosophises. Brecht and Beckett are both contained in Shakespeare unreconciled. We identify emotionally, subjectively – and yet at one and the same time we evaluate politically, objectively in relation to society. Because the profound reaches past the everyday, a heightened language and a ritualistic use of rhythm brings us to those very aspects of life which the surface hides: and yet because the poet and the visionary do not seem like ordinary people, because the epic state is not one on which we normally dwell, it is equally possible for Shakespeare with a break in his rhythm, a twist into prose, a shift into slangy conversation or else a direct word from the audience to remind us – in plain common-sense – of where we are and to return us to the familiar rough world of spades as spades. So it is that Shakespeare succeeded where no one has succeeded before or since in writing plays that pass through many stages of consciousness. What enabled him technically to do so, the essence, in fact, of his style is a roughness of texture and a conscious mingling of opposites which in other terms could be called an absence of style. Voltaire could not bring himself to understand it, and could only label it 'barbaric'.

We could take *Measure for Measure* as a test case. As long as scholars could not decide whether this play was a comedy or not, it never got played. In fact, this ambiguity makes it one of the most revealing of Shakespeare's works – and one that shows these two elements, Holy and Rough, almost schematically, side by side. They are opposed and they co-exist. In *Measure for Measure* we have a base world, a very real world in which the action is firmly rooted. This is the disgusting, stinking world of medieval Vienna. The darkness of this world is absolutely necessary to the meaning of the play: Isabella's plea for grace has far more meaning in this Dostoevskian setting than it would in lyrical comedy's never-never land. When this play is prettily staged, it is meaningless – it demands an absolutely convincing roughness and dirt. Also, when so much of the play is religious in thought, the loud humour of the brothel is important as a device, because it is alienating and humanising. From the fanatical chastity of Isabella and the mystery of the Duke we are plunged back to Pompey and Barnadine for douches of normality. To execute Shakespeare's intentions we must animate all this stretch of the play, not as fantasy, but as the roughest comedy we can make. We need complete freedom, rich improvisation, no holding back, no false respect – and at the same time we must take great care, for all round the popular scenes are great areas of the play that clumsiness could destroy. As we enter this holier land, we will find that Shakespeare gives us a clear signal – the rough is in prose, the rest in verse. In the prose scenes, very broadly speaking, the work can be enriched by our own invention – the scenes need added external details to assure them of their fullest life. In the passages in verse we are already on our guard: Shakespeare needs verse because he is trying to say more, to compact together more meaning. We are watchful: behind each visible mark on paper lurks an invisible one that is hard to seize. Technically we now need less abandon, more focus – less breadth, more intensity.

Quite simply we need a different approach, a different style. There is nothing to be ashamed of in changing style – look at a page of a Folio with half-closed eyes and you see a chaos of irregularly spaced symbols. If we iron Shakespeare into any one typography of theatre we lose the real meaning of the play – if we follow his ever-shifting devices, he will lead us through many different keys. If we follow the movement in *Measure for Measure* between the Rough and the Holy we will discover a play about justice, mercy, honesty, forgiveness, virtue, virginity, sex and death: kaleidoscopically one section of the play mirrors the other, it is in accepting the prism as a whole that its meanings emerge. When I once staged the play I asked Isabella, before kneeling for Angelo's life, to pause each night until she felt the audience could take it no longer – and this used to lead to a two-minute stopping of the play. The device became a voodoo pole – a silence in which all the invisible elements of the evening came together, a silence in which the abstract notion of mercy became concrete for that moment to those present.

This Rough/Holy structure also shows clearly in the two parts of *Henry* iv – Falstaff and the prose realism of the inn scenes on the one hand and the poetic levels of so much else – both elements contained within one complex whole.

In *A Winter's Tale* a very subtle construction hinges on the key moment when a statue comes to life. This is often criticised as a clumsy device, an implausible way of winding up the plot, and it is usually justified only in terms of romantic fiction; an awkward convention of the times that Shakespeare was forced to use. In fact, the statue that comes to life is the truth of the play. In *A Winter's Tale* we find a natural division into three sections. Leontes accuses his wife of infidelity. He condemns her to death. The child is put to sea. In the second part the child grows up, and now in a different pastoral key the very same action is repeated. The man falsely accused by Leontes now in turn behaves just as unreasonably. The consequence is the same – the child again takes flight. Her journey takes her back to Leontes's palace and the third part is now the same place as the first, but twenty years later. Again, Leontes finds himself in similar conditions, in which he could be as violently unreasonable as before. Thus the main action is presented first ferociously; then a second time by charming parody but in a bold major key, for the pastoral of the play is a mirror as well as a straight device. The third movement is in another contrasting key – a key of remorse. When the young lovers enter Leontes's palace the first and second sections overlap: both put into question the action that Leontes now can take. If the dramatist's sense of truth forces him to make Leontes vindictive with the children, then the play cannot move out of its particular world, and its end would have to be bitter and tragic: if he can truthfully allow a new equality to enter Leontes's actions, then the whole time pattern of the play is transformed: the past and the future are no longer the same. The level changes, and even if we call it a miracle, the statue has none the less come to life. When working on *The Winter's Tale* I discovered that the way to understand this scene is not to discuss it but to play it. In performance this action is strangely satisfying – and so it makes us wonder deeply.

Here we have an example of the 'happening' effect – the moment when the illogical breaks through our everyday understanding to make us open our eyes more widely. The whole play has established questions and references: the moment of surprise is a jolt to the kaleidoscope, and what we see in the playhouse we can retain and relate to the play's questions when they recur transposed, diluted and disguised, in life.

If we imagine for a moment *Measure for Measure* and *A Winter's Tale* written by Sartre, it would be reasonable to guess that in the one case Isabella would not kneel for Angelo – so that the play would end with the hollow crackle of the firing squad – and in the other the statue would not come to life, so that Leontes would be faced with the bleak consequences of his actions. Both Shakespeare and Sartre would be fashioning plays according to their sense of truth: one author's inner material contains different intimations from the other's. The mistake would be to take events or episodes from a play and question them in the light of some third outside standard of plausibility – like 'reality' or 'truth'. The sort of play that Shakespeare offers us is never just a series of events: it is far easier to understand if we consider the plays as objects – as many faceted complexes of form and meaning in which the line of narrative is only one amongst many aspects – and cannot profitably be played or studied on its own.

Experimentally, we can approach *Lear* not as a linear narrative, but as a cluster of relationships. First, we try to rid ourselves of the notion that because the play is called *King Lear* it is primarily the story of one individual. So we pick an arbitrary point in the vast structure – the death of Cordelia, say, and now instead of looking towards the King we turn instead towards the man who is responsible for her death. We focus on this character, Edmund, and now we begin to pick our way to and fro across the play, sifting the evidence, trying to discover who this Edmund is. He is clearly a villain, whatever our standards, for in killing Cordelia he is responsible for the most gratuitous act of cruelty in the play – yet if we look at our first impression of him in the early scenes, we find he is by far the most attractive character we meet. In the opening scenes there is a denial of life in Lear's rusty ironclad power; Gloucester is tetchy, fussy and foolish, a man blind to everything except his inflated image of his own importance; and in dramatic contrast we see the relaxed freedom of his bastard son. Even if in theory we observe that the way he leads Gloucester by the nose is hardly moral, instinctively we cannot but side with his natural anarchy. Not only do we sympathise with Goneril and Regan for falling in love with him, but we tend to side with them in finding Edmund so admirably wicked, because he affirms a life that the sclerosis of the older people seems to deny. Can we keep this same attitude of admiration towards Edmund when he has Cordelia killed? If not, why not? What has changed? Is it Edmund who has changed, through outside events? Or is it just the context that is different? Is a scale of value implied? What are Shakespeare's values? What is the value of a life? We flick through the play again and find an incident importantly situated, unrelated to the main plot, often quoted as an example of Shakespeare's slovenly construction. This is the fight between Edmund and Edgar. If we look closely, we are struck by one fact – it is not the powerful Edmund, but his younger brother who wins. In the first scenes of the play, Edmund had no trouble at all in outwitting Edgar – now five acts later in single combat it is Edgar who dominates. Accepting this as dramatic truth rather than romantic convention, we are forced to ask how it has come about. Can we explain it all quite simply in terms of moral growth – Edgar has grown up, Edmund has decayed – or is the whole question of Edgar's undoubted development from *naïveté* to understanding – and Edmund's visible change from freedom to entanglement – far more complex than a cut-and-dried question of the triumph of the good? Aren't we compelled in fact to relate this to all the evidence connected with the question of growth and decline, i.e. youth and age, i.e. strength and weakness? If for a moment we assume this point of view, then suddenly the whole play seems concerned with sclerosis opposing the flow of existence, of cataracts that dissolve, of rigid attitudes that yield, while at the same time obsessions form and positions harden. Of course the whole play is also about sight and blindness, what sight amounts to, what blindness means – how the two eyes of Lear ignore what the instinct of the Fool apprehends, how the two eyes of Gloucester miss what his blindness knows. But the object has many facets; many themes criss-cross its prismatic form. Let us stay with the strands of age and youth, and in pursuit of them move on to the very last lines of the play. When we read or hear them first our reaction is, 'How obvious. What a trite end', for Edgar says:

> We that are young
> Shall never see so much, nor live so long.

The more we look at them the more troubling they become, because their apparent precision vanishes, making way for a strange ambiguity hidden in the naïve jangle. The last line is, at its face value, plain nonsense. Are we to understand that the young will never grow up, or are we to understand that the world will never again know old men? Both of these seems a pretty feeble winding up by Shakespeare of a consciously written masterpiece. However, if we look back through Edgar's own line of action, we see that although Edgar's experience in the storm parallels Lear's, it certainly has not wrought in him the intense inner change that has taken place in Lear. Yet Edgar acquired the strength for two killings – first Oswald, then his brother. What has this done to him – how deeply has he experienced this loss of innocence? Is he still wide-eyed? Is he saying in his closing words that youth and age are limited by their own definitions – that the only way to see as much as Lear is to go through Lear's mill, and then *ipso facto* one is young no longer? Lear lives longer than Gloucester – in time and in depth – and as a result he undoubtedly 'sees' more than Gloucester before he dies. Does Edgar wish to say that it is experience of this order and intensity that really means 'living long'? If so, the 'being young' is a state with its own blindness – like that of the early Edgar, and its own freedom like that of the early Edmund. Age in turn has its blindness and decay. However, true sight comes from an acuteness of living that can transform the old. Indeed, it is clearly shown to us in the unfolding of the play that Lear suffers most and 'gets farthest'. Undoubtedly, his brief moment of captivity with Cordelia is as a moment of bliss, peace and reconciliation, and Christian commentators often write as though this were the end of the story – a clear tale of the ascent from the inferno through purgation to paradise. Unfortunately for this neat view the play continues, pitilessly, away from reconciliation.

> We that are young
> Shall never see so much, nor live so long.

The power of Edgar's disturbing statement – a statement that rings like a half-open question – is that it carries no moral overtones at all. He does not suggest for one moment that youth or age, seeing or not seeing, are in any way superior, inferior, more desirable or less desirable one than the other. In fact we are compelled to face a play which refuses all moralising – a play which we begin to see not as a narrative any longer, but as a vast, complex, coherent poem designed to study the power and the emptiness of nothing – the positive and negative aspects latent in the zero. So what does Shakespeare mean? What is he trying to teach us? Does he mean that suffering has a necessary place in life and is worth cultivating for the knowledge and inner development it brings? Or does he mean us to understand that the age of titanic suffering is now over and our role is that of the eternally young? Wisely, Shakespeare refuses to answer. But he has given us his play, and its whole field of experience is both question and answer. In this light, the play is directly related to the most burning themes of our time, the old and the new in relation to our society, our arts, our notions of progress, our way of living our lives. If the actors are interested, this is what they will bring out. If we are interested, that is what we will find. Fancy dress, then, will be left far behind. The meaning will be for the moment of performance. . . .

Source: extract from the chapter on 'The Rough Theatre' in *The Empty Space* (London, 1968), pp. 85–95.

Charles Marowitz   'The Tony Richardson—Nicol Williamson *Hamlet*' (1969)

[Marowitz adds the following prefatory comments to the reprint of his original review of the Round House production of February 1969–Ed.]:

Any play is *the play* plus its social context. Richardson's *Hamlet* was mounted in the name of some wooly-minded notion of modernity. It is like Noël Coward offering himself as lead actor with Grotowski's Theatre Laboratory. Richardson by temperament and experience was a traditional director, whose best results from *Look Back in Anger* onwards were in the tradition of solid, realistically-based, English behaviourist-acting. Commendable as it may be to wish to destroy that tradition, it is not done through the agency of press-releases. My antipathy to the commercial aura of this production may well have accelerated my ire, but none of those facts was kept secret, and they must have conditioned the attitudes of other spectators as well. A performance, of course, begins the moment you hear about it; or read about it in the press. The expectation generated by 'announcements' is the prelude to that performance, even if it happens six or eight weeks before the actual event. One can no sooner put that from the mind than one can the experience of having seen an actor in countless other roles before encountering him anew. The past impinges upon the present in a way that cannot be mitigated. This was a factor here, as was the general ennui generated by yet another rendition of *Hamlet*. There are always a plethora of Hamlets about, but at this time it was a veritable deluge, plus the fact that I had recently restructured the play for my own company. I had become so innured to the play's narrative and poetry that nothing short of a total, emotional blitz could have moved me on that subject again. This is something that actors and directors never take fully into consideration. For them, it is new and fresh and original, but for a critic, in an average season, it is that blustering old war-horse, going through its ponderous paces, yet again. It takes an enormous dedication of will to keep one's mind from splattering all over the carpet. Here, a younger critic, a greener critic, may well have derived much more from this performance that I did. Months after the event, I saw the film of the production and it was so good that one went through that self-abusing reappraisal that makes one suspect every emotional and intellectual response triggered in a theatre. There is certainly a degree of cultural-exposure which becomes injurious to the sense, and although periods of recuperation mend the tissue, at the height of that exposure can one really credit anything one says or feels?

[The review itself is now presented – Ed.]

If the planned transfer to Broadway of the Tony Richardson-Nicol Williamson *Hamlet* had fallen through, as my grapevine told me it might, New York would have been spared one of the most mindless and pretentious productions of Shakespeare ever souped up for British consumption.

The production was a striking example of the facility with which PR techniques and the right sort of media preliminaries can condition the reaction of even the most sophisticated theater-going public. Richardson, who recently banned film critics from *The Charge of the Light Brigade*, is a past-master at propelling a commodity beyond the distance it can travel on its own steam. The studied contempt against critics which preceded *Light Brigade* managed, in some quarters, to garner more upbeat notices than it would ever have received had it just turned up as the next item on the cinematic assembly-line. No great shakes as a picture, that was not the issue on its release. After the press boys had masticated the pablum specially prepared by Richardson, one's approval or disapproval of the film was hinged to one's attitude to film criticism and its effect on the public. In the less gullible journals, the subterfuge was seen through, and the film got the pummelling it deserved.

The hoopla hooched up by Richardson for *Hamlet* concerned a woolly-minded concept called 'free theater' which after the rhetoric subsided, turned out to be a plea for open staging and a blast at proscenium theater; a crusade which is almost exactly 50 years old and which, in England, has already succeeded in places as far afield as Stoke-on-Trent and Bristol, not to mention recent environmental breakthroughs at LAMDA, Donmar, the three London fringe theaters, and the Round House itself.

The only thing more irritating than Richardson's production is his fatuous program note which burps sophistries such as: 'This (the availability of theatre to new audiences) can only be done by emphasizing what is most unique in theatre; its presence'; and later, half-baked Artaudian theories echoing through the windier recesses of his mind: 'To restore impact to the theatre, it must be liberated from the tyranny of any form. Every production can have its own shape of stage and audience.'

The tenor of the note and the entire production infers a revolutionary attitude, and in the face of the tame, muddle-headed, and unresourceful work being projected, I can think of no production in recent years that does more to reinforce the stodgier traditions of English acting. The possibilities of the Round House, a marvellously open-spaced engine-shed, are totally ignored. A makeshift thrust stage is set up on traditional actor-audience geography. The setting could be transferred wholesale either to a West End or Broadway theatre, and I don't doubt for a moment that's what was in everyone's mind. The TV film of the play has already been accomplished during its London run. The smell of commercial packaging and commodity merchandizing is so strong in the air of the Round House that bleats about art and revolution are about as credible as a Cecil B. de Mille version of *Ten Days That Shook the World*.

As for the production itself, its one and only reason-for-being is the presence of Nicol Williamson, a formidable talent, now officially referred to as 'our finest actor under 40', a nomination one would not dispute, although even 'our finest actor under 40' can look gormlessly trapped in the vacuum of a thoughtless production context, which he does.

Williamson's Hamlet is a rasping, dentalized, round-shouldered lope of a performance, glorying in its North Country aggressiveness and committed to eccentricity as if only that could rescue it from the clutches of conventionality. One critic called it the only Hamlet to shake free from the influence of Gielgud and Olivier. That it does, but in so doing, lands itself in a world of posturing so removed from the demands of the text that one can analyze it only as a specimen of anti-classical behaviorism rather than a coherent interpretation of the role. Williamson's accent mangles the verse the way that relentless machine in *Goldfinger* masticated automobiles. It is temporarily exciting to see verse propelled with such force, and predictable reading shattered by unexpected inflections. For this Hamlet, the vow to revenge his father's death is a convenient excuse for venting an hostility which would have grasped at any pretext for unleashing itself. His attitude to Claudius is one of unmasked contempt; to Gertrude, unmasked contempt; to Polonius, after a few paltry attempts at sarcasm, unmasked contempt; to Ophelia, after a few bear-hugs and copped feels, unmasked contempt. In short, Williamson's reaction to both internal pressures and external events is dynamically monotonous. It is the spirit of Lear raging in the slender frame of the prince. It is neither the courtier nor the scholar, the soldier nor the glass of fashion, but a whining, neurotically suppressed, superannuated post-grad spoiling for a fight and obviously not up to licking even the shortest kid on the block.

Marianne Faithfull's Ophelia, indistinguishable from her interpretation in last year's *Three Sisters*, wrinkles her eyes and oozes vapidity.

She suggests a long-standing intimacy with Hamlet in the scenes where they are together and total unfamiliarity when they are apart. When she performs, one can hear the creaky trundling of her unlubricated machinery trying to make individual lines work with no comprehension of what the overall role is supposed to convey. She involves us mainly in her technical inadequacies; the suspense in her performance in centered entirely on whether or not she will get through speeches without turning them into the mindless drivel, which, at almost every phrase, threatens to overtake them.

The supporting cast is uniformly atrocious. Claudius is neither king nor father, villain nor neutral; he hovers around the stage like a desperate pilot signalling to land and being told to keep circling. The Queen, grossly underwritten to begin with, minces, grins, bats her eyelashes, and, utilizing every conspicious gesture in the book, managers to produce a characterization so unsubstantial it could double as the Ghost. The smaller roles are played in the rough and ready style that flourished at the Old Vic 20 years ago. The production, if by that one means the structure of the play's events and the organization of its language in an attempt to insinuate some impression of its meaning, simply does not exist.

SOURCE: review in *The Village Voice* (1969); reprinted, with additional comments, in *Confessions of a Counterfeit Critic* (London, 1973), pp. 147–51.

Michael Billington   'Nicol Williamson's Hamlet' (1969)

No doubt about it: Nicol Williamson's Hamlet undoubtedly leaves a lot out. The observer's eye is mercilessly there but scarcely the scholar's tongue or soldier's sword; 'Sweet prince' seems the strangest of appellations for this testy, penetrating member of the blood royal; and he was like, had he been put on, to have proved most costive. Not for the first time it occurs to me that I would far rather live in an Elsinore governed by Claudius than one ruled by someone as mercurial as Hamlet.

And yet, for all its excess coarseness and over-reliance on a note of unmasked contempt, this is the most exciting Hamlet since Redgrave's 1958 Stratford performance. Its secret is not that it abandons the reflectively melancholic Gielgud tradition or that it offers the kind of angry young Hamlet with whom the Roundhouse audience can identify: it is, quite simply, that it combines a relish for grandiose romantic effect with a scrupulous attention to detail and to the sheer basic sense of the lines. The text has clearly been re-thought and re-felt: at the same time the door has been left open for the use of arresting effect.

In aspect, Williamson is not your conventionally good-looking Hamlet: the leonine head with its waves of light-blond hair gives him a slightly top-heavy look and the voice combines the slimy whine of Brummagem with the slightly pinched vowel-sounds of a puritanical Scottish lay-preacher. He looks more like Gertrude's elder brother than her son and has clearly been doing post-graduate work at Wittemberg, even heading possibly for the role of militant junior don siding with student complaints. From the start he is weighed down, more onerously than any Hamlet I have seen, with a prophetic sense of doom, with a farsighted realisation that he is involved in some kind of ritualistic dance of death: thinking of his mother's marriage he warns us, emphatically and fatalistically, that 'it is not nor it *cannot* come to good'. The contradiction in Hamlet is, however (and it is this more than anything that explains the character's obsessive fascination down the centuries), that his instinct for death and destruction is combined with a paradoxical enthusiasm for life: the uses of the world may be weary, stale, flat and unprofitable but yet the players must be well-bestowed; women may be painted deceivers but 40,000 brothers could not, with all their quantity of love, make up his sum. This sublime contradiction Williamson expresses perfectly. At the news of the Ghost's nocturnal presence on the battlements he rubs his hands together in delirious anticipation and paces the stage like a demonically possessed sentry letting his words tumble over each other. And he delights in mimicry and play: he gets caught up in the emotional excitement of the 'rugged Pyrrhus' speech, abandoning it only with reluctance to the First Player, and in private converse with Horatio he fastidiously and exactly apes other people's accents and mannerisms.

The romanticism? This comes out in key moments like the leap into Ophelia's grave on 'This is I, Hamlet the Dane', cloak being flung back over left shoulder as if it were the Red Shadow finally revealing himself. The realism? *Passim.* Never before have I been made to realise that Hamlet has always been an impassioned railer, that when he advises Ophelia to betake herself to a Nunnery this is part of a familiar stream of invective at which Ophelia can indulgently smile. Never before have I seen a Hamlet who communicated such a strong sense of physical disgust: 'nay but to *live* in the rank sweat of an enseamed bed', he retchingly observes, the point rubbed home by the fact that Claudius and Gertrude seem to conduct much of their diplomatic business from a fourposter. Never before have I felt a Hamlet establish quite such a fearsome and direct contact with his audience: the soliloquies have a strong element of challenge about them ('Who does me this, HA?') and Yorick's skull is held up for our inspection so that the moral to be drawn from it ('Now get you to my lady's table and tell her, let her paint an inch thick, to *this* favour she must come') is inescapable.

This is not a complete Hamlet. On the debit side, it reminds me of Agate's description of Wolfit: 'There is very little suggestion of weakness and Hamlet's reluctance to put paid to his stepfather's account is almost as inexplicable as it would be in the case of a heavyweight boxer or Woolwich Arsenal centre forward'. It lacks irony, delicacy, gentleness. Its virtues, however, plead trumpet-tongued on its behalf. It matches the play's questing feverishness with a bottled hysteria of its own. It informs the lines with a bristling, bruising intelligence and is constantly showing Hamlet to be testing those around him—'How if I answer No?' he suddenly asks Osric when confronted with Laertes's challenge, as if genuinely anxious to get a reply. And it provides that rarest of all sensations: the feeling that the actor rejoices wholeheartedly in his presence on the stage. After David Warner's Hamlet (too lymphatic by half) and Richard Chamberlain's (a handsome head-boy with deep personal problems) it is refreshing to find a man-sized ravenously hungry attack on the part. Some actors take the stage by default: Mr Williamson invariably takes it by storm.

Source: review of the Round House Production, February 1969, reprinted in Billington's *The Modern Actor* (London, 1973), pp. 75–7.

J. L. Styan   Shakespeare, Peter Brook and Non-Illusion (1977)

[Styan first outlines the main features of important productions at Stratford after 1960, when Peter Hall took charge of the Royal Shakespeare Company – Ed.]

. . . Peter Brook's contributions to the sequence of developments at Stratford in the sixties was, however, the most far-seeing. The fullest statement of his ideas appeared in a slim volume published in 1968, *The Empty Space*,[1] although the thinking here had been initiated twenty years earlier in a notable essay, 'Style in Shakespearean Production'.[2] From the first, his sense of theatre was ritualistic. Audiences still unspoiled by the pedantic accretions of tradition, he argued, willingly accepted the flights and suggestions, the basic inconsistencies and anachronisms, of the stage, and he believed that a revitalised drama always returned to its popular source: 'I can take any empty space and call it a bare stage. A man walks across this empty space whilst someone else is watching him, and this is all that is needed to an act of theatre to be engaged.'[3] Thus Brook began his book. The Elizabethan theatre was born of a violent, vital, pioneering age, and it was 'just a place with some doors – and so it enabled the dramatist effortlessly to whip the spectator through an unlimited succession of illusions. . . . This theatre not only allowed the playwright to roam the world, it also allowed him free passage from the world of action to the world of inner impressions'.[4] Shakespeare was 'experimental, popular, revolutionary'[5] and productions of his plays in England at least had been influenced by the discovery that they 'were written to be performed continuously, that their cinematic structure of alternating short scenes, plot intercut with subplot, were all part of a total shape. This shape is only revealed dynamically, that is, in the uninterrupted sequence of these scenes.'[6] The task was to recreate Shakespeare's theatrical meaning for today's audiences.

The way was to be that of non-illusion. Brook's programme note to his production of *A Midsummer Night's Dream* in 1970 was the simple statement which concluded his chapter on 'The Rough Theatre', the popular category in which he placed Shakespeare in his book: 'We must open our empty hands and show that really there is nothing up our sleeves. Only then can we begin.' Anything more pictorial – a touch of period in the décor of the stage, a suggestion of day or night in the lighting – and the audience had at once surrendered its imagination into the director's hands. The theory had been set out twenty years before:

> When an audience enters a theatre, its imagination is completely open. If . . . it finds the curtain up, the stage bare, then the initial anti-pictorial gesture of the production makes it clear that no picture is going to be presented, and that the proscenium is merely an arch over a square of boards on which the actors will seek to create an illusion. Thus in the opening gambit the conventions are established, and the audience's imagination is liberated, leaving it both ready and capable of creating its own pictures.[7]

In one way this was a restatement of the old notion that Shakespeare's poetry should do the painting, but in another it was the most absolute assertion of the primacy of the theatrical over the literary experience of drama.

It was none other than Barry Jackson who in 1946 had introduced Peter Brook to Stratford audiences at the age of 21. Brook made a challenging and risky choice in *Love's Labour's Lost*, which he had seen that spring in Paris spoken in a French which reminded him of Molière, Marivaux and Musset. Faced with a stage from which 'actors and audience seem to be staring at each other rather pathetically through the wrong end of a pair of opera glasses' [Stephen Potter's comment], he decided to try to capture the conceited style of this comedy by pictorial means. He turned to Watteau, 'because the style of his dresses, with its broad, undecorated expanses of billowing satin seemed the ideal visual correlative of the essential sweet-sad mood of this play'.[8] In the set and costumes, the designer, Reginald Leefe, sought a pastoral chastity which was matched by Brook's delicate groupings and 'puff-ball lightness' of movement [*The Times's* comment]. Exquisite grace on the part of the lovers was balanced by the touch of harlequinade for the comics: Costard was a Pierrot dressed after Watteau, Constable Dull a doll policeman in pale blue Victorian uniform, Holofernes in mortar board with silver stencil and silver tassel. Yet in this context Marcade's black entrance in v ii,

MARCADE	The King your father –
PRINCESS	Dead for my life
MARCADE	Even so: my tale is told.
BEROWNE	Worthies away, the scene begins to cloud.

fell aptly, in Trewin's phrase like 'frost in the summer night'. The scribbles on the text of the prompt-copy convey nothing of this achievement in style: everything lay in the directing.

Brook's hunt for the 'inner vision' of a play was on. In 1947, Stratford presented his very youthful *Romeo and Juliet* (Daphne Slater was 19, Laurence Payne was 27) encircled by a stylised decoration of toy crenellated walls against a deep blue sky. In 1950, his choice was *Measure for Measure*. Awkward in the study, traditionally criticised for a disjointed structure, an uncertain 'problem comedy' as to mood, ranging in characterisation, this play needed a production which would fuse its parts and prove its coherence. Brook sought the sources of its energy and compulsion as drama. He recognised the common soil which nourished at once the depravity and dark sexuality of the city, and the zealous purity of Isabella. Without being realistic, the action was rooted in 'a very real world . . . the disgusting, stinking world of medieval Vienna'. [See above, page 126 Ed.] He found what Robert Speaight called the play's 'interior fire' especially in the street and prison scenes.

Brook designed his own permanent set of stone pillars and arches which could be backed and touched with suggestive detail of palace or street, convent or prison, and in spite of this semi-pictorial bent, the action could be swift and various and played out to the audience. But the set was less important than the costumes, in which several critics felt the grotesque spirit of Breughel and Bosch. The vigour of the crowded streets of dissolute Vienna is well conveyed by the prompt-book notes for I iii:

Crowd noise and entrance immediately lights fade
6 peasants, 1 beggar, 2 whores, 3 cripples
Barrel, table, jug and mugs, bagpiper
Squabbling, hubbub, drum-roll
To see Claudio, one jumps on to back
Mistress Overdone, Pompey exeunt L then peer round door, re-enter as
    prisoners appear
Provost leads procession on OP with drummer
Tableau and jeering
At sign from Provost, 2 take Juliet's arms and turn half circle with her, showing
    her to crowd. Jeering
Gaoler enters through soldiers with pikes, points stick at Juliet
Juliet rushes to Claudio, embraces him
2 seize Claudio, pull him back to sign from Provost
Crowd yells
Exit Claudio, jeering rising to a roar
Crowd follows jeering

For the prison, grilles and bars were set in the doors and arches, and the grim procession of prisoners themselves created the setting throughout the scene, as the prompt-book indicates:

> Prisoners take positions in silence; moan, clank chains, move uneasily at entrances and exits of Pompey, Overdone. Also, when Isabella comes out of cell, and before and after final soliloquy. Otherwise quiet throughout.

It is these prisoners whom Pompey in stocks greets in IV iii ('I am as well acquainted here, as I was in our house of profession'), but Brook missed the opportunity for the pimp/clown to embrace the house with the ironic naming of his clients. The stage was dotted with gruesome items – a block, a wheel, a weapons rack, a torture machine: T. C. Worsley commented that this production had gone 'beyond our usual Dickensian or eighteenth-century stage prisons to the wheels, the fires, the whips and the racks of a still cruder epoch'. And the orchestra pit became an extension of the stage when Barnardine was hauled up from his straw by a rope.

In such a world, Isabella's unnatural preference for her chastity before her brother's life seemed more probable. But then the temptation scenes (II ii & iv) were strongly physical, with Angelo grasping Isabella's arms, holding her against a table, squeezing her wrist, so that when the climax of the play came, it came with a most memorable pause. In V i, Brook asked Barbara Jefford as Isabella to pause before she knelt for Angelo's life, and to hold it until she felt the audience could take it no longer, a lapse of time lasting as much as two minutes. Richard David reported,

> 'He dies for Claudio.' The pause that followed must have been among the longest in theatre history. Then hesitantly, still silent, Isabella moved across the stage and knelt before the Duke. Her words came quiet and level, and as their full impact of mercy reached Angelo, a sob broke from him. It was perfectly calculated and perfectly timed; and the whole perilous manoeuvre had been triumphantly brought off.[9]

The pause was not memorable merely for its length, but because it accurately caught the implications of all the elements built into the production, cruel and Christian, death-bringing or life-giving. Brook described the device as a 'voodoo pole': 'a silence in which the abstract notion of mercy became concrete for that moment to those present'.[10] In a motionless tableau it perhaps encapsulated something of the play's inner vision.

In 1955, Brook reclaimed *Titus Andronicus* by judicious cutting and a formalised treatment designed to emphasise the tragedy's 'ritual of bloodshed'. Again he had sensed an appropriate style for an uncommon play. He was less successful in releasing Shakespeare's ritualistic energy in his first encounter in 1957 with another intractable play, *The Tempest*. It was a fussy production of transformation scenes using gauzes and traps, and accompanied by Brook's own *musique concrète* (Kenneth Tynan conjectured 'a combination of glockenspiel, thunder-sheet, Malayan nose-flute and discreetly tortured Sistine choirboy'). Not much better was the 1963 revival of *The Tempest* in collaboration with Clifford Williams. The fantasy of the play was perhaps made more obvious by a magic mirror setting in perspex, and a note by Williams in the programme hinted at the direction of R.S.C. was taking: 'At one time we thought of lifting all the scenery away at the end (as happens in one of Roland Petit's ballets), or of putting all the characters of the finale in clown's costumes, to underline the derisory nature of the play's resolution.' And in 1968 Brook took what now seems the inevitable step with *The Tempest* to meet the demands of his own creative imagination.

At the instigation of Jean-Louis Barrault and sponsored by the Théâtre des Nations, Brook produced *The Tempest* for a third time in the Round House, London. The set had become a gymnasium of high scaffolding under a tent roof. The actors wore work clothes and were accompanied by percussion instruments. The intention was not a literal interpretation of the play, but 'abstractions, essences, and possible contradictions embedded in the text. The plot is shattered, condensed, deverbalised; time is discontinuous, shifting. Action merges into collage'.[11] Ariel evoked the storm by voice and gesture, while the cast enacted both the crew and the sinking ship. Miranda and Ferdinand met, touched and made love, while Ariel and Caliban mimicked them. Caliban emerged from between the legs of a giantess Sycorax standing at the top of the scaffolding, and evil was born. He raped Miranda and became master of the island in a sexual orgy. So the play's submerged ideas were dragged to the surface, improvised and explored in terms of such clues as Shakespeare had provided. The result was mutilated Shakespeare, but original Brook: in their time colleagues had said as much of G. Wilson Knight's symbolic commentaries.

While still tussling with *The Tempest*, Brook mounted his most far-reaching assault on a Shakespeare tragedy, this time on a play which was perhaps the greatest challenge the stage could accept. In early 1962 he had read in French Jan Kott's highly charged and idiosyncratic judgements in *Shakespeare Our Contemporary*, and discussed with him the unheroic, existentialist view of *King Lear* as 'a great ritual poem on evanescence and mortality, on man's loneliness in a storm-tossed universe'.[12] Kott's chapter on *Lear* had been entitled 'King Lear or Endgame': from his experience of the horrors of war in Poland, Kott thought he recognised in the play a familiar violence to humanity, and placed the King in company with the despairing anti-heroes of Samuel Beckett, Vladimir and Estragon, Hamm and Clov. There followed the rare case of a major production directly inspired by the opinions of a literary critic.[13] Kott's assertion was that Shakespeare was like the world, in which every age found what it was looking for; it 'cannot do otherwise'. With this a director like Brook could only agree: to set any play upon a stage was to offer an interpretation for the contemporary audience. Robert Weimann reminded readers of *Shakespeare Survey* that the reason why teddy boys appeared in *Romeo and Juliet*, why a Roman mob could be presented as revolutionaries, Hamlet shown as an angry young man, Brutus presented as an existentialist, Macbeth as a Fascist ruler or *King Lear* as an absurdist play, was that '*any* Shakespeare staging has to come to terms with the tension between Renaissance values and modern evaluations'.[14]

However, in the process of coming to such contrived terms, primary Shakespearian values may be lost. Patrick Cruttwell was one of many who found Kott's thinking misbegotten and over-simplifying, and in a well-labelled article, 'Shakespeare Is Not Our Contemporary', he pointed out that 'if you ask Shakespeare the answers to the problems, you ask him the problems you yourself are obsessed with and you find the answers you yourself have already found'.[15] Jan Kott's world was bitter, brutal and erotic, and he found these qualities wherever he looked in Shakespeare, in tragedy and, comedy alike. Writing of 'The Sad Case of Professor Kott', Michael MacOwan argued that 'to sustain this misguided endeavour to cut the mind of Shakespeare to the measure of the mind of Kott, the methods of argument used are, necessarily, disingenuous and unscholarly'.[16] Comedy for this contemporary lay in the outrageous plotting, but it was also coloured by his unwillingness to see the joke; tragedy lay only in the suffering of the hero, not in his nobility of mind or sacrifice. Yet the Kott/Brook *King Lear* was received with unusual enthusiasm – in London as in Prague – much to the embarrassment of teachers: scholarly criticism was at odds with aesthetic acclaim.

The Kott/Brook *Lear* at Stratford in 1962 seemed to assert its artistic independence of scholarship and tradition by many felicities, but also by many deliberate distortions. Brook saw the play as a metaphysical farce about the blindness of man in an environment of savage cruelty. Accordingly the set and costumes were created in order to suggest a primitive mood of menace:

The set consists of geometrical sheets of metal which are ginger with rust and corrosion. The costumes, dominantly leather, have been textured to suggest long and hard wear. The knights' tabards are peeling with long use; Lear's cape and coat are creased and blackened with time and weather. The furniture is rough wood, once sturdy but now decaying back into its hard, brown grain. Apart from the rust, the leather and the old wood, there is nothing but space – giant white flats opening on to a blank cyclorama.[17]

The play began with slow deliberation and great formality of entrance and greeting, except that Lear (Paul Scofield) arrived unexpectedly from a side entrance, cutting through protocol. The declarations of the daughters were made with much ceremony and emphasised by the royal orb, as the prompt-book record:

Goneril rise x cs. Curtsey, Take orb from Kent. Move DSOP corner throne ros. Extend orb. Goneril return orb to Kent. Kent bow. x cs. Curtsey. x sit DSPS. Regan repeats business.

Meanwhile Lear sat with grizzled head erect, eyes narrowed dangerously and a cause for fear. He was described by J. C. Trewin as 'a figure of cold arrogance, set in tarnished gold, his hands clenched upon the arms of a crudely fashioned throne'.

The first innovation was a hunting scene of rowdy knights, following Goneril's admonishment of her father. Charles Marowitz noted: 'Incensed by her words, Lear overturns the dinner-table and storms out. This is the cue for general pandemonium as the knights, following their master's example, tip chairs, throw plates and generally demolish the chamber.'[18] He recorded that in rehearsal the stage 'exploded' in the improvisation, tankards flying through the air, hitting actors, ricocheting off the stage. The scene remained dangerously unpredictable in performance. This Lear, according to Harold Hobson, was not a myth, but 'a man capable of tramping twenty miles in a day over sodden fells, and arriving home at nightfall properly tired and in a filthy temper'. And Hobson added, 'In his rage he throws over his daughter's dinner table, and in its enormous revenge the universe overthrows his reason'. All this had the perverse effect of diminishing sympathy with Lear and increasing it with Goneril at the very moment when Shakespeare wishes to modify our first-act revulsion against him. However, not everyone found the King's capriciousness inappropriate, and Kenneth Tynan thought the effect 'revolutionary':

Instead of assuming that Lear is right, and therefore pitiable, we are forced to make judgements to decide between his claims and those of his kin. And the balance, in this uniquely magnanimous production, is almost even. . . . He is wilfully arrogant, and deserves much of what he gets.

Conversely, his daughters are not fiends. Goneril is genuinely upset by her father's irrational behaviour, and nobody could fault her for carping at Lear's knights, who are here presented as a rabble of bellicose tipplers. After all, what use has a self-deposed monarch for a hundred armed men? Wouldn't twenty-five be enough? We begin to understand Regan's weary inquiry: 'What need one?'[19]

It also followed that the beloved Kent of tradition became no less than a bully when he tripped poor Oswald. Tynan argued that these were correct alienation effects, making the familiar strange. But doesn't Shakespeare supply a full charge of alienation effects of his own when the King and his company are thrust upon the enigmatic heath?

Non-illusion dominated the scenes of storm on the heath. Marowitz reported that the rusted thunder-sheets had been fitted with motors which made them vibrate, and the actors mimed the storm to their orchestration.[20] J. C. Trewin wrote,

Brook always asks for our imagination. Consider the storm scene: a bare stage, the slow descent of what resemble three bleak rusted metal banners that aid the thunder's reverberation, the appearance of men crouching and huddling against the storm, and the sight of Paul Scofield's Lear striding and lunging on through the gale. Then he defies the elements with a mighty and sustained cry of 'Blow winds'.[21]

As these scenes moved to their crisis of madness, only the metallic screens were left on stage with the two pitiful figures of Gloucester and Lear. The descent of the thunder-sheets coincided exactly 'with a stylistic change in performance': the acting became 'starkly non-naturalistic'.[22] Kent and the Gentleman of III i ('Who's there besides foul weather?') staggered, fell, ducked and crouched beneath these sheets, and the prompt-book made a careful notation of Lear's voice and the sound effects:

Blow winds, and crack your cheeks (*short*) rage, blow (*longish*).
You cataracts, and hurricanoes spout,
Till you have drench'd our steeples, drown'd the cock (*short*).
You sulphurous and thought-executing fires,
Vaunt-couriers of oak-cleaving thunderbolts,
Singe my white head (*short*). And thou all-shaking thunder,
Strike flat the thick rotundity o' th' world,
Crack Nature's moulds (*short*), all germens spill at once
That makes ingrateful man (*longish + watch Scofield gesture*).

At this point Scofield, hands to his head, staggered back a pace. These sounds seemed to speak to Lear like a supernatural voice rather than be a general background of noisy opposition, and it was this storm that was heard rumbling a further threat at the fall of the curtain.

Rehearsal and performance suffered somewhat from Brook's mistaken urge to see the Fool and Edgar as fully rounded, motivated characters rather than functional role-players. Marowitz reported an actual improvisation designed to establish the Fool's 'offstage character', no less. He was to explore an affectionate relationship with Cordelia, and behind his mask be 'a worried man and terribly tired of all the desperate foolery that he has to carry on all day long'.[23] In performance, the Fool (Alec McCowen) was treated brutally by Lear, and when the storm broke he chose not to huddle under the King's robes, but crouched apart upstage. The role of Edgar puzzled the director, who found it hard to make consistent a character who had to change his job so frequently: Brook had not yet grasped the full implications of non-illusory theatre.

The most heated criticism was prompted by Brook's treatment of Gloucester in the scene of his blinding (iii vii). Robert Speaight had properly condemned Kott for ignoring the play's great redemptive moments: 'It is easy to present Lear as a tragedy of absurdity and despair if in forty pages you leave out any mention of Cordelia.'[24] Brook was likewise determined to create a cruel and hostile world for Lear by cutting what signs of pity and hope he dared. Thus, Cornwall's servants were omitted, and with them their balancing compassion for a Gloucester who had been blinded first with Cornwall's golden spur, then with his fingers ('out vile jelly'). Instead, a cold Brechtian light came up and [in Bamber Gascoigne's comment] the audience was given the unforgettable visual image of 'a hunched Gloucester, his eyes just out and a ragged cloth thrown over his head, trying to find his way off the stage among the servants who are clearing the set'. One actor was instructed to be sick, presumably to encourage the audience, who were denied 'all possibility of aesthetic shelter' and forced to 'take stock of the scene before being engulfed in automatic applause'.[25] By the same impulse the harmonious music Shakespeare called for to wake Lear from his madness ('louder the music there', iv vii) was made harsh upon the ear.[26] The prompt-book has 'horns off'. And the dying Edmund was not permitted to try to save the royal prisoners at the end ('some good I mean to do/Despite of mine own nature', v iii); instead, he died on stage and was dragged off ignominiously by Edgar.

These flaws notwithstanding, highly respected critics joined in a chorus of praise. Thinking perhaps of the ancient belief that *Lear* was unactable, Tynan wrote of 'this incomparable production'; Philip Hope-Wallace found it 'the most moving production of the play' he had seen since the war; and W. A. Darlington thought it would go into theatrical history 'as the best all-round performance of this tremendous play in modern times'. But perhaps the most acute comment came from an American scholar, Michael Goldman, who observed that all the alienation finally made the play less painful and more manageable: 'It succeeded in giving us the impression of going through a great deal of horror without having to digest it'; but with a nicely balanced judgement he conceded that Peter Brook 'shows us more of Shakespeare's meaning when he is wrong about it than most of us do when we are right'.[27]

All-white sets of plain curtains or flats date back to J. B. Fagan in the twenties. They encouraged a non-realistic image for Shakespeare, but the tired eyes of the spectator inhibited attention as well as illusion. The practice matured somewhat with the three-sided white box design, lit harshly from above, conceived by Christopher Morley for Trevor Nunn's Stratford season of 1969, particularly for *Pericles* and *The Winter's Tale*. Nunn's professed purpose was to focus upon the actors and their relationships in 'a kind of chamber architecture'[28] which must have made the open stagers shake their heads. In *The Winter's Tale*, the set served to symbolise a white nursery world of innocence as well as to mark reality from illusion by a lighting change from yellow to blue for Leontes's first-act asides, unhappily suggesting that in his jealousy he was also subject to schizophrenic hallucinations. Peter Brook had moved in a similar direction, notably with his violently Artaudian production of Peter Weiss's *Marat/Sade* (1964), where his plain cold set was planned primarily to achieve a Brechtian effect of alienation. The ultimate setting of this kind was demonstrated by Sally Jacobs for Brook's Stratford production of *A Midsummer Night's Dream* in 1970.

After Kott's essay, 'Titania and the Ass's Head', erotic versions of *The Dream* had proliferated, the most notable example being John Hirsch's production at Stratford, Ontario in 1968. Brook, however, did not seek the key to the play in its sexual theme, but in its element of magic. In his *Orpheus* essay of 1948 he had long before attacked the tradition of 'gauzes, ballets and Mendelssohn' associated with this play, and by coincidence a Regent's Park Open Air Theatre production in the summer of 1970 had disproved the idea that a pastoral setting provided a fitting background: 'The main casualty, of course, is magic. You cannot have magic in an environment loud with passing aircraft and where actors are obliged to trumpet their lines to reach the back row. [Irving Wardle's comment]. Brook sought the magic not in the fairies, who could as well be stage hands as ballet dancers, but in the play itself, as Helen Dawson observed:

> The key to this production comes when Theseus rebukes Hermia for refusing to marry Demetrius. 'Take time to pause', he tells her, and in the pause before the new moon, the play (the dream, the magic) takes place, peopled by the subconscious personalities of Theseus and Hippolyta before their wedding; of Hermia, Lysander, Demetrius and Helena before they finalise their love.[29]

Brook's problem was to find the appropriate substitutes for gauzes and ballets in all the visual and aural elements of his stage, and in the total style of performance. The result? 'The traditions of a lifetime have been torpedoed into infinity! Every accepted canon of stage-mounting has been thrown to the winds. And for what! The quaint simplicity of a child's Christmas toy-box.' But this was the response of *The Stage* to Granville-Barker's *Twelfth Night* in 1912.

Sally Jacobs's set was variously seen as a three-sided white box with white carpet, a squash court, a clinic, a scientific research station, an operating theatre, a gymnasium and a big top. Two doors were cut in the back wall, two slits in the sides, two ladders set at the downstage edges, and a gallery or catwalk round its top allowed the musicians and fairies to gaze down at the players fifteen feet below in the box. Dawson found it to be 'not only a valid device, but one which bursts with invention', and Irving Wardle thought it 'removes the sense of being earthbound: it is natural here for characters to fly'. Into this space the immortals could indeed descend on trapezes or manipulate flexible metal coils on the end of rods to suggest trees. For John Russell Brown, 'this was a machine for acting in',[30] and at the same time the actors acting in it were the visible puppets of the machine.

The box was lit with a fierce white light, and when drums rolled the whole company swooped into the arena in long white capes: not unlike the actors in Williams's *The Comedy of Errors*, their entrance bluntly declared that they were performers, and that thereafter the audience would be participants in their game. Capes flung off, the actors suddenly became characters in primary colours, Theseus in purple, Hippolyta in green, Egeus in blue, Philostrate in black with a tall cap, the lovers mostly in white. Philostrate later became Puck in billowing yellow silk breeches and a little blue cap, while the fairies were less than characters in their baggy grey judo pyjamas. With a great scarlet feather hammock hanging high above them, awaiting an occupant, the purple and yellow figures swung loosely on trapezes in their white open space.

The audience was to look into this magic box, not only to see the magic, but also to be shown what was up the magician's sleeve. Brook explained, 'Today we have no symbols that can conjure up fairyland and magic for a modern audience. On the other hand there are a number of actions that a performer can execute that are quite breathtaking. So we went to the art of the circus and the acrobat because they both make purely theatrical statements.'[31] For a month Brook had made the actors practise their tricks in improvisation and rehearsal, and in this setting the audience willingly accepted any invention of the company. The show was indeed breathtaking. The purple flower became a twirling plate on a juggler's wand, passed spinning from Puck to Oberon, a magic image in itself (II i). 'L'imagination n'a pas de forme', Brook stated in an interview with Guy Dumur for *Le Nouvel Observateur*:

Doit-on montrer une fleur plus extraordinaire qu'une autre, comme on le ferait dans la vitrine d'une boutique de modes? Non, la magie, c'est agir sur un être, opérer un changement. Aussi ai-je choisi de montrer l'opération magique par une scène d'acrobatie qui, jouée avec humour et virtuosité, prend la forme de quelque chose que tout le monde peut voir – un dépassement.[32]

'The plate does not *become* the flower', Peter Thomson commented; 'instead the act of passing it becomes the *magic* of the flower.' Thus, for her nightmare, Hermia was shown frantic in a jungle of the coiled wire (II ii). For his assignation with Titania, Bottom was carried to her scarlet bower of feathers in a shower of streamers and paper-plate confetti, backed by the blare of Mendelssohn's Wedding March as Oberon swung across the stage on a rope (III i). The lovers were more athletes and tumblers than dancers, chasing up and down the ladders and round the gallery. On Lysander's 'Withdraw and prove it too' to Demetrius, Hermia threw herself sideways across a door to prevent his going, and as if by a miracle he saved her from falling to the floor. Thereupon he hung her on a trapeze and her 'O me! You juggler! You canker-blossom!' was screamed to Helena as she dangled and kicked the air helplessly (III ii). At the end of the scene, Puck's teasing of Lysander and Demetrius in the wood had them chasing in confusion round the legs of giant stilts, on which Puck seemed to have a supernatural power to control their movements. In an interview with Ronald Hayman for *The Times*, Brook made this point: 'Where someone in a library uses intellectual and analytical methods to try to discover what a play is about, actors try to discover through the voice, through the body, through experiment in action.'[33]

Through all this, the players who were not on stage watched those below, on occasion shooting blue and silver darts across the space and making sounds with musical saws and plastic tubes. Richard Peaslee's two small percussion groups provided an intermittent accompaniment of music from bongo-drums, guitar, autoharp or zither, bed-springs and tubular bells. Frequently the verse lines shifted into mock-operatic arias, as for Lysander and Hermia on 'Fair love, you faint with wandering in the wood' (II ii), Demetrius's 'So sorrow's heaviness doth heavier grow', Puck's 'Up and down' and Helena's 'O weary night' (III ii), and 'Sixpence a day' by the mechanicals (IV ii). One would think that in all this the lines would be drowned. True, the text was often at variance with the action,[34] but J. W. Lambert was not alone in reporting a 'subtle sculpting of phrase'[35] and J. C. Trewin decided that 'the more closely we watched the actors' unexpected virtuosity, the more we heard of the play, better spoken than most people had ever known'.[36]

The fairies were no longer thought of as decorative, but as functional. They appeared as hefty circus hands when they swept up the confetti,[37] as familiar spirits when they physically controlled the movements of the lovers and demoniacally trapped them in their steel forest, and as amoral trolls when they stripped Snug of his trousers and created an obscene phallus for Bottom. Yet throughout the proceedings and all their busy interventions they remained calm and casual as puppet-masters should.

The mechanicals were very sober workmen, no longer the butts of the play, but keen amateur actors whose play was important to them. The customary laughs were missing, and Quince's tears of joy when Bottom returned in time to play Pyramus were genuinely moving. For his ass's head, Bottom wore no smothering fur, but a button nose, ear muffs and clogs, so that while he looked like a circus clown his facial expressions remained realistic to a degree: at least in this respect, the imagination was not free to run riot. Quince's men were treated as individuals, not stereotypes, so that their rehearsals were afforded an unusual dignity. Consequently, the play scene was unfunny, and Snug's lion really did alarm the ladies. Miriam Gilbert carefully noted the effect of Pyramus's dying speech:

Pyramus's death speech is fairly sincere. When Theseus says, 'This passion, and the death of a dear friend, would go near to make a man look sad', he looks across at Hippolyta, as if he's testing her. And she responds, as I think he wants her to, with 'Beshrew my heart, but I pity the man'. Theseus smiles. After Pyramus dies, there are again flip remarks, but Theseus remembers something else as he says, 'With the help of a surgeon, he might yet prove an ass', and the second half of the speech is directed out to the audience, slowly, musingly, challenging us to remember that Pyramus is Bottom who was an ass in the forest.[38]

When in earnest Bottom spoke his line, 'No, I assure you, the wall is down that parted their fathers' (v i), it was as if he were speaking the solemn moral of the piece for the benefit of all the lovers on the stage. So much sobriety among so much revelry seemed a curious contradiction, but the integration was strongly assisted by a controlling device of the director's. In *The Merry Conceited Humours of Bottom the Weaver* (1646), the pre-Restoration droll derived from *A Midsummer Night's Dream*, Theseus had doubled with Oberon and Hippolyta with Titania; it is probable that this was also the practice of the Lord Chamberlain's Men in the first production (*c.* 1595), since perforce they regularly doubled the roles in a play whose characters exceeded their number.[39] Although Benedict Nightingale declared that the doubling in Brook's production was done 'for no clear reason except economy', it was apparent to many that his intention was to suggest that the dream in the wood near Athens was a premarital fantasy of the Duke and his bride. The result was that the different groups within the play, the lovers, the fairies and the mechanicals, whose activities are usually set in contrast with one another, seemed more of a kind. The idea of the doubling was made neatly theatrical: Theseus and Hippolyta simply shed their white cloaks at 'dusk', and assumed them again at 'daybreak', by standing in each door to be dressed. Philostrate, Theseus's master of the revels, also became Puck, master of Oberon's magic.[40] The device was made visible: the audience was to participate as omniscient observers.

The new unity of the court and the wood scenes in addition introduced an unaccustomed and darker mood into the comedy. The high spirits of the dream were constantly undercut by the memory of the real problems facing the mortal lovers. Thus, Oberon's desire to punish, even degrade, the Titania he loved became a sobering issue. And Helen Dawson was careful to report that the wood scenes were 'not all fun':

As in a dream – and in a circus – there are moments of stark terror, at times reminiscent of Brook's *Marat/Sade*, when the tent turns into the high walls of an institution, when characters scuttle in fear through Puck's grotesque stilt legs. The fairies are streaked through with cruelty; an uneasily ambiguous bunch who seem to be warning, 'Don't meddle in illusion'.[41]

Theseus's melancholy extended to the last act, when his grave tone underscored the central concept of the imagination which 'bodies forth/

The form of things unknown'. Dawson considered that Brook's inter-
pretive idea cut through the play like a laser: 'In this extra-terrestrial
world we meet that part of ourselves which we bury under social
convention', and upon Theseus's rebuke to Hermia, 'Take time to
pause', all parties to the play were submitted to Shakespeare's idiom of
the supernatural.[42]

Needless to say, opinions about Brook's *Dream* were radically
divided. Those who disliked it could not see past the surface of the
production, Kenneth Hurren finding it 'a tiresomely self-indulgent
display of directorial gimmickry' and J. W. Lambert was troubled that
the director's 'commentary' on the play 'though often stimulating and
enriching, may swamp its subject'. David Selbourne, who watched
rehearsals, summarised this position when he argued that the production was 'technically brilliant', but a 'director-shaped commodity'.[43] However, a leader in *The Times* sought to resolve the
contradiction between the eccentric setting and performance, and the
shrewd and thought-provoking ideas many spectators perceived. The
article asked the question, 'How, beyond an identity of text, is Mr
Brook's production related to William Shakespeare's play?', and
answered,

This is not the kind of production that seeks to reconstruct the performance that
Shakespeare and his company are most likely to have devised. There have been
such essays in theatrical scholarship. Being original, the Stratford production is
not one of them. Being also appropriate, it is not at the opposite pole either,
where the play is treated as if it were no more than an idea, or a structure, or a
source of invention, rather in the way Joyce or Sartre has made use of Greek
myth. In versions of that kind the producer does not respect the natural limits
imposed by the text. He feels free to contrive situations and to characterise the
dramatis personae as he fancies. Being appropriate, the Stratford production is not
of that kind either. . . .

A good Shakespeare production is true to the original in a sense other than
textual accuracy or resemblance to how it might have been at the Globe. One
begins to see why Plato needed his doctrine of Forms. The question is easily
resolved if one is allowed to have a Form of the *Dream* laid up in heaven.
Productions of the play to be good would have to resemble the Form of it, the
resemblance being not one of copying but of congruence. So it would come
about that for all the trapezes, juggling, helical wire trees, and general non-
Elizabethanism, the Stratford production is not just good theatre but a true
production of the *Dream*.[44]

Just as the poet cannot explain his meaning in terms other than those of
the words of his poem, so Brook could not express his sense of a play in
terms other than those of performance. The Platonic Form lay hidden

there, valid and (one would think) scholarly, awaiting discovery. How close are we here to Wilson Knight's concept of 'interpretation'? . . .

SOURCE: extract from chapter II, in *The Shakespeare Revolution* (Cambridge, 1977), pp. 211–30.

NOTES

[These have been renumbered, with some deletions, from the original – Ed.]

1. Peter Brook, *The Empty Space* (London, 1968).
2. Peter Brook, 'Style in Shakespearean Production', *Orpheus*, I (1948), 139–46: reprinted in Daniel Seltzer (ed.), *The Modern Theater: Readings and Documents* (Boston, Mass., 1967).
3. *The Empty Space*, p. 9.
4. Ibid., pp. 78–9.
5. From an address at the UNESCO Shakespeare Quatercentenary, Paris, 1964; cited in J. C. Trewin, *Peter Brook: A Biography* (London, 1971). p. 148
6. *The Empty Space*, p. 78.
7. 'Style in Shakespearean Production', pp. 252–3.
8. Ibid., p. 254.
9. Richard David, 'Shakespeare's Comedies and the Modern Stage', in Allardyce Nicholl (ed.), *Shakespeare Survey 4* (Cambridge, 1951), p. 137.
10. *The Empty Space*, p. 81.
11. Margaret Croyden, 'Peter Brook's *Tempest*', *TDR The Drama Review*, 13, no. 3 (New York: Spring 1969), p. 126.
12. Martin Esslin, Introduction to Jan Kott, *Shakespeare Our Contemporary* (London, 1964; Anchor Books edition, New York, 1966), p. xxi.
13. The Alec Guiness/Simone Signoret *Macbeth* of 1966 was founded on Kott's chapter, 'Macbeth or Death-Infected'. Kott's essay 'Shakespeare's Bitter Arcadia' was possibly influential in the National Theatre's decision to produce an all-male *As You Like It* directed by Clifford Williams in 1967. . . . The chapter 'Titania and the Ass's Head', with its stress on female sexuality, has spawned several morbid *Dreams*, notably John Hancock's in San Francisco and Pittsburgh in 1966 and Theatre de Lys, New York in 1967; in this the fairies were strange flitting creatures and the lovers' codpieces were luminous. Graham Murray's 69 Theatre Company at Manchester University tried out Kott's hunched and lecherous fairies.
14. Robert Weimann, 'Shakespeare on the Modern Stage: Past Significance and Present Meaning', in Kenneth Muir (ed.), *Shakespeare Survey 20* (Cambridge, 1967), p. 115.
15. Patrick Cruttwell, 'Shakespeare is Not Our Contemporary', *Yale Review* LIX (1969), 49. See also Maynard Mack, *King Lear in Our Time* (Berkeley, Calif., 1965), for a similar attack.

16. Michael MacOwan, 'The Sad Case of Professor Kott', *Drama*, 88 (Spring 1968), 31.

17. Charles Marowitz, 'Lear Log', *Encore*, 10, no. 1 (Jan/Feb. 1963), 21. Marowitz was Brook's assistant director, and his 'Log' usefully documents the details of rehearsal. It is reprinted in *Tulane Drama Review* (Winter, 1963), pp. 103–21, and in C. Marowitz and S. Trussler (eds), *Theatre at Work* (London, 1967).

18. Ibid., p. 18.

19. Kenneth Tynan, *Observer*, 11 Nov. 1962.

20. Marowitz, op. cit., p. 27.

21. J. C. Trewin, *Birmingham Post*, 7 Nov. 1962.

22. Marowitz, op. cit., 27. See also Carol Carlisle, *Shakespeare from the Greenroom* (Chapel Hill, N. Carolina, 1969), p. 291.

23. Marowitz, op. cit., 26.

24. Robert Speaight, 'Shakespeare in Britain', *Shakespeare Quarterly*, XIV (1963), 421.

25. *The Empty Space*, p. 67.

26. See F. W. Sternfeld, 'Music in *King Lear* at the Royal Shakespeare Theatre', *Shakespeare Quarterly*, XIV (1963), 486–7.

27. Michael Goldman, *Shakespeare and the Energies of Drama* (Princeton, N.J., 1972), pp. 95–6 and footnote.

28. Trevor Nunn, interview with Margaret Tierney, *Plays and Players* (Sept. 1972), 27. See also John Russell Brown, *Free Shakespeare* (London, 1971), pp. 23–5.

29. Helen Dawson, *Observer*, 30 Aug. 1970.

30. John Russell Brown, op. cit., p. 27.

31. Cited by John Barber, *Daily Telegraph*, 14 Sept. 1970, and by Peter Thomson, 'A Necessary Theatre: The Royal Shakespeare Season 1970 Reviewed', in Kenneth Muir (ed.), *Shakespeare Survey 24* (Cambridge, 1971), p. 126.

32. Peter Brook, in *Le Nouvel Observateur*, 18 Sept. 1972.

33. Peter Brook, in *The Times*, 29 Aug. 1970.

34. See especially John Russell Brown, op. cit., pp. 43–4.

35. J. W. Lambert, *Drama* (Autumn 1971), p. 30.

36. Trewin, op. cit., p. 184.

37. In 1968 William A. Ringler Jr had argued that the fairies had probably been doubled with the mechanicals in Shakespeare's time. See his essay 'The Number of Actors in Shakespeare's Early Plays', in G. E. Bentley (ed.), *The Seventeenth-Century Stage: A Collection of Critical Essays* (Chicago, 1968), pp. 133–4. According to K. M. Briggs, the Elizabethans thought of fairies as both large and small: *The Anatomy of Puck* (London, 1959), pp. 13–16.

38. Miriam Gilbert, in a letter to the author after seeing performances in both New York and Chicago, 1971.

39. Frank Dunlop has also doubled these parts in a recent production at a Oxford Playhouse.

40. Egeus also became Quince, probably to give a leading actor a larger part.

41. Helen Dawson, *Observer*, 30 Aug. 1971.

42. Peter Brook, in *Le Nouvel Observateur*, op. cit., remarked: 'Shakespeare ne s'est servi des fées, comme, dans d'autres oeuvres, des rois et des reines, que pour en dire davantage. Tout est langage chez lui: les fées, les rois et les reines ne sont que les signes de ce langage.'

43. David Selbourne, 'Brook's *Dream, Culture and Agitation* (London, 1972), pp. 13–28.

44. *The Times*, 29 Aug. 1970.

3. MODERN AND CONTEMPORARY DRAMA: STUDIES AND REVIEWS, 1924–1976

James Agate   'Not an Ounce of Sensation' – Saint Joan (1924)

[Comment on Shaw's Preface]

Mr Shaw's preface to the newly printed version of *Saint Joan* is compact, as all this writer's prefaces are, of awful sanity, incredible erudition, and unbelievable flippancy. There is enough horse-sense in these sixty odd pages to keep the solar system going for a twelve-month. There is enough imaginative and reconstructive stuff about the Middle Ages to suggest that the author's power of divining the past is at least as great as Mr Wells's capacity to guess the future. The joking is first-rate.

Mr Shaw is at enormous pains to prove that Joan was really one of Mr Arnold Bennett's heroines born some five hundred years before her time. 'She was very capable; a born boss.' He makes us believe in the actuality of this Joan, mainly by adducing the wrong reasons. Joan is sane because the modern woman who allows her child to be vaccinated is insane. She is nineteen and healthy-minded because the people who in their old age take to monkey glands are diseased. We are to believe that she heard voices because people of a later date have been what is known as 'Galtonic visualisers'—like, one supposes, the folk who play blindfold chess. And so on, and so forth, at a fascinating length. Watch the brilliant fellow lay about him. The 'legal compulsion to take the doctor's prescription, however poisonous, is carried on to an extent that would have horrified the Inquisition and staggered Archbishop Laud'. Burning at the stake, breaking on the wheel, drawing and quartering did not inflict on the victims 'the misery, degradation and conscious waste and loss of life suffered in our modern prisons, especially the model ones'. The reason people formerly believed that the earth was flat 'is because their senses told them so'. Their senses told them nothing of the sort. What about boats hull-down on the horizon? But perhaps Mr Shaw is alluding to the days before boats. The preface is called 'a sober essay on the facts', though you might not call it that off-handedly.

The Main in Literature gives Mr Shaw his head. Shakespeare's Joan is 'as little authentic as the popular English view of the German Crown Prince in 1915 or Lenin in 1917'. Voltaire and Schiller are laughed off the page. Mark Twain's heroine 'skirted to the ground, and with as many petticoats as Noah's wife in a toy ark, is an attempt to combine Bayard with Esther Summerson from *Bleak House* into an unimpeachable American school-teacher in armour'. If Twain was a street arab, Andrew Lang was a simpleton who, like Walter Scott, 'enjoyed mediaeval history as a string of Border romances rather than as the record of a high European civilisation based on a catholic faith'. Anatole France is 'anti-clerical, anti-mystic, and fundamentally unable to believe that there ever was any such person as the real Joan'. In other words, Mr Shaw's Joan must be right because everybody else's has been wrong. One would rather say that the latest Joan is right by virtue of her own truth. The others have nothing to do with the case.

But one would not, in short space, undertake to discuss either comprehensively or in detail this closely packed piece of argument. As a piece of reasoning it is both wayward and flawless; as a piece of writing it is first-rate. It is all so extraordinarily 'cute. The difficulty now is not the mud which Shakespeare, or some other, threw at Joan, but the dirt which, later and for some hundreds of years, has been allowed to bespatter her judges, and the whitewash with which it became fashionable to coat their victim. This is so obvious that only a big man would have thought of saying it. Shakespeare's kings, Mr Shaw points out a little later, are not statesmen, and his cardinals have no religion. His world is not governed by forces in the shape of religions and laws, but by vulgarly ambitious individuals who make rows. This is perfectly true; but who else would have thought it noteworthy?

There follows a good passage showing that essential truth may demand an inexact picture of accidental facts:

It is the business of the stage to make its figures more intelligible to themselves than they would be in real life; for by no other means can they be made intelligible to the audience. Cauchon and Lemaître have to make intelligible not only themselves but the Church and the Inquisition, just as Warwick has to make the feudal system intelligible, the three between them having thus to make a twentieth century audience conscious of an epoch fundamentally different from its own. Obviously, the real Cauchon, Lemaître, and Warwick could not have done this: they were part of the Middle Ages themselves, and therefore as unconscious of its peculiarities as of the atomic formula of the air they breathed. But the play would by unintelligible if I had not endowed them with enough of this consciousness to enable them to explain their attitude to the twentieth century.

Well, they *do* explain it, and the author regrets that he cannot have twelve hours to do it in instead of three and a half. Will Mr Shaw never realise that the better the stuff the less you can stand of it? The scene in the Cathedral failed with me for the simple reason that my mind had been exhausted in the precedent struggle to cope with the aforesaid Church, Inquisition and Feudal System. Mr Shaw defends his epilogue on the ground that it is essential. One would attack it on the ground that it is redundant; to the perceptive it is implicit in all that has gone before. But perhaps all playgoers are not perceptive. Perhaps some of them are like the average jury, to whom counsel must say everything three times over. Once, because the box hears that counsel is speaking but does not distinguish the words. Twice, because it distinguishes the words but does not grasp their meaning. Three times, because, with luck, the jury may at last understand who is speaking to whom and what is being said. Mr Shaw's epilogue is for those who are hard both of hearing and understanding.

'It is always hard for superior wits to understand the fury roused by their exposures of the stupidities of comparative dullards.' To which the correct retort is: 'Art thou there, true-penny?' Cannot Mr Shaw understand the fury roused in the devout breast on reading that Joan is the most notable Warrior Saint in the Christian Calendar, and the 'queerest fish' among the eccentric worthies of the Middle Ages?

[Review, 30 March 1924, of the first performance.]

The thing to do with a new work by Mr Shaw – and, indeed, with any new work – is to find out its particular quality of interest, enlightenment, ecstasy, and provocation, to discover the exact kind and degree of emotion which that particular work, and not some other, contains. The point is to get at an author's meaning, and not to attempt to discover corroboration of your own conceptions. What like is Mr Shaw's *Joan?* For the moment nobody else's matters. You are not to find yourself aggrieved because her memorialist has not seen fit to bathe his subject in the sentimental mysticism of M. Anatole France, or to make her the central figure of some romantic melodrama, all gilt armour and mellifluence, unfurling her replies to her judges in words silken as the banner of France. Incidentally, if ever you saw Sarah's Maid, half angel and half bird – who, to the charge of being a witch, retorted, 'Si je l'étais, je ser-r-r-ais déjà loin!' with a gentleness and ineffability unknown to celestial choir or cooing dove – incidentally, if you remembered this most pathetic impersonation, the thing to do was to forget it and put it out of your consciousness altogether.

You are not, I suggest, to 'worrit' because Joan is not really the principal personage in the play, nor yet because the drama does not pan out quite as you would have it. Let me admit that it is a trifle disconcerting to see Joan plunged at the rising of the curtain into so very much the middle of things, ordering a noble lord about as though she were one of Mr Arnold Bennett's 'managing' young women. It would have been pleasant and romantic to find Joan tending sheep in her native fields of Domremy; hearing her 'voices', and rejecting some loutish suit. It is, to the conservative playgoer, distressing to have no glimpse of the coronation in Rheims Cathedral – what a 'set' they would have made of it in the old Lyceum days! – and to be fobbed off with the less important cloisters, and what for a time looks like mere desultory chatter. But I must not waste space in describing what the play is not, but rather try to make plain what it is.

Saint Joan seems to me – and I stand open to any amount of correction – to be a history of privilege. It is in seven scenes. The first sets the play going in so far as it establishes the immaculacy and immunity of the Maid, and provides her with armour, horses, men, and means of access to the Dauphin. The second scene shows her conquest of the Court. Let me say here, since I may not have space later on, that the Dauphin was beautifully played by Mr Thesiger, who showed beneath his astonishing grotesquerie the pity and pathos of all weakness. It is during this scene that Mr Shaw strikes one of his very few false notes. Joan is challenged: 'You tell us that Saint Catherine and Saint Margaret talk to you every day?' 'They do!' comes the retort. 'Through your imagination?' they suggest to her, and she replies, 'That is the way God talks to us'. Now Joan never said that and never believed it. If I am wrong, then we must deem her to have been five hundred years in advance of her time. Similarly, an Archbishop who defines a miracle as 'an event which creates faith', in contradistinction to a supernatural happening which has to be believed whether you like it or not – such a cleric has read rather more Herbert Spencer than is good for, or probable in, a fifteenth-century divine. The third scene shows a miracle – the change of wind – happening before Joan prays for it, which seems to indicate that Mr Shaw would have belief follow in the wake of reason. But I would not be dogmatic here. Throughout the play the author is at his old trick of what in music I think they call 'over-tones'. Simpler, perhaps, to say that he runs two hares at once, and that the value which accrues when old speeches are informed with present-day meaning must obviously be at some cost of authenticity.

The real play begins with the fourth scene, in which the Bishop of Beauvais, the Earl of Warwick, and Chaplain de Stogumber assemble round a table and 'get down to it'. The English peer wants Joan burned, not so much because her continued prestige is a danger to English arms, but because, by going direct to the Dauphin and not through the intermediacy of the Court, she has struck at the very existence, and reason for being, of the peerage. The Bishop wants Joan burned because she pretends to the ear of God by ways other than through his Ministers. This scene is enormously long; we lose sight of Joan; and there is danger, as the trio review the whole field of religion and politics from 1429 to the present day, and we sit and hope in vain that each fresh turn in the argument will be the last – there is danger, I repeat, of both physical and intellectual cramp. Will Mr Shaw never learn to distinguish between length and significance? Cut this scene in two and you double its meaning; quarter it and you quadruple its effect. One was so weary of the flood of talk that the ensuing colloquy in the Cathedral hardly got the attention it deserved. There was great pathos in the repeated warnings of Archbishop, General, and King that not one prayer, man or louis would be expended on Joan's salvation, should she fall into enemy hands. Joan had her second opportunity here, and her passage comparing the loneliness of the human soul with the loneliness of God was immensely fine.

After the much-needed interval came the Trial scene in the Hall at Rouen. In an Author's Note on the programme, Mr Shaw states that Joan's confessions, recantation, relapse, and execution, which actually occupied several days, on the stage occupy forty minutes. This is inaccurate. The scene lasts forty minutes, but for the first half of it Joan is still in her cell, and the time is taken up with an exhaustive and exhausting disquisition on heresy. It may be true that all evil begins in good, but the lecture, or so much of it, held up the action and ultimately became a weariness. However good the cackle – and it *was* good – one was conscious of a growing impatience for the 'osses. The trial and all that followed was masterly. When Warwick entered, called for attendants, and received no answer, the silence betokening that all that little world had gone to the burning, you realised that the theatre was being put to its proper purpose. And this was reinforced when Stogumber rushed in with the horror of the accomplished martyrdom written on his face, its terror quaking in his voice, his whole soul shaking with the sudden realisation of cruelty. There was another sermon here – one-tenth the length of the others and ten times more effective.

The play then draws rapidly to what ought to be its close. Warwick ascertains from the executioner that not a nail, not a hair, not a vestige which might become a relic remains. The legend of Joan is destroyed. But the priest who held the Cross before her dying eyes avows that it has just begun. 'I wonder!' says the English murderer as the curtain falls. This should have been the end. There is a faintly jovial, quasi-satirical, and wholly unnecessary epilogue, conceived in a vein of lesser exaltation. Mr Shaw excuses this on the ground that without it the play would be 'only a sensational tale of a girl who was burnt'. Do not believe it; Mr Shaw does himself injustice here. There is not an ounce of sensation anywhere in his piece, and the epilogue is implicit in all that has gone before. It is the greatest compliment to this play to say that at its tragic climax every eye was dry, so overwhelmingly had its philosophic import mastered sentiment. None in the audience would have saved Joan, even if he could.

The production was beyond any praise of mine. The scenery; designed by Mr Charles Ricketts, was neither frankly representational nor uncompromisingly expressionistic, but a happy blend of the two. The dresses made a kind of music in the air, and at the end Joan was allowed to stand for a moment in all that ecstasy of tinsel and blue in which French image-makers enshrine her memory. As Joan Miss Thorndike had three admirable moments: when she said 'They do!', when she listened in the Ambulatory to the pronouncement of desertion to come, and when she listened to the reading of her recantation. May I beseech Mr Shaw to allow her to drop her dialect? Whatever the quality of Lorraine peasant-speech, it cannot have been Lancashire, and there was too much the smack of Oldham about such sentences as 'Ah call that muck!' and 'Th'art not King yet, lad; th'art nobbut t'Dauphin!' Apart from these eccentricities, which were not of the actress's seeking, Joan was excellent – boyish, brusque, inspired, exalted, mannerless, tactless, and obviously, once she had served her turn, a nuisance to everybody. The part is one which no actress who is leading lady only and not artist would look at. But Miss Thorndike is a noble artist, and did nobly.

It is in keeping with the spirit of the play that the character which remains most with me is not Joan. Since Thursday I find myself thinking continually of Mr Lyall Swete's Warwick, who was the materialistic fox of the Middle Ages come to life, and of Mr O. B. Clarence's Inquisitor, about whose silver serenity there was real awe, and whose long speech was a very notable performance. Mr Casson, in his outburst on cruelty, gave one more proof of those talents as to which he is altogether too modest; and there should be good words for Messrs Robert Horton, Eugene Leahy, Lawrence Anderson (very sincere and moving as Joan's comforter), Victor Lewisohn, Milton Rosmer, Bruce Winston, Raymond Massey, and Shayle Gardner.

SOURCE: extract from 'New Plays', in *Red Letter Nights* (London, 1944), pp. 211–18.

Barrett H. Clark 'Producing and Acting Shaw' – *Candida* (1936)

Candida is a shaft aimed at current conceptions of what is moral, right, and fitting. It has always been accepted as commonplace that the father is the respected head of the family, yet Crampton in *You Never Can Tell* indicates that all fathers are not and should not be such. In *Candida* Shaw attempts to shatter the ideals of the 'sanctity of the family', and shows a weak man and a strong man – each at first appearing to be the reverse – with a woman between them. The woman finally clings to the weaker, as he needs her most; not, Shaw implies, because she happens to be his wife.

As an acting play *Candida* is one of Shaw's best works. Not radically different in form from the 'well-made' play, it takes the old conventions and turns them into new channels, and promulgates ideas which are for the most part strictly germane to the story, and sets forth characters with vividness in a highly entertaining manner. Shaw had not as yet freed himself from those elements of 'Sardoodledom' against which he had so vigorously protested in his early days as a critic. . . . *Man and Superman* marked a great advance toward technical freedom, while *Getting Married* and *Misalliance* at length bridged the gap.

> [Clark then enumerates points of special interest in the production and understanding of the play – Ed.]

1. The plays of the past fifty years differ strikingly from those of earlier times in the matter of stage directions. The Greeks, the Latins, and the Elizabethans wrote primarily for the simplest of stages, so that the merest suggestion (Entrances, Exits, and so on) sufficed for the director. There are few indications of 'business.' Since it has become the fashion

to issue plays in book form, certain dramatists feel the need of amplifying and expounding. Ibsen was among the first to do this, and Shaw has followed in his steps. With the development of the drama, which has been extraordinarily rapid since Ibsen's day, has come the need of commenting upon the more complex settings and subtler characters, which are comparatively new. In general, the earlier plays were simpler, they treated characters more as types. With the advent of Ibsen, stock actors found that such indications as 'First Lead,' 'Villain,' and 'Ingénue' were not sufficient. Therefore Ibsen told something about his characters in stage-directions. Not satisfied with this, Shaw told a great deal.[1] He carried the practice almost to an extreme, but he was practically forced to do so. Shaw has said that when he published his first two volumes of plays 'nobody dreamed of reading plays, which were usually printed in acting editions only, with frankly technical stage-directions, very useful to producers, but utterly destructive to the imagination of a reader.' Nobody 'would touch' his plays, so that he was compelled to 'make people read them.'

Determine, after a careful reading of the stage-directions in this play, which among them can be utilised by the actor, manager, and stage-carpenter, and which are for the reader alone. Compare the stage-directions of Granville Barker in *The Voysey Inheritance* or *The Madras House*, and of Barrie in *The Twelve-pound Look*, with those in *Candida*.

2. It is often said that the characters in Shaw's plays are merely puppets, without life and emotions, set in action by a clever thinker and craftsman. In his *Dramatic Portraits*, P. P. Howe states of the characters in *Mrs Warren's Profession*, and makes the remark applicable to Shaw's characters in general:' . . . They are puppets at the end of wires, and the wires are attached to a battery, and Mr Shaw is in charge of the current.' Usually, Shaw is so much in earnest, so 'full of his message,' that he cannot adopt an aloof attitude such as, for instance, is found throughout the work of Galsworthy, and allow his personages to speak and act in accordance with their own thoughts, passions, and beliefs. Still, how far does Mr Howe's criticism apply to *Candida*? To Lady Cecily Waynfleete in *Captain Brassbound's Conversion*? To Dick Dudgeon in *The Devil's Disciple*? Are these people human beings, or are they only puppets?

3. Shaw speaks of the occasional obscurity in Ibsen's plays resulting from a lack of proper stage-directions. What is the value of Shaw's own stage-directions in *Candida*? Especially in the latter part of the first act? Would that scene between Marchbanks and Morrell be quite intelligible without them? Could the dramatist have made it so without them? Has he failed, using the novelist's method in default of dramatic

dialogue? What, at the end of the final act, was 'The secret in the poet's heart'?

4. During his early days Shaw waged a merciless war against the conventions of the 'well-made' play; and yet he not infrequently made use of those same conventions in his own plays. As one critic put it, he fell in love with his own medium, and it finally mastered him.

Determine in what respects *Candida* is 'well-made.' Are the 'curtains' effective? What of the exposition? Is it sufficient? Obvious? And the development? Compare this play, structurally, with Sudermann's *Magda* and Björnson's *Gauntlet.*

A still more 'old-fashioned' play of Shaw's is his first, *Widowers' Houses*. Notice the 'asides,' the soliloquy, and the numerous stilted speeches in that play.

SOURCE: extract from *A Study of the Modern Drama* (New York, 1936), pp. 255–8.

NOTE

1 'It is astonishing to me,' says Shaw in his preface to *Plays, Pleasant and Unpleasant*, vol. 1, 'that Ibsen, who devotes two years to the production of a three-act play, the extraordinary quality of which depends on a mastery of characterisation and situation which can only be achieved by working out a good deal of the family and personal history of the individuals represented, should nevertheless give the reading public very little more than the technical memorandum required by the carpenter, the gasman, and the prompter. Who will deny that the resultant occasional mysteriousness of effect, enchanting though it may be, is produced at the cost of intellectual obscurity? Ibsen, interrogated as to his meaning, replies, "What I have said I have said." Precisely, but the point is that what he hasn't said he hasn't said.'

T. C. *Worsley* Poetry Without Words: Miller's *Death of a Salesman* (1949)

Death of a Salesman, the new play by the American Mr Arthur Miller (whose *All My Sons* we saw last year) is at the moment, if we may trust reports, setting all New York weeping. At the Phoenix Theatre last week I did not observe any snuffling nor did I myself, though a ready enough snuffler, have to reach for my handkerchief once. I think it fairly describes the effect of the play to record that there was in the middle a good deal of that shifting of position and creaking of seats which indicate that attention is slipping: but that at the curtain fall the applause was long, loud and sincere. It was one of those comparatively rare plays, too, about which you are prepared to go on talking for two or three hours. But you may very likely find that you are not so much discussing the impact of the play itself as trying to account for the fact that the impact is so much smaller than it somehow ought to have been. Somehow much more expectation has been generated than ever gets satisfied. Immense care, elaboration, skill have been employed, and yet at the end we go away hungry. It is rather as if we had been invited to what promises to be a very grand dinner indeed. Jewels flash: starch gleams: the flowers on the table are exquisitely arranged: and heavens, we are dining off gold plate! And yet and yet . . . the soup when it comes: doesn't it strike us as being a little thin? And how slow the service is! It takes a long time to reach the sole. At least 'sole' is what it is called on the menu. But doesn't it taste suspiciously like plaice? And only one minute fillet each! No doubt something more substantial will arrive presently. But no, what's this? The ladies are already rising and now the coffee essence is going round. Still, even if we are a little empty we cannot but admire immensely the ravishing little coffee cups in which it is served, all green and gold – Russian, don't you think they must be, in origin?

Mr Miller in this play has joined the school of American playwrights (Saroyan, Thornton Wilder, Tennessee Williams) who are trying to break out of the constrictions of the naturalistic play form while at the same time retaining the realist contemporary subject. It is an attempt to make a poetic approach to every-day life without using poetry – or even heightened speech. The characters are to remain as inarticulate as they are in real life; the 'poetry' is to be supplied by symbols, by the handling, the time-switches, the lighting; the production, in short, is expected to do most of the work of evoking the heightened mood. Thus the Salesman of this play is living in a three-roomed Brooklyn house with his wife and two gone-to-the-bad sons. The stage design for this is skeletal; we see all three rooms at once, and we see, even more important, looming up behind, the great lowering claustrophobic cliff of concrete skyscraper in which their living space is embedded. A highly effective design this, by Jo Mielziner. He is also responsible for the lighting which focuses our attention on one room or another as the little scenes shift to and fro. Or he may bring us to the front of the stage for the 'flashbacks' into the idealised past when the boys were young and loved their father and he could still hope for himself and for them; and this is 'symbolised' by the leafy fringe projected in these scenes by a lantern on to the backcloth, shutting out the barren city landscapes to which their lives have now been reduced.

Willie Loman, a travelling salesman, is at the end of his career. He is only sixty, but his life is sagging. He is worn out, worn out with travelling and with hoping and promising. The hopes have never materialised, the promises haven't been fulfilled, the travels are coming to an end – he is to lose his job this day. He still talks by habit as if he believed in a future, in turning some corner, in its all coming right. But the talk has already begun to fail to convince even himself. It is on his elder son, Biff, that his highest hopes have always centred – Biff, who adored him too, who was the star of the school football team, who was excused all his faults, adored and worshipped (all shown us in flashbacks). Why is Biff now at thirty a failure, and why does he now hate his Pop? Why did he suddenly stop loving him somewhere around seventeen? And why, the boys themselves wonder – Biff and Happy spotlighted in their bedroom on the first floor – has the old man started to go to pieces? He talks to himself all the time now, and all the time about the past and Biff. And why does he keep smashing up the car? This at least their mother can tell them – he is trying to kill himself and it's their fault; he's old and tired and disappointed in them. It takes the first half of the play to get us so far. But after the interval the pace does begin to quicken, through a final disappointment in Biff, to the climactic reconciliation between father and son. This releases Willie Loman ('He likes me . . . He likes me . . . Remarkable, most remarkable') to walk out and kill himself.

There is no doubt that this play, episodic and rather rambling as it is, has a certain power. It creates a world and takes us into it. It gives off the feel of sincerity; it has evidently been deeply, even solemnly felt. On the other hand it is altogether slighter than the author or the producer seem to have any idea of. The whole atmosphere in the theatre is heavily scented with self-importance. There is a sad lack of contrast; there is hardly one moment's relief. The little theme is made to take itself much too seriously. In this sense it is sentimental: all the time it is being made to live far above its emotional and intellectual station.

The slightness derives partly from the fact that there are only one and a half characters to carry us along. The wife and the younger brother are on stage much of the time, it is true. But they aren't worked. They are really stooges, each given a character – she the perfect wife, he a girl-hungry bum – but they have no real part in the emotional texture of the drama. The elder son, Biff, comes alive only on the occasions when he comes in conflict with his father. Mr Kevin McCarthy makes a very vivid character then of the young man fighting through the densities of the family optimism to try to discover himself behind them. But conflict only rises in the last quarter of the play and meanwhile the burden has fallen, too heavily, on Mr Paul Muni as the salesman. I don't quite see what more he could have done for this character than he has, except perhaps to hasten the pace and insist on cutting his part. He gets the shallow, weak charm perfectly, the craving to be liked, the intoxication of optimism and the shuffle and sag of failure. But he has to go on repeating these without either words or actions to help him. In the end it gets repetitious. We begin to shift in our seats, even while we admire.

A contributory cause for this is the episodic time-switching and place-switching. A friend of mine said to me recently of this school of playwrights: They've discovered the secret of American audiences who, when they are in the theatre, would much rather be in the cinema. These devices belong to the cinema (and even at the cinema we have begun to groan when the flashbacks start). The playwright's ace is concentration of interest and the Unities are the principle behind that concentration. These switches keep dispersing the tension, which then needs to be laboriously built up again time after time. I hope this play will demonstrate to young playwrights here the barrenness of such tricks.

But in the end it all boils down to one thing only – words. Poetry is made with words; and in the poetic approach, nothing but words will in the last analysis bring success. Mr Kazan may produce as brilliantly as he likes; he may bring out every device of lighting, grouping, stylising, timing and designing to evoke the play's moods. But none of them is an adequate substitute for the words which just aren't there.

SOURCE: review of the first London production in 1949; reprinted in *The Fugitive Art* (London, 1952), pp. 93–6.

Tyrone Guthrie Is There Madness in the Method? (1957)

The Method is now the most talked-about approach to acting in the American theatre, its temple is the Actors' Studio, its high priest is Lee Strasberg. The Actors' Studio has attracted some distinguished adherents; some extravagant claims for it are advanced with ardour and as warmly rebutted. It has been a valuable force for thought and discussion about the art of the theatre, about the craft of acting and about the philosophy and technique of self-expression. Its influence is widely felt in contemporary acting, not just in New York, but in every English-speaking theatre. That cannot be questioned. The value and the performance of this influence are a matter of controversy.

Let me begin by saying that I have no first-hand experience of the Method. I have met and worked with zealous Method-ists; I have heard descriptions of rehearsals and demonstrations of the Method; but I have never attended any of the Gospel Meetings.

I am under the impression that Lee Strasberg, a wonderful teacher, is inculcating an approach to acting derived from that of Stanislavsky, the founder and director of the Moscow Art Theatre. The basis of this is that the actor must derive his characterisation from his personal experience. He must imagine a given situation so strongly that he can 'feel' himself in it. His own experience being necessarily limited, he must also feel it legitimate to derive at second-hand from the real experience of other people, but not from other acting.

With little of this could any sensible person disagree. My own disagreement with the Method is limited, and under two heads: theoretically, it is in rebellion against conditions which have ceased to exist and, consequently, is out of date. Practically, it places too much emphasis upon self-analysis and too little upon technique.

First, let us consider the theoretic side. The professional context in reaction to which Stanislavsky founded the Moscow Art Theatre and his own acting method belonged to the *fin de siècle* and the very early years of the twentieth century, and no longer exists. It has been liquidated by the social, political and economic revolutions which have occurred all over the world. Stanislavsky was reacting against a theatre which was still in aim very much concerned to please an audience of the socially élite and its imitators; a theatre very concerned with inherited conventions, largely derived from the artificial comedy of manners of the eighteenth century, transmitted through the Parisian Boulevard comedies and dramas, which had dominated Europe for more than a century.

Stanislavsky preached a method based upon first-hand observation, rather than upon imitation of other acting. He also advocated the production of plays which reflected contemporary Russian life in a real way, rather than as a romantic image of elegant manners abroad. The Moscow Art Theatre, while not at all political, was nevertheless strongly nationalist.

Although it was never of any great popular or commercial account – the theatre was tiny and by no means always full – the Moscow Art Theatre became the most powerful influence on the stage of its time. The 'poetic naturalism' of Chekhov, in supplement to the prosaic and didactic quality of Ibsen and Shaw, has been the dominant influence on serious playwrights of the last fifty years, not only in Russia but all over the occidental world; and the acting and direction at the Moscow Art are still the dominant models, although possibly a little less so now, since the impact of Bertolt Brecht.

Stanislavsky did not really hit the American theatre until after the publication in English of his book *My Life in Art*. He then found enthusiastic disciples in Mr Strasberg and Harold Clurman, founders of the Group Theatre. The Group, like the Moscow Art before it, found itself in reaction against the theatrical *status quo*. It was opposed to the conventional themes and methods of the commercial theatre, which to the young people of the Group seemed extremely reactionary. It was opposed also to foreign domination of the American stage, particularly by London's West End, with its insistence upon elegance and gentility to the exclusion of almost all other content.

This was the period of depression, the end of one epoch and the beginning of many radically new political, social and economic ideas. The Group Theatre was in the *avant-garde* of this ferment; and I hope that a non-American may be forgiven for emphasising something which in subsequent political ferments has been either overlooked or misinterpreted: this literary and theatrical movement was an earnest and conscious expression of American nationalism. The Group was trying, early in the comparatively brief history of the American theatre, to look at indigenous American problems and characters through American eyes, and to express them in an indigenous way, not in a manner imitative of dominant – and imported – conventions.

Harold Clurman in *The Fervent Years*, one of the best books of theatrical reminiscence which I know, has described the aims, impact and some of the inner stresses and strains of the Group. Its activity, compared to that of the Moscow Art Theatre, was confined to a very brief period. Its artistic achievement has been less than its influence. The Group, I venture to believe, has been an all-important influence in the evolution of the Method. The ideas which brought the Group into being are the source of the Method's greatest value; but I suggest that they still express youthful revolt against a social and political environment which has now ceased to exist.

In 1930 there was some point in young actors and actresses proclaiming by their dress, speech and bearing that they were of the

Proletariat. In 1930, there was some important political and social purpose to be served by depicting faithfully the efforts of the inarticulate American masses to express themselves. In 1930, this required some serious political faith, not in Leninism, but in the future of American democracy. Artistically it was ground which, outside Russia, had hardly been trodden, and demanded a serious effort to evolve a new technique because the current fashions in acting and directing were no guide.

But today the burning issues of 1930 are ashes, and other issues burn. Even in America, comparatively so little affected by the events of 1939–45 (a fact which is to many Americans bewilderingly hard to grasp, so accustomed are they to believe themselves in the vanguard rather than the rearguard of historical context), the political, social and economic changes have been immense. Meantime, the young iconoclasts of the early Odets period are now middle-aged; the prominent ones are well-to-do and securely seated upon the very thrones under which twenty-seven years ago they were placing the dynamite.

But the Method-ists do not seem to have quite got around to this. In blue jeans, with dirty nails and wild hair, they are busy proclaiming themselves Proletarian – but members of a vintage Proletariat. While in 1930 it was new, and even dangerous for artistes to announce that they were also Proletarians, it is now cliché; especially when more than one prominent associate of the Method has been at pains to dissociate this type of Artistic Proletarianism from any taint of political subversion, from the faintest tinge of red. In 1930, adequately to present an inarticulate proletarian upon the stage required some innovation of acting technique; but this too has now become cliché.

This brings me to the second issue on which I part company with the Method: technique. In 1930, it was necessary to seek new means of expressing new ideas about people whom it was a novelty to see depicted on the stage. Until then, stage conventions had required that, with amazingly few exceptions, plays were about the Upper Orders. If members of the Lower Orders appeared at all, it was as character parts – Faithful Retainers, Roughs, Prostitutes, Little Matchgirls or, most frequently, just 'Comics'. Then plays began to have as their chief figures Taxi Drivers and Boxers shown, not as the expression of natures more rough and inarticulate than their former 'betters', but as people who had been denied the privileges of the more fortunate.

It can readily be seen that the new school of playwriting required a new school of acting, less conventional, less romantic, less elegant, but, in compensation, more 'real'. Now, oddly enough, most of us in the theatre, as in other avocations, are nearer in environment to the Proletariat than to Grand Dukes. Hence, when the new school required of the actor that he unlearn a lot of fancy ways and fancy speech, which had been thought necessary in the portrayal of Grand Dukes, it seemed as though he were being required to revert to 'behaviourism', to just Being Himself.

Incidentally, isn't it just middle-class sentimentality, and a very 'superior' attitude, to imagine that it is more 'real' to be rough than to be genteel, more 'real' to wear blue jeans than a neat Ivy League number, more 'real' to look like a whore than a Junior Miss? Surely it is not more real, but less expensive. The proletariat does not dress and speak and behave as it does, nor live where it does, from choice, but because it cannot afford to do otherwise. In America today it is only eccentric 'intellectuals' who are 'prole' by choice.

In 1930, however, the Group believed that good acting consisted in Being Yourself and, consistently enough, aimed to make its members better actors by making them more Aware of Themselves. Remember that this epoch coincided with the first great popular impact of psychoanalysis. At the confluence of two rivers – popular psychology and 'behaviourist' acting – like Pittsburgh, stood the Group. At the same confluence stands the Method. But twenty-seven years have passed and the waters of both streams are now less turbulent, but also far less clear and fresh.

In my opinion, the Method now means Behaviourist acting, which is cliché, and which is inadequate to express any wide range either of character, environment or style. It is suited only to express the very limited field of the actor's own, and his friends' experience, and in a naturalistic style. It is stylish acting (by which I do not, of course, mean merely elegant) which now needs cultivation.

The search by actors for the Truth Within Themselves has now gone too far. They are in grave danger of forgetting two more objective elements of truth which no artiste should dare to ignore: first, each of us is not only himself, but a member of the Human Race; second, it is the duty of an artiste to develop the Means of Communication of the truth within himself, so as to share it with fellow members of the race.

The Method-ists overprize the Search For Truth as opposed to the Revelation Of Truth. They have neglected the means of communication. Now the actor's principal means of expression is the voice. The expression of eyes, of the whole body, is important, too; but it is on the breathstream and by means of sounds and, more particularly, the organisation of sounds into, first, syllables, then words, then sentences, that the most subtle and the most articulate communication occurs between human creatures.

Until recently the Actors' Studio has tended to pay but little attention to matters of technique. But now Mr Strasberg has said that this has been a mistake. Lessons in Voice Production and Diction are now part of the curriculum. No reasonable person but will applaud when error is admitted and amendment begun. But amendment has only just begun, so it is rather too early to look for the fruits of this Revised Method. Also it is a radically new idea that anything so self-conscious and artificial as Vocal Technique, so unspontaneous, so remote from the animal life of the individual, or the social life of the group, should be admissible as part of the Method. And so influential has the Method become in the contemporary theatre that it is going to be very hard to eradicate the notion that any cultivation of this Craft can only be to the detriment, not only of an actor's Art, but of his Psyche.

This notion has led the Method-ists into one very awkward dilemma: none of the great classics of the theatre – the Greek tragedies, French tragedy, Shakespeare, Molière, Schiller or Goethe – can be adequately performed without a real battery of technical accomplishment. An untrained beginner, however gifted, just cannot do justice to great rhetorical poetry any more than an untrained beginner in music can sit right down and play a Bach fugue. So far the Method has not suggested that it aims beyond a very highly developed Behaviourism. I am not denying that in this field remarkable results have been achieved. But mere Behaviourism will not take an actor far on the way to King Lear, Andromache or Faust.

A world-famous and justly eminent director, who is also a supporter of the Method, has avoided this dilemma by declaring that the classics are all bunk; that he, thank God, has never directed a classic; and, please God, never will. This rather immature point of view is certainly not that of Mr Strasberg.

I guess that a great deal is talked and written about the Method by persons, including myself, who have only been indirectly concerned with it. And while this is not quite fair, it is absolutely inevitable. The Method is a popular talking-point and, as such, has gained extraordinary prestige. But fame and success carry their own penalties as well as rewards. That Marlon Brando, Marilyn Monroe, and so on, have been associated, has been, in one sense, a great boost for the Actors' Studio, but in another it has been detrimental. Neither of these gifted alumni could be described as an accomplished actor; their fame rests upon other qualities. And the sort of publicity which their connection has generated has blown up a serious professional effort into a sensational stunt, with many of the stigmata of quackery.

To sum up: it is my opinion that Mr Strasberg is a serious teacher and no quack. The Actors' Studio is genuinely and laudably trying to break away from theatrical clichés, but has gone too far in the direction of self-analysis, and away from a sensible pursuit of craftsmanship, particularly vocal technique. The great professional and popular success of the Method has resulted in a rather grave lack of humility on the part of many of its adherents. Statements on the lines of the classics being all bunk are not unusual; and there's a tendency to forget that people of my age do not find anything new in the theory. On the contrary, we remember when it was new to us in the mouth of Stanislavsky; people a little older remember the same theories being applied still earlier at the Abbey Theatre in Dublin and in the folk theatres all over Europe; still older people recall the *Quintessence of Ibsenism*. And so on, back and back.

Looking forward, I see reason to believe that, like every popular craze and like so many Progressive Movements whose adherents become unduly excited by success, today's Method may all too easily become tomorrow's Dodo.

SOURCE: article in *Encore* (November 1957); reprinted in Charles Marowitz, Tom Milne and Owen Hale (eds), *'Encore' Reader: Chronicle of the New Drama* (London, 1970), pp. 29–36.

Katherine J. Worth 'Revolutionary Eliot' (1972)

At first glance Eliot's progress as playwright seems to be a movement away from experiment. His most modern-looking piece, a jazz melodrama, was published in 1926; his last play, produced in 1958, looks more like a piece of staid neo-Ibsenism. Many of his critics saw the postwar plays as a regression: even Martin Browne, who produced them all and was deeply in sympathy with his playwright, was inclined to take that view. He thought them an unconscious reversion to the style of theatre Eliot had known as a young man. Eliot did jokingly say himself about some improvement suggested for *The Cocktail Party* that every step seemed to take him nearer to Lonsdale.

But experiment of some kind is going on all the time in Eliot's drama. He had an extraordinarily keen sense of new theatrical possibilities. *Sweeney Agonistes*, his most radical experiment (of the plays not written for religious occasions) was so far ahead of orthodox theatre practice that for years it was thought of as a poem rather than as what it now clearly looks to be, an exciting (if unfinished) piece of theatre. *The Cocktail Party* has a claim to be considered the first black comedy in the postwar English theatre and *The Confidential Clerk* indicated some interesting new directions for farce. Both these plays, and in its own way *The Elder Statesman*, explore subjects that fascinate the modern theatre – role playing, the search for identity – with techniques that foreshadow those of Albee and Pinter.

Eliot's central characters suffer from a troubling sense of division between their real and their acted selves. 'Real' self is a concept that still has force in his drama – here he separates from successors like Pinter – but the performing self is very much in the foreground, uneasily conscious of its liability to be taken over by the 'speechless self', the mute, tough one.

Eliot finds some interesting answers to the problem of how to represent these selves, with their different voices. To a great extent, of course, he relies on the traditional means of verse drama, imagery. There is a tremendous amount of acting imagery in the plays, a fact that Martin Browne draws attention to in his absorbing account of his collaboration with Eliot; an indispensable book, this, for anyone concerned with the drama of the period as well as with Eliot's work.[1] Through all the plays runs a chain of nightmarish images to do with losing one's part, being in the wrong play, having a sense of existing only in a part.

The Chorus in *The Family Reunion* resent being summoned to 'play an unreal part in some monstrous farce, ridiculous in some nightmare pantomime'. Harry comes home prepared for one part and finds 'another one made ready – The book laid out, lines underscored, and the costume/Ready to be put on', and Lord Claverton, who describes himself as a broken-down actor, dreads the moment when he will have to walk off the stage 'without his costume and makeup./And without his stage words.'

Other more direct methods are tried out too. In one interesting sequence from an early draft of *The Cocktail Party*, much cut down in the final version, Peter Quilpe is invited by the other characters to imagine roles for them in the film he is supposed to be making about a country house murder. 'Very few people can act the thing they are', he says, and goes on to cast accordingly. Edward can't be a lawyer in the film, though he is in the play, because he doesn't look secretive; neither does Alex, so he can be the Secret Service character; as for Reilly and Julia, they can't be in it at all: nothing about them is ordinary enough for what an 'ordinary' murder film requires. The effect of this – trying to imagine characters as characters – is unsettling. Even in the unsatisfactorily verbose form it has in the draft, the scene takes us to the edge of the phantasmagoric region where Edward exists, not sure whether he is really there, except in his role as husband to Lavinia: 'Without her, it was vacancy./When I thought she had left me, I began to dissolve,/To cease to exist.'

The feeling of being an actor is closely related to the feeling of being spied on which Eliot's characters suffer from. Roles, false names and identities are protection against being known. The characters are terribly repressed and inhibited by the polite society they live in: the point is made in that way in *The Family Reunion*. They have to be shocked into opening up and revealing themselves . A violence comes in here which takes Eliot's drama very close to Pinter's. Characters are subjected to painful, mysterious inquisitions, the Furies appear at a window, bringing their victim near to total nervous collapse; an uninvited guest arrives at a cocktail party; with the aid of two spies he manoeuvres three of the characters to a consulting room for 'treatment'[2] which ends in the violent death of one of them; two unwanted visitors decend on an elderly man taking a 'rest cure'[3] and badger him into confessing past faults; he collapses and dies.

Of course these summaries are misleading, omitting as they do the 'bright angle' aspect of the inquisitors and the emphasis Eliot puts on conversion and reconciliation. But perhaps all the same they hint at a truth about the plays, that their greatest theatrical vitality is just in those dark and icy areas where they draw so near to Pinter's drama. *The Birthday Party* seems to take over where they leave off: it's a very live connection.

Eliot is certainly good at suggesting suppressed violence. He manages at times to look like a forerunner of the theatre of cruelty without ever allowing an act of physical violence to erupt on his stage. He can manoeuvre the audience into a worrying sense of complicity with sadism, for instance with the jokes in *The Cocktail Party* about Christians eating monkeys and pagans eating Christians. They are nasty jokes but the audience usually laughs at them, to their embarrassment when they learn that Celia was one of the victims. Martin Browne was relieved when Eliot agreed to cut out some of the horrific detail[4] that outraged the first audiences in Edinburgh. He was surely right in thinking that the emphasis on physical horror would distract attention from Celia as a person. I'm not so sure, though, that Eliot did think of Celia as a person in quite the way Browne himself did: it was he who had advised Eliot to build up sympathy for her: 'She is the character whom above all we want to love – the heroine, the play's necessary focus of sympathy.'[5] But that last scene was first written as an epilogue: the germ of the play was the marriage of Edward and Lavinia and, to my mind, it's in that Strindbergian dance of death relationship that the strongest dramatic interest lies. The prevailing mood is grotesque; masked actors in a cruel harlequinade, decidedly in tune with the modern spirit which encourages the rewriting of *The Dance of Death* in the near-farcical terms of Dürrenmatt's *Play Strindberg*.

I began by referring to the extremely modern look of Eliot's first dramatic piece, the unfinished *Sweeney Agonistes*. If he had continued to write in that vein he would have been in the front ranks of the anti-realists and I would probably have been discussing him now along with O'Casey and Arden and other makers of the alternative tradition rather than in relation to Pinter and Priestley.

Even as it is, *Sweeney Agonistes* has had some influence on the playwrights who have made the sharpest break with realism, on Auden and Isherwood, and on John Arden, who tells us that his first schoolboy attempt at dramatic writing was a play inspired by the death of Hitler written in the style of *Sweeney Agonistes*.

It's odd that this seminal piece should still be included among the poems in the collected edition of 1969, especially as it has had a number of interesting productions. In Peter Wood's 1965 production[6] – with Cleo Laine as Dusty and jazz by Dankworth – it came over as an exhilaratingly open piece of theatre, with its evocative changes of rhythm, its easy, swinging movements out of dialogue into soft shoe turns and musical comedy numbers like 'My little island girl.' Osborne seems to be recalling this in *Look Back in Anger* when he has Jimmy and Cliff go into one of their turns as T. S. Eliot and Pam, 'Bringing quips and strips to you'. There's the same feeling here that knockabout is a blessed means of breaking out from an oppressive atmosphere of sexual tension – what Pinter's characters, for instance, can't ever do – nor Eliot's own in later plays.

Sweeney is very much a play of breaking out and acting out rather than talking out. There's a feeling that anything could happen: it's in key for an old gentleman looking like Father Christmas to turn up, as he did in Peter Wood's production, with an alarm clock in one hand and a champagne bottle in the other, to close down the proceedings.[7] Violence is *in* the action, not just something heard about. Sweeney's tale of his friend who did a girl in and pickled the body in a bath of Lysol comes over as a kind of sleep-walking preliminary to the real thing, the murder of a woman such as Dusty by a man driven by a mysterious loathing of women: 'Any man has to, needs to, wants to,/Once in a lifetime, do a girl in'. It's the world of Jack the Ripper, or of the Grand Guignol theatre – which was active in London in the twenties[8] – illuminated by the understanding of a poet who is deeply involved in Sweeney's complex feelings about women and violence.

Whether because the method of *Sweeney* was too direct and physical for the subject he wanted to handle or because he saw no hope of getting the right production for this style of play in the theatre of the time – these are questions to which there are as yet no answers. Certainly there wasn't a regular theatre company in London in 1926 (the year *Sweeney* was published) geared to the style of production the play needed. Eliot knew this well: it was in these years that he was enthusing in the pages of *The Criterion* about the superior training in bodily discipline and expressiveness that ballet dancers had; the ballet was the great potential source of the truly modern drama of the future (a remark which seems to point straight to Beckett's mimes and the ritualistic movements of *Endgame* and *Krapp's Last Tape*). The other acting qualities he admired – and aimed to bring into *Sweeney* – came from another kind of non-realist theatre, the music hall. Eliot was fascinated by the directness of entertainers like Marie Lloyd, their openness to their audience, their capacity for improvisation. His account of her 'searching in her handbag' turn[9] shows a feeling for the music hall art that makes one understand why a writer like John Arden should have been so drawn to *Sweeney*: something of that feeling got into the play.

It seems rather sad that Eliot couldn't find an outlet for these sympathies in the theatre of the twenties and that *Sweeney* had to remain for so long a fragment on a page. When he did see it performed by the Group Theatre[10] in 1935 he apparently wasn't very enthusiastic: one can't tell whether it was because the production was poor or because his interest in the method had waned.

Perhaps the closed form of the fourth wall play better expressed his state of mind at that time. Certainly one feels that the special force of *The Family Reunion* comes from the sense of the lid being held on so tight: the moments when the repressed feelings trickle through in delicate verbal music are poignant just because the context is so stiff and anti-musical.

Eliot has, I think, a stronger interest in the 'ordinary' part of his material, the non-mystical part, than he's usually credited with. There are striking resemblances of detail between his play and the typical family plays and detective plays of the thirties, and some interesting indications that he was aware of experiments being made with the material by contemporaries such as Priestley.

The first audiences of *The Family Reunion* had an opportunity of seeing the standard family play and Eliot's adaptation of it playing almost side by side. Dodie Smith's *Dear Octopus*, the epitome of the popular family drama, opened at the Queen's Theatre on 14 Sept 1938, while Eliot was finishing his play. For a time there was even the entertaining possibility that Gielgud who was playing Nicholas Randolph in *Dear Octopus* might take on Harry as well in matinée performances of *The Family Reunion*. Harry in the afternoon, Nicholas at night – a mind-boggling prospect, as the advertisements for *The Mousetrap* have it! Gielgud was looking forward to bringing out the contrasting treatments of 'the same characteristics, the family theme, the return of the prodigal etc. . . .'[11] He would have had plenty to work on.

In each play, as he indicates, a prodigal returns home for a family anniversary: in *Dear Octopus* it's a daughter who, like Harry, has been kept abroad for years by an unhappy sexual relationship. Both have to come to terms with fiercely possessive mothers and with families obsessively taken up with their own past. About here the resemblances end and the obviously much more important differences begin. One wonders how Gielgud's performance as Nicholas would have survived the cold light thrown on that cosy family from the other one. Just occasionally the irony might have gone the other way, perhaps: one of Dodie Smith's child characters has a line nicely pointing out to *The Family Reunion*: 'I wish we didn't have any dead people in the family. It sort of spoils the party.' But it seems safe to assume that *Dear Octopus* would have been the play to shrivel under the comparison!

The uncanny thing about it – viewed alongside *The Family Reunion* – is its deep unselfconsciousness. The characters manage to evade real scrutiny, as they do in most of the family plays of the time, even those, like Van Druten's *After All*, which ask to be taken rather more seriously than *Dear Octopus*. Eliot seems to provide the critical focus for the whole genre, to give it full selfconsciousness for the first time.

His way of forcing his characters to examine themselves is to put them in the framework of an amateur detective play, borrowing from another popular type of thirties drama, which was represented in the London theatre at the time he was writing by Anthony Armstrong's *Mile-Away Murder* (1937). He sets the play up as a probe into the causes of Harry's breakdown; witnesses come forward in turn – Agatha, Mary, the family doctor, the chauffeur – even the stolid country policeman is brought into the scene, and we hear of the off-stage brother getting into trouble with the police. Some of the conventional elements – the bucolic sergeant, for instance – make an uneasy fit, but they function usefully as a means of keeping some sort of connection with the outside world – clearly important for Eliot – and of emphasising the family's dread of publicity, the strength of their will to keep everything closed and hushed. One after another of the witness brings out this governing principle:

WARBURTON
Harry, there's no good probing for misery.
There was enough once: but what festered
Then, has only left a cautery.
Leave it alone.

CHORUS
Why should we stand here like guilty conspirators, waiting for some revelation
When the hidden shall be exposed, and the newsboy shall shout in the street?
When the private shall be made public, the common photographer
Flashlight for the picture papers: why do we huddle together
In a horrid amity of misfortune? why should we be implicated, brought in and brought together?

In applying pressure from the detective play to the 'matter' of the family drama Eliot had hit on a technique with rich possibilities. He was taking up where Joyce left off in *Exiles* but going much beyond him into the area where feelings are nameless, the sense of guilt obscure and undefined.

His true heir in this sphere is Pinter. Contemporaries seem to have picked up hints too, though: Priestley in *An Inspector Calls* (1947) uses the detective technique in a similar way. And Eliot in turn picks up from Priestley, to judge from the striking similarities between *The Family Reunion* and *I Have Been Here Before* (1937)....

SOURCE: extract from chapter IV, 'T. S. Eliot', in *Revolutions in Modern English Drama* (London, 1972), pp. 55–62.

NOTES

1. E. M. Browne, *The making of T. S. Eliot's Plays* (1969).
2. M. C. Bradbrook draws attention to this anticipation of Monty's in *The*

Birthday Party in her *English Dramatic Form* (1963).

    3. *The Rest Cure* was Eliot's original title for *The Elder Statesman*.

    4. There were references to Celia's body being smeared with a 'juice attractive to ants' and to its decomposition.

    5. Browne, op. cit., p. 176.

    6. Globe Theatre, 13 June 1965; in a memorial programme, 'Homage to T. S. Eliot'.

    7. A transcript of this scene (discarded from an earlier draft) was included in the programme to the 1965 production.

    8. See G. Sutton's 'The Shocking Business in the Adelphi', in his *Some Contemporary Dramatists* (1924) for an account of these Grand Guignol seasons.

    9. T. S. Eliot, 'Marie Lloyd', *Dial*, 73 (1922); reprinted (revised) in *Criterion* (1923) and in his *Selected Essays* (1932).

    10. See J. Isaac's account in his *An Assessment of Twentieth Century Literature* (1951), pp. 135–6.

    11. See his letter to Martin Browne in E. M. Browne, op. cit., pp. 145–6.

John Russell Brown The Dramatist's Theatre – Pinter, Osborne, Wesker, Arden and Beckett (1972)

The latest plays by all four dramatists [Pinter, Osborne, Wesker, Arden] strain the resources of theatre. At the beginning of their careers each writer recognised a comparatively simple purpose. Harold Pinter alerts attention so that the audience becomes more aware and more questioning. He can present each element of theatrical experience – speech, presence, gesture, sound, grouping, movement, rhythm and progression – with such precision that the audience becomes attentive and perceptive. But as he does this, the demands upon his actors for honesty in performance and the ability to relate element to element become ever more taxing. Pinter's imagination in his later plays encompasses a wider range of behaviour and social reality than before, but the means whereby the 'relaxed' and inwardly realised dramatic illusion is created have never asked for so much hidden work from the actors in their task of creation and elimination. Moreover, the audience is left without the comparatively easy excitements of *The Room* or *The Birthday Party*, where the unexpected is expressed in entries and exits, actual violence and physical transformations. Pinter has discovered drama in the smooth and ordinary surface of life. His plays reveal violence, helplessness and momentary joys of sensation and thought in forceful confrontations and with almost titanic measure, but always the everyday scale and confusions of life are expressed as well. By becoming engrossed in the minutiae of theatre language, Pinter has increased the range of his perceptions, and has insisted on actors, designers, directors and audiences sharing a similar, demanding (and rewarding) journey towards finesse.

John Osborne started by setting his characters to fight themselves and each other, and gave them arias, songs and close combat in which to make magnificent 'fusses' or simple, deep-touched stands. Actors could stretch themselves in these roles, and audiences were confident that, in one turn after another, the performance would be alive with energy and invention. Words were used resoundingly and pathetically, and physical performances were clear and varied. But, for *Inadmissible Evidence*, one actor is kept on stage throughout the long play, and part of this character's dilemma is his almost total lack of new resources when belief in his social and personal roles fail him. In later plays, the scale of performance is greatly reduced, the action being restricted to exchange of news or opinion, very few entrances and exits, a number of drinks and a series of consultations about past, future or possible activity. Verbally and physically, the actors' tasks are still demanding and, since the obvious excitements are removed or lessened, they must hold attention more by the quality of performance and a pervasive sense of an undesired and unavoidable unreality. Osborne has not chosen 'show-biz' characters in order to evade the presentation of ordinary human confrontations, but to represent the small, sharp edge of the continuing yet intermittent sense of disbelief that he experiences in and around himself. Either he is forcing theatre language to change with his own mind, or possibly the theatre is drawing him on to a sharper recognition of the bases of his life. Both ways, the going is more difficult, despite Osborne's undiminished zest.

Arnold Wesker, who starts by using the theatre to represent life and as a platform for argument and assertion, becomes increasingly concerned to make the theatre 'demonstrate' the values in human involvement in a form more bare, bold and inescapable than life. Argument is still an element in the later plays, but more and more the demonstration relies on a particular and highly charged moment in which the actors have to hold attention. In *The Four Seasons*, Wesker's purposes would founder completely if his actress were incapable of giving precise and varying 'meaning' to twenty minutes of silence. In *Their Very Own and Golden City*, the leading actor must stand on his head to express joy and a basic seriousness. Speeches have become more operatic without losing a continuous echo of ordinary speech.

John Arden's later plays include a whole-day's Carnival for the students of New York University in which he himself took part, and in which the audience were enlisted in opposing sides of a War Game. One of his own long speeches announced that he had created the dramatic event as part of his job as a secret agent, to provide 'Washington watchdogs with a firm list of suspect students'.[1] In later, fully scripted plays, the strength, variety, freedom and commitment that he demands from his actors have increasingly led him to be dissatisfied with professional theatre-makers. He now works chiefly on his own, in collaboration with his wife and with casts of his own choice and under his own direction.

Besides increasing their demands upon their interpreters, each dramatist has moved towards increasingly idiosyncratic forms of drama. From the first they have felt free to experiment whenever they saw the need. Ordinary rules about exposition have been flouted, especially by Pinter and, in *The Kitchen*, by Wesker. Time and place have been free to change, so that Archie Rice moves from home to nightmare or Pinter uses a blackout to change the characters' alignment artificially. Narrative is often a small element, and character is sometimes defined by the play's action as much as by a fully imagined background, physique or temperament. Style changes from imitation of ordinary behaviour to soliloquy, oration, dance, proverb, song, interrogation, ritual, physical activity or sustained silent tableau. These dramatists all know that the theatre can be free from the constraints of what used to be called a well-made play. On occasion they feel no need to reproduce an illusion of life, or even to give life-likeness of detail.

They were fortunate in that Samuel Beckett's *Waiting for Godot*, first performed in English in London in 1955, had made all these claims in one evening's entertainment. Words and actions were here controlled by a new dramatist who was already a practised and confident writer. Echoes of long-accepted religious and philosophic thought and an exciting ambiguity in the use of language both caught attention. Words and actions were often very funny. But more than this, the whole play was sustained by a steady, clear-eyed appreciation of the nature of human consciousness, so that it carried conviction by unity of thought and feeling, as well as by the confidence of its artifice. No young dramatist could have commanded his audience as Beckett did, nor taken their expectation so far in one stride.

The setting of *Waiting for Godot* is fantastic: a road, or a bog, with a single tree, and the audience recognisable, from time to time, out in front. The moon rises at the end of each Act, promptly on cue. The two main characters, Estragon and Vladimir, meet and separate, unaware of time or place, and giving only a sketchy impression of lonely and persecuted life outside the confines of the play. Pozzo and Lucky are joined together as master and servant; when first seen, they are due to part, but they return still more dependent on each other, the one in self-willed slavery and the other through incapacity. The ordinary business of living is scarcely represented, save in hunger, pain, fear, apprehension and occasional, short-lasting happiness or satisfaction.

Other dramatists could show the way towards fantasy, especially Ionesco, whose *Lesson* was first seen in English in the same year as *Godot*. His plays are 'realised dreams': their source is: 'not submission to some predetermined action, but the exteriorisation of a psychic dynamism, a projection onto the stage of internal conflict, of the universe that lies within: . . . it is in the deepest part of myself, of my anguish and my dreams, it is in my solitude that I have the best chance of rediscovering the universal, the common ground.'[2] His characters may have several noses, may fly into the air, turn into rhinoceroses or unconcernedly pick poisoned mushrooms in the drawing-room. Ordinary actions, like the serving of coffee or taking a pupil through a lesson, may become exaggerated through repetition or through unreasonable or climactic emphasis, so that the ordinary becomes fantastic, comic or terrifying.

In some measure, the four younger English dramatists have followed Beckett and Ionesco towards fantasy as a means of giving dream-like intensity and range, but none has been so surrealistic as Ionesco or attempted the same kind of timelessness and generality as Beckett. Pinter is the most fantastic of the four, but he has never cut free from all representations of ordinary living.

In *Waiting for Godot* another important claim was made on the audience's perception. Even as the play is being given, there are reminders that the characters are truly actors in a theatre. So theatrical performance becomes, in itself, an image of human activity. Often this is presented by implication alone: Estragon and Vladimir engage in cross-talk reminiscent of music-hall comedians or circus clowns; they do a trick with three hats; Pozzo 'explains the twilight', and expects attention and then appreciation. But there is more specific treatment as well: Lucky is called upon to entertain by dancing or thinking, and Estragon and Vladimire talk about their theatre audience. After the audience's interest has been caught by Pozzo and Lucky, the two tramps spell out the theatrical image:

VLADIMIR: Charming evening we're having.
ESTRAGON: Unforgettable.
VLADIMIR: And it's not over.

ESTRAGON: Apparently not.
VLADIMIR: It's only the beginning.
ESTRAGON: It's awful.
VLADIMIR: It's worse than being at the theatre.
ESTRAGON: The circus.
VLADIMIR: The music-hall.
ESTRAGON: The circus.

(1st edn, p. 34)

The reference to the circus is illuminating. Pozzo is the ring-master with his whip, who flogs the weakest, dependent clown. Estragon and Vladimir appear as the superior or dignified clown and 'He who gets slapped'. Estragon says Lucky 'played the fool', and in the French version Pozzo calls him a 'knouk' which is defined as a kind of 'bouffon' kept for entertainment. Even the Boy may be the boy who customarily interrupts the clowns' act with a message from the landlord of the tavern 'around the corner'. At the close of the play, when the tramps end another day with another resolve to commit suicide, they effect, apparently by accident, a further routine clown's trick of trousers falling down; immediately after this piece of traditional comedy, they make their final gesture by not moving from the stage as both verbally agree to do so. The characters' 'performances' are seen as habitual attempts to exist, without too much consciousness or too much pain. The characters put on an act, for themselves as for others; they are amused, when they let themselves 'go' and think of nothing but the immediately available entertainment.

The effect of this element in Beckett's writing is harder to discern in the four younger dramatists. But both Osborne and Pinter introduce music-hall routines, sometimes with the characters' consciousness of theatrical impersonation. Each of them, on occasion, directs a character to 'take the stage' and to put over a performance, a claim for attention or an attempt to impersonate some other character, stronger, more successful, or more assured than he himself can expect to be. Osborne's characters are commonly caught between belief and disbelief. Arden's main characters are all speech-makers, and have the unbounded vitality of theatrical illusion. In later plays he sets the action moving with the speed, variety and colour that have more connection with carnival than with life. Wesker is the least ostensibly theatrical, but the Interlude of *The Kitchen*, the party of *Chips with Everything* and the public meetings of *Their Very Own and Golden City* are like plays-within-plays. In these episodes the characters speak for their 'dreams', not their realities or, in the later plays, for their attempted compromises and not their true failures. All four dramatists seem committed to the theatre partly because of its ability to present an illusionary element that they find in life, to define pretence and disbelief, and to show the effort needed to sustain commitment in private or in public.

In his language, Beckett also showed the way ahead. Pinter's debt is the most obvious, though indirect: he has said that he admires Beckett's work 'so much that something of its texture might appear in my own'.[3] The 'texture' springs from Beckett's sense of verbal ambiguity – so in *Endgame*, a painter is said to be an 'en*graver*', being 'ap*pall*ed' and seeing only 'ashes' in all the 'rising corn'[4] – but even more from his awareness of subtextual meanings and misunderstandings. The ambiguities allow words or phrases to stand out from the rest of the dialogue to awaken impressions in the audience's minds which may well be supposed absent from the speakers'. In a letter, Beckett spoke of the ability of the words in *Endgame* to 'claw' at the mind.[5] At rehearsals of a revival of *Waiting for Godot* in 1964, he is reported to have said: 'This is a play full of implications, and every important statement may be taken at three or four levels. But the actor has only to find the dominant one; because he does so does not mean the other levels will be lost. All that matters is the laugh and the tear.'[6] But the comic and the pathetic are not always easy to identify on first reading, for Beckett's sense of subtextual implications enables him to mask involvement, so that what is truly comic may be expressed pathetically, and vice versa.

In his study of *Proust* (1931), Beckett described an artist's use of dialogue and reaction in terms that are applicable to his own plays: 'He was incapable of recording surface. . . . The copiable he does not see. He searches for a relation, a common factor, substrata. *Thus he is less interested in what is said than in the way in which it is said.* . . . The verbal oblique must be restored to the upright: thus "you are charming" equals "it gives me pleasure to embrace you".'[7]

There are substrata in actions as well as words, and what is heard and seen depends on the hearer and onlooker at least as much as on the doer. Beckett recounts how Proust's narrator hears his grandmother's voice on the telephone and, because it is not accompanied by her physical presence to which he is accustomed, he hears the voice 'for the first time, in all its purity and reality', so that he does not recognise it at first. He rushes to Paris and surprises his grandmother reading a book: 'the notion of what he should see has not had time to interfere its prism between the eye and its object', and now he sees a 'mad old woman', not the face 'mercifully composed' by his own 'solicitude of habitual memory'.[8]

Beckett also notes the moment when Odette says to Swann, her

husband, that Forcheville, her lover, 'is going to Egypt at Pentecost'.
Because of Swann's feelings of 'doleful resignation', it is as if he hears
other words; he effectively translates the remark into 'I, Odette, am
going with Forcheville to Egypt at Pentecost'. For this hearer, the future
of the speaker seems already present, and his suffering is acute: he has
infected the speaker with his own mobility of thought. Beckett takes
more examples to show that: 'When it is a case of human intercourse, we
are faced by the problem of an object, whose mobility is not merely a
function of the subject's, but independent and personal: two separate
and imminent dynamisms related by no system of synchronisation.'[9]

In Beckett's plays the characters change for each other, and so do
objects, the past and the effects of words. Mostly the characters speak
ordinary words that neither represent them accurately nor carry
definition; when they seem to agree, they may severally be thinking of
different objects or resolving on opposed actions; when they seem to
differ they may well be of the same mind. But occasionally their
perception is sharpened by a word that, as if by chance, breaks through
habitual responses. Almost any passage in *Godot* might be quoted as
example:

VLADIMIR   How they've changed!
ESTRAGON   Who?
VLADIMIR   Those two.
ESTRAGON   That's the idea, let's make a little conversation.
VLADIMIR   Haven't they?
ESTRAGON   What?
VLADMIR   Changed.
ESTRAGON   Very likely. They all change. Only we can't.
VLADIMIR   Likely! It's certain. Didn't you see them?
ESTRAGON   I suppose I did. But I don't know them.
VLADIMIR   Yes you do know them.
ESTRAGON   No I don't know them.
VLADIMIR   We know them, I tell you. You forget everything. [*Pause
To himself.*] Unless they're not the same . . .
ESTRAGON   Why didn't they recognise us, then?
VLADIMIR   That means nothing. I too pretended not to recognise
them. And then nobody ever recognises us.
ESTRAGON   Forget it. What we need – Ow! [*Vladimir does not react.*]
Ow!
VLADIMIR   [*to himself*]   Unless they're not the same . . .
ESTRAGON   Didi! It's the other foot! [*He goes hobbling towards the
mound.*]
VLADIMIR   Unless they're not the same...   (pp. 48–9)

Vladimir starts by trying to understand, but Estragon joins him to pass the time. Vladimir talks of Pozzo and Lucky, but Estragon thinks of others and of himself. Vladimir agrees, but is beginning to doubt his own eyes. Estragon begins to speak of their needs, but becomes conscious of his own pain. He makes a direct appeal to Vladimir, but Vladimir does not hear.

Here is drama that is independent of unambiguous statement or sustained eloquence, that shows the results of feelings obliquely, that moves from dialogue to solo-speech at any moment, that has talk to hide silence, and silence as eloquent as talk. Language is laughable and pathetic, necessary and inessential. Within the freedom of such a style, other dramatists could find encouragement for expressing their own sense of subtextual energies, the hide-and-seek of personal relationships, and the changing motivations and forms of expressiveness.

But the greatest step that Beckett made in *Waiting for Godot* was still more basic: to write a play that did not tell the audience what it was about. Who is Godot, why do the characters persist in acting as they do, what could they do, or what might they do, to change their predicament and ameliorate their suffering, or is this even possible? There are many clues, often at variance with each other: is the tree the tree of life or a symbol of renewal; is it a willow, reminiscent of forlorn lovers and of Judas, or is it a 'shrub' or 'bush', or is it reminiscent of the 'Tree' on which Christ died, to which Vladimir explicitly refers? When Estragon 'does the tree', he stands as if crucified on one foot with arms spread out, and he asks, 'Do you think God sees me?': closing his eyes as he is instructed he '*staggers worse*', stops and cries '*at the top of his voice*': 'God have pity on me! . . . On me! On me! Pity! On me!' (pp. 76–7). Elsewhere a barefooted Estragon explicitly compares himself to Christ: but the similarity is faint and momentary. He is also selfish, suicidal, cruel, spiteful, stupid, deceitful, ungrateful. Besides other characters are also, momentarily, Christ-figures. Lucky is the suffering servant, or fool, who is being taken to the fair to be sold: in the French version this destination is named, specifically: '*Saint-Sauveur*'. Even Pozzo, returning blind, is helped up by Vladimir and Estragon whom he takes to be highwaymen – the sufferer between two thieves. Godot, who never appears, may seem more meaningful, especially to English audiences who hear echoes of 'God' in his very name. He keeps sheep and goats, sends messengers to say he will appear, and probably has a white beard. Vladimir believes that Godot can both save and punish. But he cannot be identified with the Christian God: he shows no sign that, like Lucky's hypothetical 'personal God', he 'loves us dearly'. Vladimir, who seems most assured of Godot's existence, speaks of him consulting his family, agents and books before taking a decision, as if this were 'the normal thing'; besides, Vladimir has other gods, the 'Saviour' who forgives, for some unknown reason, from the cross, the 'cruel fate' which consigns men among a 'foul brood', and, perhaps, the 'reinforcements' of other men which put an end to waiting for Godot.

Waiting for Godot is mainly about a state of being, that cannot be defined except by the play, but which seems to relate from time to time to many notions about what life is and might be. In performance, the audience is stimulated to question and remember, to laugh and pity, and slowly a 'common factor', a relation, develops in their responses, gaining strength from the 'substrata' of the interplay. Beckett has shown that theatrical illusion can communicate, by its hidden structure, the unifying and creative vision of its author, which never speaks directly. He has encouraged other dramatists to use the theatre for expressing what they sense rather than what they say in words. The danger is incoherence, if the writer's responses are not based in experience, and settled in manner of working. The opportunity is that of by-passing limitations and barriers of language, of presenting a whole reaction to life, instinctive and subconscious as well as conscious and explicit.

No other dramatist has followed Beckett all the way, but few, if any, can remain unaffected by his achievements. He has restored the theatre as a necessary art, a form which allows a specifically twentieth-century consciousness to be explored and presented. No other art form has both the mobility and the physical reality of the theatre as Beckett used it. No other could so nakedly and consistently show man, involved with himself and with others in time, operating in all his faculties or with suspended consciousness.

The younger dramatists have not shown Beckett's rigour, being unwilling to limit theatrical means to so few and so unaccommodated human figures. But, while employing a closer imitation of ordinary life and greater variety of incident and character, those who have worked in the theatre for ten years or more have all proved to be pioneers and experimenters, using the medium with increasing boldness and for specifically theatrical effect. Unfortunately this has made their work progressively more specialised, more difficult for audiences as well as performers. . . .

SOURCE: extract from chapter 7 in *Theatre Language* (London, 1972), pp. 235–47.

NOTES

1. 'John Arden's NY War', *Flourish*, vol. 9 (1967), 1, 8, 9, 16.
2. Ionesco, 'Foreword', *Plays*, vol. 1, trans. D. Watson (London, 1958), pp. viii–ix.
3. 'Harold Pinter Replies', *New Theatre Magazine*, vol. II, no. 2 (1961), 9.
4. S. Beckett, *Endgame* (London, 1958), p. 32.
5. S. Beckett, Letter to Alan Schneider, *Village Voice* (March 1958).
6. Report by Kenneth Pearson, *Sunday Times*, 20 Dec. 1964.
7. S. Beckett, *Proust* (New York, 1931), pp. 63–4.
8. Ibid., pp. 14–15.
9. Ibid., pp. 5–7.

Andrew Kennedy   Shaw and Naturalism (1975)

Shaw only gradually recognised his distance from naturalism in his attitude to dramatic language – explicitly only relatively late in his development. In 1923, he wrote:

Neither have I ever been what you call a representationist or realist. I was always in the classic tradition, recognising that stage characters must be endowed by the author with a *conscious self-knowledge and power of expression* . . . and a freedom from inhibitions, which in real life would make them monsters of genius. It is the power to do this that differentiated me (or Shakespeare) from a gramophone and a camera. The representational part of the business is mere costume and scenery.[1](my italics)

Here Shaw comes near to claiming the kind of expressive power that Dryden had in mind when he stated that 'serious plays ought not to imitate conversation too nearly'. Though Shaw may have been the first dramatist to exploit the comic potentialities of a phonograph on stage, he certainly had less use for that invention than any of the great prose realists. Not that the latter reproduce conversation, but they write from and against the felt pressure of 'men speaking to men'. Despite differences, this is true of Ibsen and Chekhov; and Synge's eavesdropping or Pinter's 'ear for dialogue' does, at one level, mean storing in the mind speech fragments ready for patterning in dialogue. Instead, Shaw carried in his mind a prodigious gallery of known rhetorical models ready to be drawn on for 'power of expression'. It is a process of heightening from without, essentially different from Pirandello's definition of *spoken action*: 'immediate expressions inseparable from action . . . words, expressions, phrases impossible to invent but born when the author has identified himself with his creature to the point of seeing it only as he sees himself'.

This takes us to the essential distinction between 'spoken action' and 'verbal theatricality' . . . The former goes with authentic self-expression under the pressure of action; the latter with 'endowing' a character 'with conscious self-knowledge', or costume-speech. At its simplest this takes the form of comic-didactic bravura speech for a 'ventriloquist' like Doolittle, in *Pygmalion*, Act II. Shaw first prepares a kind of rostrum for such a character, the stage directions announce that he has 'a remarkably expressive voice' and that he adopts a *pose* on entry. Next a link is established with superficial naturalism; Higgins savours one of Doolittle's early flourishes:

This chap has a certain natural gift for rhetoric. Observe the rhythm of his native woodnotes wild. 'I'm willing to tell you: I'm wanting to tell you: I'm waiting to tell you.' sentimental rhetoric! that's the Welsh strain in him.

Finally Doolittle is told the 'floor is yours', and the dialogue gives way to the dustman's tirades, including the well-known disquisition on middle class morality.[2] ('What am I governors both? I ask you what am I? I'm one of the undeserving poor: that's what I am'). Here Shaw is exploiting, with the gay linguistic consciousness that fits in well with a comedy on the mechanics of speech,[3] the simple comic tension in 'natural . . . rhetoric', vulgar eloquence. It does not wear well – it is too obvious – but it is certainly controlled. But in Shaw's more ambitious plays the pull of verbal theatricality against naturalism goes with a complex and often imperfectly controlled tension.

Shaw's inability to distinguish critically between naturalism (or 'natural history') as an ideology and naturalism as a style has, it seems, never been noted. It is widely recognised that in *The Quintessence of Ibsenism* Shaw misunderstood Ibsen; it is less well-known how difficult Shaw found it to understand his own art. The *Quintessence* – the first (1891) edition, that is – was, after all, intended to be nothing but a vigorous defence of the 'realist' *Weltanschauung*; there was no confusion there, only a conscious if mistaken omission of 'Ibsen the poet'. Similarly, whenever Shaw talks about the basis of the new drama as a new 'natural history' the stress is, deliberately, on the message, not the medium.[4] It is in the later writing, in the chapters added to the enlarged edition of *The Quintessence* in 1913, that we can discover how central – and once again how unresolved – is the tension between the 'naturalist' vision and the non-naturalistic language in Shaw. (The discussion of Ibsen's four last plays, with its sympathetic awareness of how Ibsen's art had changed, and its insight into the death-in-life of the aged Ibsen 'like a child trying to learn again how to write', in itself demonstrates a characteristic duality in Shaw even in the years before the First World War: he writes of disturbed modes of being and language with the old robust symmetry.) But it is the ten-page argument entitled 'The Technical Novelty of (Ibsen's) Plays' that tells us most about the tension we are concerned with. For it is here that Shaw singles out *discussion* – as first manifested in the final act of *A Doll's House* – as the principal innovation of the post-Ibsen drama; and, in effect, he equates the drama of discussion with a minimum of the bad old theatricality (not just Scribe, but Othello's handkerchief and even the tragic *dénouements* of Ibsen)[5]. Indeed, the play Shaw now most admires for its absence of forced stage action is *The Cherry Orchard*, written by a 'hand no less deadly than Ibsen's because more caressing'. No doubt Shaw was at this time feeling his way towards a new creative method – the *supposed* Chekhovian elements in *Heartbreak House* – and he can so far forget his own actual practice as to define the post-Ibsen drama as 'really the inevitable return to nature which ends all the merely technical fashions. Now the natural is mainly the everyday; and its climaxes are, if not everyday, at least everylife, if they are to have importance for the spectator.'[6]

But what kind of dialogue does Shaw envisage in this 'return to nature' in dramatic art? The answer is the use of 'what has been used by preachers and orators ever since speech has been invented . . . rhetoric, irony, argument, paradox, epigram, parable'. And as if to underline how final this answer is, the chapter ends with a resounding restatement of what is to be substituted for the 'old stage tricks': 'a forensic technique of recrimination, disillusion, and penetration through ideals to the truth, with a free use of all the rhetorical and lyrical arts of the orator, the preacher, the pleader, and the rhapsodist'.[7]

It is really the case that Shaw was, simultaneously, drawn to verisimilitude and driven to all the known forms of eloquence in dialogue by a contrary impulse. The linguistic gap that separates 'the natural that is mainly the everyday' and 'the free use of all the rhetorical and lyrical arts' fairly epitomises the duality found in all the plays. That is why one finds a hesitancy under the seemingly robust critical statements; and we are enabled, as if reading a code, to see how, whenever Shaw makes the attempt to come near to everyday speech, the dialogue is soon transposed into quite another key.

This is true even in those plays which are most nearly naturalistic in intention. Thus *Widowers' Houses*, the nearest thing in Shaw to the thesis-play, was, in Shaw's own words, 'distorted into a *grotesquely realistic* exposure of slum landlordism';[8] and to the stylistic incongruity Shaw himself noted in his apprentice work, we may add an early example of dialogue where theatricality repeatedly triumphs over Shaw's intention to expose reality and move the audience to 'conviction of sin'. Sartorius, for example, reels off this little litany of objects as he defends the view that his tenants are not fit to live in proper dwellings:

My young friend: these people do not know how to live in proper dwellings: they could wreck them in a week. You doubt me: try it for yourself. You are welcome to replace all the missing banisters, handrails, cistern lids and dusthole tops at your own expense; and you will find them missing again in less than three days: burnt, Sir, every stick of them. I do not blame the poor creatures: they need fires . . . (Act II, *Plays Unpleasant*, Penguin ed., 1946, p. 69).

A 'Dickensian' voice in a supposedly 'Ibsenite' play; yet in the first Preface Shaw explains – has to explain – that Sartorius is no Pecksniff but a typical citizen; and elsewhere he argues that 'the Dickens–Thackeray spirit is that of a Punch-and-Judy showman . . . in contrast to Ibsen's power to move through every character'.[9] If we turn to a sociological play with a markedly personal centre – *Mrs Warren's Profession* – we find that in such scenes as the confrontation between mother and daughter in the final act, the personal emotion is diluted by Shaw's preservation of melodramatic speech in a play written against melodrama. Mrs Warren – naturalistically portrayed as the high-class prostitute and conventional woman – speaks with the posed voice of 'the fallen woman' and 'the grief-stricken mother'.

The violent style-shifts from quasi-naturalism to hybrid modes of heightened expression can be best seen in *Major Barbara* and *Heartbreak House*, two central plays in Shaw's search for a theatre of parables. More extended study would show how the texture of either play is made up of continuous, and sudden, modulations from one key to another; the principle of selection is often arbitrary, for Shaw is relying, above all, on what Francis Fergusson has called the 'perpetual-emotion machine of the dialogue', and on his own expectation that the plays will be interpreted by actors displaying 'great virtuosity in sudden transitions of mood'.[10] Here two scenes must suffice to clinch the point.* The shelter scene in *Major Barbara* (Act II) starts with superficial naturalism, including the attempt at authentic Cockney accents; and Shaw's descent from the Edwardian conversation scene (of Act I) into the world of the socially damned might make one expect something approximating Gorky's *Lower Depths*. But the language of the poor turns out to be melodramatic stage-Cockney – Bill Walker derives from Bill Sikes. As for the climax of the scene; we had better look at it before attempting to say what it is:

> BARBARA: (*almost delirious.*) I can't bear any more. Quick march!
> CUSINS: (*calling to the procession in the street outside.*) Off we go. Play up, there! Immenso giubilo. (*He gives the time with his drum . . .*)
> MRS BAINES: I must go, dear. You're overworked: you will be all right tomorrow. We'll never lose you. Now Jenny: step out with the old flag. Blood and Fire!·(*She marches out through the gate with her flag.*)
> JENNY: Glory Hallelujah! (*flourishing her tambourine and marching.*)
> UNDERSHAFT: (*to Cusins, as he marches out past him easing the slide of his trombone*). 'My ducats and my daughter!'
> CUSINS: (*following him out.*) Money and Gunpowder!
> BARBARA: Drunkenness and Murder! My God: why hast thou forsaken me? (*She sinks on the form with her face buried in her hands. The march passes away into silence. Bill Walker steals across to her.*)
> BILL: (*taunting.*) Wot prawce selvytion nah?

Caught up in a whirl of 'scoring' we have here in quick succession: the voice of Barbara's anguish; brisk colloquial orders and the cue to a wedding march from Donizetti; a clash of slogans over drum, tambourine and trombone ('Blood and Fire' versus 'Money and Gunpowder' being central to the play); the slogans merge into ironic quotation (Shylock's line) and despairing quotation (the words from the Passion which, in another context, sum up an entire culture's tragic sense); and finally the Cockney phrase of Bill which, three times repeated in the scene, is used like one of the Cries of London. What is

---

* Since writing this I have seen new productions of *Major Barbara* (R.S.C., Oct. 1970) and *Mrs Warren's Profession* (National Theatre, Dec. 1970), and I feel bound to report that in each play the posed and the personal, the melodramatic and the natural tone were given a unity. The very scenes and speeches I discuss here were controlled by the *authentic-sounding* melodramatic tone of the leading actress (Barbara: Judi Dench; Mrs Warren: Carol Browne).

intended? Almost certainly a theatrical equivalent for what an earlier
stage direction calls a 'convulsion of irony' at the spectacle of
Undershaft (whom Cusins calls 'Mephistopheles! Machiavelli!' in an
aside in the same scene) buying the Salvation Army. What is the effect?
The potential personal reality is killed (Barbara's anguish, requiring
'empathy'); for there is no centre, phrases are used like stage properties.
At the same time the irony (requiring more classic detachment or
'alienation') overflows into the orchestrated clash of voices, the operatic
tour-de-force.[11]

But if in *Major Barbara* (1905) Shaw still used melodrama as a ground
bass for the 'Socratic dialogue' structure of the play, in *Heartbreak House*
(1913–16) he is for the first time consciously aiming at a play – fusing
leisurely discussion, 'fantasia' and parable – with a natural-sounding
dialogue, dependent – in his own words – on 'nuances and subtleties'.
Indeed, any good production of the play confirms that much of the
dialogue has a spontaneity, a casual yet compelling rhythm, rare in
earlier plays by Shaw. Yet in the presumably central scenes dealing
with felt experience – the sequence of heartbreaks and the sense of being
stripped naked – Shaw cannot decide whether to give such experience
natural or posed expression. For example, Ellie, the *ingénue* turned
Shavian heroine, is intended to speak with the voice of authentic
experience, as in her long duologue with the Captain in Act II where she
makes this inward discovery after a heartbreaking experience: 'I feel
now as if there was nothing I could not do, because I want nothing.'[12]
Yet in the same Act we have Mangan's writhing and sobbing
heartbreak in the midst of the trilling voices of the Captain's demon
daughters (Hesione invoking the 'night in Tristan and Isolde'); and in
Randall's shouting-foaming-weeping, Shaw falls back on an *opera buffa*
heartbreak. The transitions from the expression of feeling to its parody
are very precarious. And throughout the play the voices of personal
experience are stylised in a manner barely distinct from the love-poses of
the 'equestrian classes' – their galloping language predominates. (As
Hector says, 'In this house we know all the poses.')

The 'spiritual marriage' of Ellie and the sleeping Captain is another
operatic climax.[13] First a quartet of voices exclaiming all together
'Bigamy!' and asking lucid questions that merge into stage 'rhubarb';
then Hector intoning Shelley:

> Their altar the grassy earth outspread,
> And their priest the muttering wind.

There follows Ellie's vow:

Yes: I, Ellie Dunn, give my broken heart and my strong sound soul to its natural captain, my spiritual husband and second father.

And, as the Captain awakes, Ellie intones a litany of blessings:

There is a blessing on my broken heart. There is a blessing on your father's spirit. Even on the lies of Marcus there is a blessing; but on Mr Mangan's money there is none.

Of this incantation Ellie herself says that she does not understand it, though she knows it means something. It seems that Shaw intends to switch from the ironic operatic mode to something like a personal epiphany. But he is only master of the operatic mode, as in the *Götterdämmerung*-like ending, with the desperate yet frivolous voices celebrating the explosion. If the 'extravaganza' or 'fantasia' elements are stressed, as in the theatre they often are, the play lives; if the personal theme is stressed, we find a waste of spirit in an expense of words. The inwardly controlled *subtext* and expressiveness of Chekhovian comedy, half-attempted by Shaw, are not within the range of his dramatic language.

After *Heartbreak House* Shaw's drama becomes, with a few exceptions, much more deliberately non-naturalistic. But the exception, *Village Wooing* (1933), is worth brief consideration. For in this play Shaw does attempt to reproduce conversation; the playlet is a succession of three conversations. But what is striking is, firstly, that these duologues are between two cyphers: A, a literary gentleman who becomes a grocer, and Z, a bored young lady who becomes his 'slave' in the village shop; secondly, where the naturalistic dialogue has most vitality it anticipates Ionesco's later use of clichés in cross-talk as an assault on human reason:

z   I never cared much for geography. Where are we now?
a   We are on the Red Sea.
z   But it's blue.
a   What did you expect it to be?
z   Well, I didn't know what colour the sea might be in these parts. I always thought the Red Sea would be red.
a   Well, it isn't.
z   And isn't the Black Sea black?
a   It is precisely the colour of the sea at Margate.
z   (*eagerly*) Oh, I am so glad you know Margate. There is no place like it in the season, is there?
a   I don't know: I have never been there.
z   (*disappointed*) Oh, you ought to go. You could write a book about it.

A   (*shudders, sighs, and pretends to write very hard.*)
    A pause.
Z   I wonder why they call it the Red Sea.[14]

By the Third Conversation the conversational dialogue is too much for
Shaw. And without any apparent change in the situation, merely
letting A draw on his being 'a poet' and not a 'materialist', the key
changes into:

A   We shall get quite away from the world of sense. We shall light up for one
    another a lamp in the holy of holies in the temple of life; and the lamp will
    make its veil transparent. Aimless lumps of stone blundering through space
    will become stars singing in their spheres. Our dull purposeless village
    existence will become one irresistible purpose and nothing else. An
    extraordinary delight and an intense love will seize us. It will last hardly
    longer than the lightning flash which turns the black night into infinite
    radiance . . .[15]

The emphatic rhythm, the repetition and balance, the near-pastiche
poetic diction in A's speech all emerge from the conversation piece.
Such a transition is almost an indulgence; an uneasy mixture between
'the thrilling voice' of the higher love in *Arms and the Man* and the
earnest speculative rhetoric in *Methuselah*.

    That Shaw had aspirations to naturalism is clear; it is equally clear
that his attempts at naturalism were deflected by his emphatically
different use of language. The early documentary plays turned into
something else; melodrama when inverted – or used as the basis for
discussion play – left solid blocks of melodramatic dialogue in an
otherwise changing form. And in his most memorable play on a
contemporary theme, the rhythms of contemporary speech are like one
thin voice in a many-voiced assembly.

    To command many voices is one of the primary talents of the
dramatist. (Children begin by mimicking voices and gestures.) All
tension, and comic tension in particular, springs from a clash of
discordant worlds, unexpected collisions. A dramatist who has more
than one style is potentially able to voice every style of speech, to present
or parody every voice. But the crucial question in Shaw is the extent to
which he can *command* his mixture of styles; the extent to which his use of
traditional rhetoric in an art of parody and pastiche is controlled. . . .

SOURCE: extract from *Six Dramatists in Search of a Language* (Cambridge, 1975), pp. 53–62.

NOTES

[These have been renumbered, and in some cases abbreviated, from the original – Ed.]

1. Letter to Alexander Bashky, written in 1923; published in the *New York Times*, 12 June 1927; reprinted in *Shaw on Theatre*, p. 185.

2. Shaw himself compared Doolittle's disquisition on morality to Falstaff's discourse on honour: *Shaw on Theatre*, p. 132.

3. Shaw writes from the standpoint of a superior Higgins: received pronunciation versus eccentric dialects. . . . Shaw's linguistic stance finds an easy outlet in parody, most often using lower-class accents as *buffa* voices in operatic scoring . . . . The underlying linguistic ideology is perhaps best summed up by Shaw's desire to 'nationalise . . . the existing class monopoly of orthodox speech', in *Morning Leader* (16 Aug. 1901), reprinted in W. F. Bolton and D. Crystal (eds), *The English Language* (Cambridge, 1969), vol. 2, pp. 80–5.

4. (1) Preface to *Plays Pleasant* (1898) – conclusion. (2) Preface to *Three Plays for Puritans* – conclusion. (3) Preface to *Three Plays by Brieux* (1911), pp. xiii ff., where the context is scientific factuality against 'romance' and writing on hitherto tabooed subjects, including sex.

5. In the Preface to *Three Plays by Brieux*, Shaw more than half agrees with Judge Brack's comment on Hedda's suicide: 'people don't do such things'. He prefers 'slices of life' as the material for the dramatist; and yet, he says, 'life as it occurs is senseless' (pp. xvii and xxvi).

6. Shaw, *Major Critical Essays*, p. 139.

7. Ibid., p. 146.

8. Preface to *Plays Unpleasant* (1898): Penguin edn (1946), pp. x–xi; Standard edn, pp. x–xi. Shaw goes on: 'The result was revoltingly *incongruous* . . . The farcical trivialities in which I followed the fashion of the times became silly and irritating beyond all endurance when intruded upon a subject of such *depth, reality, and force* as that into which I had plunged my drama.' (My italics.)

9. *Prefaces*, pp. 701–6; and *Major Critical Essays*, pp. 131ff.

10. Francis Fergusson, *The Idea of a Theater* (1949; New York, 1953), p. 194, and *Shaw on Theatre*, p. 185, respectively. . . . The climax of *Major Barbara*, Act II, is interpreted as genuinely Dionysiac by Margery Morgan in *The Shavian Playground* (London, 1972), pp. 142ff.

11. In a comparative study of Shaw and Brecht I would argue that Shaw needed a cooler principle of alienation for his drama of parables; and that the romantic irony – and the intrusion of personal-melodramatic language – in a play like *Major Barbara* cuts across his intention to demonstrate that it is a mistake to be either poor or merely charitable. But then Brecht in *St Joan of the Stockyards* – which is derived from *Major Barbara* – also fails to give any degree of reality to either the capitalist or the workers. . . .

12. *Heartbreak House*: Penguin edn (1964), pp. 130–1; Standard ed., p. 115.

13. Ibid.: Penguin ed., pp. 148–50; Standard ed., pp. 131–2.

14. '*Too True to be Good*', '*Village Wooing*' and '*On the Rocks*': Standard edn, p. 112.

15. Ibid., p. 137–8.

John Elsom   'Distilled Naturalism': Pinter's The Homecoming (1976)

. . . The menace in Pinter's plays . . . operates on three levels, of physical violence, of the labyrinthine problems set by the outside world and of the dreaded loss of emotional security. Pinter took the now familiar theme of social alienation and presented it in emotional terms which both transcended and explained the other, more limited explanations. He knew what it felt like to be a real outcast in society, not just someone who was suffering from 'divine discontent' or an Oedipal rebel. His plays, however, are rarely grim, although they can be frightening. His dialogue provides a ripple of constant pleasure, which partly derives from the actual jokes and partly from the sheer accuracy with which the underlying emotions are conveyed. His language is mainly naturalistic: Bamber Gascoigne has termed it 'distilled naturalism', in that much ordinary explanation has been omitted and that the strong sub-text has to be grasped or felt through fragmentary lines. When, for example, Ruth in *The Homecoming* (1965) meets the sexual aggression of one of her husband's brothers, Lenny, the conflict between them which Ruth wins is expressed casually but intensely through a disagreement over a glass of water:

LENNY   Just give me the glass.
RUTH   No.
         (*Pause*)
LENNY   I'll take it then.
RUTH   If you take the glass . . . I'll take you.
         (*Pause*)
LENNY   How about me taking the glass without you taking me?
RUTH   Why don't I just take you?

The Homecoming can be regarded as a transition play in Pinter's development in that it is the most complete statement of one constant theme, the search for emotional security, but also suffers from the trend towards ellipsis which sometimes becomes a Pinter mannerism. The title, *The Homecoming*, has several meanings. Teddy, a college professor in the United States, returns after a six-year absence to the house in North London where he was reared: his wife, Ruth, also from North London, comes with him. But Teddy's mother, Jessie, is dead, and the house (now scarcely a home) is run by his father, Max, his uncle Sam and his two brothers. Ruth's arrival in this all-male ménage is greeted with a mixture of hostility (from Max) and sexual longing. Her presence means the restoration of a mother-wife to the family, hence in another sense the coming of home. Ruth accept these male emotions with an unexpected calm, as if she too had come into her own as a woman. The final irony is that Teddy, whose homecoming it should have been, returns suddenly to the United States, leaving Ruth behind. Teddy is someone who has lost his roots, both by being educated in a manner which has lost him an accent and a strange, rough sub-culture and by becoming too 'rational': he distrusts and fears the instinctive emotions which surround him.

The Homecoming suffers from Pinter's desire to work out his theme on many levels, all at once. The few critical moments at the end of the play reveal an intense consciousness which scarcely leaves room for any single event to work with a full dramatic impact: not Sam's death, not Max's dethronement as head of the house, not Ruth's enthronement as Queen Bee. The abruptness affects the tone of the play, as well as the plausibility of the plot, and for once Pinter's instincts in assessing the theatrically practicable effects seems to desert him. His later plays, *Landscape* and *Silence* (1969) and *Old Times* (1971), on the other hand, reveal a remarkable constancy of tone which sometimes takes precedence over his undoubted talent for controlled shock. In these plays, Pinter does not push around his characters to make them fit his themes, and a controlled allusiveness of language extended the limits of his 'distilled naturalism', bringing the sensitivity towards verbal rhythms and images closer to that of Beckett. The humour, delicacy and seriousness of Pinter's plays cast a spell over many of his contemporaries. The word, Pinteresque, was coined to cover those many half-humorous, inconsequential, elliptical strips of dialogue which cropped up in plays by many writers, from Johnny Speight to Joe Orton. But this was surface mimicry. Unlike Osborne, Pinter uncovered no ideas which writers other than he could explore in greater depth, and his best plays, notably *The Caretaker* and *Old Times*, are complete statements of situations requiring neither commentary nor appendices. Those commentators who argued that the sudden and rich growth of dramatists in Britain during the late 1950s and early 1960s was more apparent than real, that the colourful blossoms did not imply deep roots, were nevertheless often prepared to concede profundity to Pinter. He was the first major dramatist to have been produced by the change in theatrical climate.

SOURCE: extract from *The Post-War British Theatre* (London, 1976), pp. 109–11.

PART THREE

The Drama Critic

Leigh Hunt Rules for the Theatrical Critic of a Newspaper (1807)

In the first place. Never take any notice whatever of the author of a play, or of the play itself, unless it be a new one: if the author be living, it is most probable you will have no reason to speak of him more than once, and if he be not living, you have no reason to speak of him at all, for dead men cannot give dinners.

Secondly. Indulge an acquaintance with every dramatic writer, and with every action, and you will have a noble opportunity of showing your fine feelings and your philanthropy, for you will praise every play that is acted, and every actor that plays; depend upon it, the world will attribute this praise solely to your undeviating benevolence, which is a great virtue.

Thirdly. If an audience should not possess this virtue equally with yourselves, but should barbarously hiss a new piece merely because it could not entertain them, say in your next day's criticism, that it would have been infinitely more entertaining if a little had been added, or a little had been taken away, a probability which few will dispute with you. No man of real feeling will think of damning another merely because the latter cannot succeed in every attempt to please him. If the exclamation *bravo!* will make a man enjoy his supper and put a few pounds into his pocket every winter, who would not cry out *bravo?* Suppose an ugly, whimsical fellow were to accost you in the streets and to say, 'Sir, I'd thank you to tell me I am handsome, or I shall be miserable for months to come', you would undoubtedly say, 'Sir I am enchanted with your appearance, and entreat you to be perfectly happy.' In the same manner it is easy to say to Mr Reynolds, or Mr Dibdin, or Mr Cherry, 'Your play was excellent', and the poor fellow will be as comfortable as if it were really the case.

Fourthly. If you do not exactly understand how to conceal your evil opinion of men's writing or performances, but find yourself occasionally apt to indulge in maliciously speaking the truth, always say the direct contrary of what you think. The following little glossary, collected from the most approved critics, may be of service to you in this case; you will of course make use of the first column:

A crowded house – a theatre on the night of a performance when all the back seats and upper boxes are empty.

An amusing author – an author whose very seriousness makes us laugh in spite of himself.

A good author – the general term for an author who gives good dinners.

A respectable actor – an insipid actor; one who in general is neither hissed nor applauded.

A fine actor – one who makes a great noise; a tatterdemalion of passions; a clap-trapper: one intended by nature for a town-crier. This appellation may on all occasions be given to Mr Pope, who has the finest lungs of any man of the stage.

A good actor – the general term for an actor who gives good dinners.

A charming play – a play full of dancing, music and scenery; a play in which the less the author has to do the better.

Great applause – applause mixed with the hisses of the gallery and pit.

Unbounded and universal applause – applause mixed with the hisses of the pit only. This phrase is frequently to be found at the bottom of the play house bills in declaring the reception a new piece has met with. The plays announced in these bills are generally printed in red ink, an emblem, no doubt, of the modesty with which they speak of themselves.

There was once a kind soul of an author who could not bear to use a harsh word, even when speaking of villains; he used to call highway-men *taxgatherers*, pickpockets *collectors*, and ravishers *men of gallantry*. This gentleman would have made an excellent theatrical critic; he would have called Reynolds, Congreve, and Cherry, Shakespeare, and everybody would have admired his invention.

Fifthly and lastly. When you criticise the performance of an old play, never exceed six or seven lines, but be sure to notice by name the fashionables in the boxes, for such notices are indispensably requisite to sound criticism; there is a choice collection of sentences which have been in use from time immemorial with newspaper critics, and are still used by common consent, just as we universally allow one style for a note of hand or a visiting letter. Your observations, therefore, will generally be such as these:

DRURY LANE. Last night the *beautiful* comedy of *The Rivals* was performed with great éclat to an *overflowing* house: Bannister was excellent – Mrs H. Johnston looked *beautiful*. Among the company we observed the Duchess of Gordon, the Duke of Queensbury, Lady Hamilton, and many other *amiable* and *beautiful* personages. There was a quarrel in the pit.

What can be more concise, more explanatory, more critical, than such a criticism? Grammarians undertake to teach a language in five months, musicians, the whole theory of music in five weeks, and dancing-masters all sorts of steps in five hours, but by these rules a man may be a profound critic in five minutes. Let Aristotle and Quintilian hide their huge volumes in dismay, and confess the superiority of a criticism, which, like the magic word *Sesame* in the Arabian Nights, opens to us a thousand treasures in a breath!

SOURCE: essay in *Critical Essays on the Performers of the London Theatre* (1807).

A. B. Walkley Dramatic Criticism (1903)

. . . The plain truth is that the playgoer who is merely seeking his pleasure and the playgoer who has to appraise and to justify his pleasure of necessity take somewhat different views. For the one there is the sole question: Am I pleased? For the other there is that question too, but coupled with another question – a question which, by the way, was one of Matthew Arnold's many borrowings from Sainte-Beuve–Am I right to be pleased? Stendhal's precept, 'Interroge-toi quand tu ris', is nothing to the public, but it is everything to the critic. Or the public may say, 'we were bored', and forget the play as quickly as they can. The critics have to say why they are bored, and that is a bore, so that they are sure to be less charitable to a bad play than the public. The wound is kept open. Then it has to be remembered that good plays, plays which rightly please the public, often make bad 'copy' – that is to say, unworkable material – for the critic. A play that presents no variation of type may be interesting enough in itself, but vexes the critic, to whom it offers no 'purchase'. And, to go a little further into technical particulars, there are certain classes of play – for example, melodramas and farces – which always come out worse on paper than on the boards. The critic is generally tempted to describe melodrama by the ironic method – which is a perfidy – and to narrate the plot of a farce is, at the best, to decant champagne. It is for a kindred reason that the 'drama of ideas' is apt to be overpraised in print – which is a good medium for ideas. In brief, criticism, being a form of literature, can do justice to the literary elements in drama; but in drama there are many other elements, and criticism is often at fault with these, because of a purely technical difficulty, the difficulty of transporting the effects of one art into the effects of another. Criticism can give the reader a very fair idea of *Hamlet* or *Paolo and Francesca,* of *Le Demi-Monde* or *A Doll's House,* of *Iris* or *The Admirable Crichton.* It can give only an inadequate account of the pleasure afforded by *A Midsummer Night's Dream* or *La Locandiera* or *L' Enfant Prodigue.* With *Box and Cox* or *Charley's Aunt* it can do nothing.

And we have seen the reason why. It is because the critic, like the piece of furniture in Goldsmith's poem, has 'a double debt to pay'; because he is at once consumer and producer, at once parasite and independent, substantive artist. In the very act of describing and appraising the methods of another art he has to follow the methods, the very different methods, of his own. A criticism is a picture with its own laws of perspective and composition and 'values', and the play which furnishes the subject for this picture has more often than not to be 'humoured' a little, stretched here and squeezed there, in order to fit into the design. The salient points in the pattern of the play may not suit the salient points in the pattern of the criticism–though, no doubt, the good critic is he who most often gets the two sets into perfect coincidence. The critic must have his 'general idea', his leading theme, which gives his criticism its unity, something to hold it together. The general idea, however legitimately it may have been derived from the play critisised, will very likely get exaggerated, will assume a much more important part in the criticism than it actually did in the play itself. Or the critic may take some significant phrase or catchword of the play as a 'refrain' for his article, or he may perform a *fantasia* on some leading theme of the play (for example, the 'nose' theme in *Cyrano de Bergerac*), until he has exhausted all its possible permutations and combinations. These are devices permissible in criticism, because criticism is literature, an art intended to interest, to give pleasure, in itself; but their effect is to warp the genuine first-hand impression of the play, to alter its proportions. Thus criticism tends to systematise what may not be systematic, to follow out its own logic and to expand its own formulas, rather than to conform strictly to the outline and proportions of the thing criticised. That is so, because, in a sense, all art is not only a transformation but a deformation of its subject-matter. It is the old difficulty of the portrait painter. The sitter asks, 'Is it like?'; the connoisseur, 'Is it a good piece of painting?' There are whole elements of a play which are ignored by the critic, for the simple reason that they will not work into his scheme. One has even heard of cases where the name of some meritorious actor has been passed over in silence, because mention of it would spoil the hang of the critic's sentence; but that is immoral.

One must not be lured into betraying all the secrets of the craft. Enough has been said, perhaps, to show why the critic and the public differ in their opinions of the same thing, and why this difference is widened in the very process by which the critic records his opinions. It is often widened still further by what may seem a purely mechanical accident – the interval of time which elapses between the critic's

impression and his record of it. The objection is often raised against 'first
night' criticism, that it is bound to be hasty, undigested, more or less of
an improvisation. Apart from the fact that newspaper readers, in any
case, insist upon having it, I believe that it is on the whole the criticism
most advantageous to the play. The critic's sensations are vivid, his
mind is full of his subject, he still has the proportions and details of the
play in his eye. Writing after an interval, he is apt to remember his
general impression of the play rather than the play itself, and his
impression has lost in truth by the fading of minor detail, to the
consequent exaggeration of a few prominent features – a process which
may lead the most conscientious critic to unconscious caricature.

Now I trust I have not been showing you a glimpse of the critic at
work without at the same time suggesting to you his professional
drawbacks, his besetting sins. For one thing, I have said that he has
often to give an appearance of system to subject-matter which is not
really systematic. And so he is apt to become what Joe Gargery would
call too 'architectooralooral'. Then again, having to deal perpetually in
formulas, he is in danger of becoming their dupe. He is apt to indulge in
what another character in Dickens calls 'poll-parrotting'; to repeat
mechanically cant phrases – 'objective' and 'subjective', 'classic' and
'romantic', 'organism' and 'reaction'. These are the things which Sir
Leslie Stephen, with his wonted manliness and homeliness of sense,
brands as 'the mere banalities of criticism. I can never hear them', he
says, 'without a suspicion that a professor of Aesthetics is trying to
hoodwink me by a bit of technical platitude. The cant phrases which
have been used so often by panegyrists, too lazy to define their terms,
have become almost as meaningless as the complimentary formulae of
society.' And that is just it; the man of letters is here showing the same
weakness as the man of the world. For there are fashions in the library
just as there are fashions in the *salon*; and the desire for imitation for
imitation's sake, is common to all humanity.

And when the critic is apt to theorise 'in the air', because of the
constant tendency towards divorce between literature and life. Walter
Bagehot makes some characteristic remarks on this point: 'The reason
why so few good books are written, is that few people that can write
know anything. In general an author has always lived in a room, has
read books, has cultivated science, is acquainted with the style and
sentiments of the best authors, but is out of the way of employing his own
ears and eyes. He has nothing to hear and nothing to see. His life is a
vacuum. . . . He sits beside a library-fire, with nice white paper, a good
pen, a capital style, every means of saying everything, and nothing to
say. . . . How dull it is to make it your business to write, to stay by

yourself in a room to write, and then to have nothing to say.' Something
like that is very often the fate of the dramatic critic. For there are many
plays which are absolutely null and void. The general playgoer settles
the matter quite comfortably by falling asleep over them. The critic has
to say something, and in reality there is nothing to be said.

So much by way of confession of critical sins. There remain two
charges constantly brought against critics which may be admitted to the
full, but which, instead of being to their discredit, are really the best
evidence of their good faith and their good work. These two charges are:
first, lack of unanimity – the critics disagree with one another – and,
second, lack of consistency – the critic will often disagree with himself.
Critics, it is said, not being unanimous, cannot be representative of
public opinion. As though public opinion about a play was ever
unanimous! We must not be fooled by a noun of multitude. 'Public' is
one word; it does not denote one thing. I know I spoke in my first lecture
of the crowd as a whole, and sketched the general aspects of the
collective mind. But the public, of course, is extraordinarily disparate in
its parts. It comprises the people who applaud a play, the people who
hiss it, the people who slumber through it, the people who don't know
what to think about it, the people who like it because dear Angelina does,
the people who dislike it because they had to forego their after-dinner
coffee in order to see it, and the people who would stay away from it if
they were not paid to go. So that when criticism is unanimous, then, and
only then, shall we be able to say confidently that it is not representative. But fortunately that time – that monotonous time – will never
be. For in that time there will have to be absolute rules for judging works
of art, applied by everybody in the same way; all critics will possess
the same principles, taste, temperament, intellectual education, moral
standard, the experience of life. Meanwhile, 'with such a being as man
in such a world as the present' – as Bishop Butler used to phrase it – no
two critics who are thinking and feeling for themselves can be in
complete agreement. We might as well complain that their faces are not
alike! There is, no doubt, often a certain appearance of unanimity
among critics who are not thinking for themselves but are trying to
think what they suppose they ought to think or what they guess other
people to be thinking, so as to shout, on Mr Pickwick's principle, with
the largest crowd. But these are critics who have mistaken their
vocation. So that when Mr Sidney Grundy asks, 'When critics fall out,
who shall decide?' and when Sir Henry Irving refers to 'the rapture of
disagreement which is served up by the dramatic critics', they ought in
reality to have been gratified by the lack of unanimity which they
deplore. It is evidence that the plays of the one and the acting of the

other are stimulating enough to force the critics into thinking for themselves.

We have seen that while criticism as to its substance is opinion, as to its form it is art. No two opinions can be the same, because no man has the same perceptive apparatus – eye, ear, nerves, brain – as another man. Is it not notorious that no two people will agree in describing the simplest fact, the pace of an omnibus, the number of cats in the back garden? But while criticism is bound to vary, as mere record of fact, its variation is enormously increased because it is an art. Did you ever see two identical pictures of the same subject by different hands? Did you ever hear two pianists play the same sonata in the same way? Of course not, and yet there are people who seem to expect different souls to have the same adventures among the masterpieces. And if they were the same, there would still remain the variations of ability to describe them. The critic's real difficulty is that he never does describe them adequately. To adjust language with exactness to one's thoughts and impressions is an impossible feat; critics, like other writers, spend their lives in practising it, and, like other writers, never bring the feat off.

As to the critic's want of self-consistency, that is apt in this country to bring him into sad trouble. In 1902 a provincial jury mulcted a newspaper in the sum of £100 and costs for a certain theatrical 'notice', and two of the jurors wrote to the newspapers to say that the main ground of their verdict was the consideration that the notice was inconsistent with a former notice of the same play in the same quarter. If these gentlemen had been philosophers – instead of jurymen – they would have congratulated this inconsistent critic on the plain proof that he was not a mechanical recording instrument – a barometer or a pair of scales – a dead thing, but a human being with the principle of growth and life within him. They would have recognised, with a pure natural joy, that the soul never has the same adventures twice over. Nothing – to take perhaps a less humble literary example – nothing could be more interesting than to note the mental development of the well-known Danish critic, Dr George Brandes, in studying the works of Ibsen *pari passu* with their production. He says himself, after noting how Ibsen at different stages of his work was not the same Ibsen: 'But neither was the critic quite the same. He had in the meantime gone through a great deal, and had consequently acquired a larger outlook upon life, and a more flexible emotional nature. He had dropped all the doctrines that were due to education and tradition. He understood the poet better now.' A great historical instance of development in the reverse direction is that of Voltaire in regard to Shakespeare. Voltaire began by blessing Shakespeare (with reservations), and ended by (quite unreservedly) cursing him. That was by no means because he understood the poet better; but for reasons extraneous to his critical development, reasons connected with his objections to the course which he found the French drama was taking without his leave. And the moral of that little affair is that the critic should remain content to be an artist, and not set up for a literary dictator. . . .

SOURCE: extract from *Dramatic criticism: Three Lectures Delivered at the Royal Institution in February 1903* (London, 1903); reprinted in G. Rowell (ed.), *Victorian Dramatic Criticism* (London, 1971), pp. 365–9.

George Jean Nathan 'The Dramatic Critic' (1922)

. . . To ask the dramatic critic to keep himself out of his criticism to detach himself, is thus a trifle like asking an actor to keep himself out of his rôle. Dramatic critics and actors are much alike. The only essential difference is that the actor does his acting on a platform. But, platform or no platform, the actor and the dramatic critic best serve their rôles when they filter them through their own personalities. A dramatic critic who is told to keep his personality out of his criticism is in the position of an actor who, being physically and temperamentally like Mr John Barrymore, is peremptorily directed by a producer to stick a sofa pillow under his belt, put on six extra heel-lifts, acquire a whiskey voice and play Falstaff like the late Sir Herbert Tree. The best dramatic critics from the time of Quintus Horatius Flaccus (*vide* the '*Epistola*') have sunk their vivid personalities into their work right up to the knees. Not only have they described the adventures of their souls among masterpieces, but the adventures of their kidneys, spleens and cœca as well. Each has held the mirror of drama up to his own nature, with all its idiosyncrasies. And in it have been sharply reflected not the cut and dried features of the professor, but the vital features of a red-alive man. The other critics have merely held up the mirror to these red-alive men, and have reflected not themselves but the latter. Then, in their vainglory, they have looked again into the the handglass and have mistaken the reflection of the parrot for an eagle.

A third rubber-stamp: the critic must have sympathy. As properly contend that a surgeon must have sympathy. The word is misused. What the critic must have is not sympathy, which in its common usage bespeaks a measure of sentimental concern, but interest. If a dramatic critic, for example, has sympathy for an actress he can no more criticise her with poise than a surgeon can operate on his own wife. The critic may on occasion have sympathy as the judge in a court of law may on occasion have it, but if he is a fair critic, or a fair judge, he can't do anything about it, however much he would like to. Between the fair defendant in the lace baby collar and a soft heart, article x, section 123, page 456, absurdly interposes itself. (In example, being a human being with a human being's weaknesses before a critic, I would often rather praise a lovely one when she is bad than an unlovely one when she is good – and, alas, I fear that I sometimes do – but in the general run I try to remember my business and behave myself. It isn't always easy. But I do my best, and angels and Lewes could do no more.) The word sympathy is further mishandled, as in the similar case of the word enthusiasm. What a critic should have is not, as is common, sympathy and enthusiasm *before* the fact, but *after* it. The critic who enters a theatre bubblingly certain that he is going to have a good time is no critic. The critic is he who leaves a theatre cheerfully certain that he *has* had a good time. Sympathy and enthusiasm, unless they are *ex post facto*, are precisely like prevenient prejudice and hostility. Sympathy has no more preliminary place in the equipment of a critic than in the equipment of an ambulance driver or a manufacturer of bird cages. It is the caboose of criticism, not the engine. . . .

SOURCE: extracts from *The Critic and the Drama* (New York and London, 1922), pp. 120–4.

John Arden Telling a True Tale (1960)

Cruel, cruel was the war when first the rout began
And out of Old England went many a smart young man.
They pressed my Love away from me likewise my brothers three.
They sent them to the war, my love, in the Isle of Germany.

To use the material of the contemporary world and present it on the public stage is the commonly accepted purpose of play-wrights, and there are several ways in which this can be done. Autobiography treated in the documentary style (Wesker). Individual strains and collisions seen from a strongly personal standpoint and inflamed like a savage boil (Osborne). The slantindicular observation of unconsidered speech and casual action used to illuminate loneliness and lack of communication (Pinter). Tough analysis of a social disease (Ibsen/ Arthur Miller). And so on. What I am deeply concerned with is the problem of translating the concrete life of today into terms of poetry that shall at the one time both illustrate that life and set it within the historical and legendary tradition of our culture. I am writing in English (British English) and primarily for an English (British English) audience. Therefore I am concerned to express my themes in terms of British (English British, but not exclusively) tradition. This is not chauvinism but a prudent limitation of scope. Art may be truly international, but there are dangers in being too wide open to unassimilated influences from north, south, east and west.

The English public has regrettably lost touch with its own poetic traditions. There are many reasons for this – one which is often suggested is the passing of Anglo-Saxon power into the hands of America. After politics follows culture, and there is a large deploring of the flood of American Pop that has clearly caught the imagination of youth to the exclusion of anything native. In one way, however, this may be not so bad. The bedrock of English poetry is the ballad. These ballads have been preserved more vitally in America than anywhere else and now they are coming back. Let me sketch a quick line of writers who have always built close to the bedrock. Chaucer, Skelton, Shakespeare, Jonson, Defoe, Gay, Burns, Dickens, Hardy, Joyce. All these men have known, almost as an unnoticed background to their lives, the enormous stock of traditional poetry, some of it oral, some of it printed and hawked at street-corners, some of it sung from the stages of the music-halls. They are naturally not the only important writers of our history; but they form a line with strongly defined hereditary features, and they wrote from a basic unvarying poetic standpoint. (I have included a Scotsman and an Irishman for the sake of completeness – those nations of course have produced many others as firmly attached to the central thread.) It seems to me that this tradition is the one that will always in the end reach to the heart of the people,[1] even if the people are not entirely aware of what it is that causes their response. Brecht was always alive to this, and, from the German point of view, he consistently worked upon the same principle.

The theatrical poet must be general in his appeal. If he is too private his plays will only be valued for reading, or (like most of Yeats's work) will only be found actable before small private audiences in a drawing-room theatre. England is a country which is at present sick with 'tradition'. But the truer legends and histories are not those which are acted out by the Beefeaters or the cottage-thatchers for the benefit of the tourist trade. As seen through the eyes of the sort of writers I have mentioned, the English prove to be an extraordinarily passionate people, as violent as they are amorous, and quite astonishingly hostile to good government and order.

> Sally, my dear, shall I come to bed to you.
> She laugh and reply I'm afraid you'll undo me.
> Sing fal the diddle ido, sing whack fal the diddle day.

Or –

> So young Johnson beat the seven of them,
> And the rest he did not mind,
> Till this cruel-hearted woman
> Took a knife from her side and ripped him up behind.

If the modern idea of a sludgy uninterested nation, married to its telly and its fish and chips, has any truth in it (and I'm afraid it has a little) it is the business of the dramatists to cry out against it even if there seems to be no hope of his ever being heard. That there is no hope, I do not believe.

In the ballads the colours are primary. Black is for death, and for the coalmines. Red is for murder, and for the soldier's coat the collier puts on to escape from his black. Blue is for the sky and for the sea that parts true love. Green fields are speckled with bright flowers. The seasons are clearly defined. White winter, green spring, golden summer, red autumn. The poets see their people at moments of alarming crisis, comic or tragic. The action goes as in Japanese films – from sitting down everyone suddenly springs into furious running, with no faltering intermediate steps.

What does this mean in terms of the theatre? To start with – costumes, movements, verbal patterns, music, must all be strong, and hard at the edges. If verse is used in the dialogue, it must be nakedly verse as opposed to the surrounding prose, and must never be allowed to droop into casual flaccidities. This is the Brechtian technique, more or less. I would suggest a further analogy. The ancient Irish heroic legends were told at dinner as prose tales, of invariable content but, in the manner of their telling, improvised to suit the particular occasion or the poet's mood. When, however, he arrived at one of the emotional climaxes of the story such as the lament of Deirdre for the Sons of Usna or the sleep-song of Grainne over Diarmaid, then he would sing a poem which he had by heart and which was always the same. So in a play, the dialogue can be naturalistic and 'plotty' as long as the basic poetic issue has not been crystallised. But when this point is reached, then the language becomes formal (if you like, in verse, or sung), the visual pattern coalesces into a vital image that is one of the nerve-centres of the play. A medieval city, built upon one or two hills, will have in it several tall church towers which stand up proud from the spread of low-roofed houses, which in turn are cramped in by the surrounding walls. Carry the simile further, and we find a river running through the town and looping round to divide the buildings as a play is split up into acts.

The themes of traditional poetry are always the same. Simple basic situations – a pregnant girl is abandoned by her lover – a soldier is recruited for the war –

> I met with Serjeant Atkinson in the market going down
> And he said, 'Young man, will you enlist and be a Light
>   Dragoon?

– a sailor returned from the sea finds his wife re-married – the raggle-taggle gipsies at a castle gate carry off the lady and are hunted down and punished –

> O England is a free country, so free beyond a doubt,
> That if you have no food to eat, you are free to go without.

The Turkish Knight kills St George, only to find an interfering doctor who raises him from the dead again. . . . There is no need to be afraid of being corny in choice of a plot. When the stories are as firmly grounded as these, there is scarcely any limit to the amount of meaning and relevance a writer can insert into them. They are themes which can carry any strength of content from tragedy through satire to straightforward comedy, and neither be drowned in it nor seem too portentous. Social criticism, for example, tends in the theatre to be dangerously ephemeral and therefore disappointing after the fall of the curtain. But if it is expressed within the framework of the traditional poetic truths it can have a weight and an impact derived from something more than contemporary documentary facility.

This kind of theatre is easily misunderstood. I have found in my own very tentative experiments that audiences (and particularly critics) find it hard to make the completely simple response to the story that is the necessary preliminary to appreciating the meaning of the play. Other habits of playgoing have led them to expect that they are going to have to begin by forming judgements, by selecting what they think is the author's 'social standpoint' and then following it to its conclusion. This does not happen in ballads at their best. There we are given the fable, and we draw our own conclusions. If the poet intends us to make a judgement on his characters, this will be implied by the whole turn of the story, not by intellectualised comments as it proceeds. The tale stands and it exists in its own right. If the poet is a true one, then the tale will be true too.

SOURCE: article in *Encore* (May 1960); reprinted in C. Marowitz (ed.), *'Encore' Reader: Chronicle of the New Drama* (London, 1970), pp. 125–9.

NOTE

1. Not only the English people – other countries have similar traditions; so without deliberately straining for it, the effect of the poetry *becomes* universal.

SELECT BIBLIOGRAPHY

This listing is more than usually partial. Anything to do with theatre and/or drama is dramatic criticism. Unfortunately, much theatre-based criticism remains on the level of gossip, while a good deal of drama-based criticism treats the play as if it were just another piece of literature. In the following list I have tried to suggest examples of dramatic criticism which cover the wide variety available, seeking either to capture the ephemeral or enshrine the universal. Moreover, criticism is a parasitic art: one reads it for what it tells about something rather than for itself.

Titles of Works excerpted in this Casebook are not included in this list.

BIBLIOGRAPHIES

E. H. Mikhail, *Contemporary British Drama, 1950–76* (London, 1976).
Helen B. Palmer (compiler), *European Dramatic Criticism, 1900–75* (Hamden, Conn., 1977).
Stanley Wells (ed.), *Shakespeare: Select Bibliographical Guides* (London, 1973).
———— (ed.), *English Drama (Excluding Shakespeare): Select Bibliographical Guides* (London, 1975).

ANTHOLOGIES AND WORKS OF GENERAL REFERENCE

James Agate, *The English Dramatic Criticism 1660–1932* (London, 1932).
Eric Bentley (ed.), *The Theory of the Modern Stage* (Harmondsworth, 1968).
John Russell Brown (ed.), *Modern British Dramatists: A Collection of Critical Essays* ('Twentieth Century Views' ser., Englewood Cliffs, N.J., 1968).
John Russell Brown and B. Harris (eds), *Contemporary Theatre* ('Stratford-upon-Avon Studies', no. 4, London, 1962).
Terence Hawkes (ed.), *Coleridge on Shakespeare* (New York, 1959; Harmondsworth, 1969)
R. W. Corrigan (ed.), *Theatre in the Twentieth Century* (New York, 1965).
Martin Esslin (ed.), *Illustrated Encyclopaedia of World Theatre* (London, 1971).
Clifford Leech and T. W. Craik (General Eds), *The Revels History of Drama in English* (London, various dates: vols III, V, VI and VIII available).
Charles Marowitz, Tom Milne and Owen Hale (eds), *The 'Encore' Reader* (London, 1965).
J. McFarlane, *Henrik Ibsen* ('Penguin Critical Anthologies', Harmondsworth, 1970).
A. M. Nagler (ed.), *Sources of Theatrical History* (New York, 1952).
G. Oppenheimer (ed.), *The Passionate Playgoer* (New York, 1962).

G. Rowell, *Victorian Dramatic Criticism* (London, 1971).
A. C. Ward (ed.), *Specimens of English Dramatic Criticism* (London, 1946).

INDIVIDUAL WORKS

David Addenbrooke, *The Royal Shakespeare Company* (London, 1974).
James Agate, *The Contemporary Theatre, 1944–45* (London, 1946).
William Archer, *English Dramatists of Today* (London, 1882).
John Arden, *To Present the Pretence* (London, 1977).
Antonin Artaud, *The Theater and Its Double* (New York, 1958).
Eric Bentley, *The Playwright as Thinker* (New York, 1955).
——————, *The Life of the Drama* (London, 1965).
Madeleine Bingham, *Henry Irving and the Victorian Theatre* (London, 1978).
E. Martin Browne, *The Making of T. S. Eliot's Plays* (Cambridge, 1969).
Terry Browne, *Playwrights' Theatre* (London, 1975).
Judith Cook, *Directors' Theatre* (London, 1974).
S. W. Dawson, *Drama and the Dramatic* ('Critical Idiom' series, London, 1970).
Barry Duncan, *The St James's Theatre* (London, 1964).
John Elsom and Nicholas Tomalin, *The History of the National Theatre* (London, 1978).
Martin Esslin, *The Theater of the Absurd* (New York, 1961).
——————, *An Anatomy of Drama* (London, 1976).
——————, *Artaud* (Glasgow, 1976).
G. L. Evans, *The Language of Modern Drama* (London, 1977).
Francis Fergusson, *The Idea of A Theater* (Princeton, N.J., 1949).
R. Findlater, *Banned! A Review of Theatrical Censorhip in Britain* (London, 1967).
James Forsyth, *Tyrone Guthrie* (London, 1976).
John Gielgud, *Early Stages, 1921–36* (London, 1939).
Jerzy Grotowski, *Towards a Poor Theatre* (London, 1969).
Eugene Ionesco, *Notes and Counter Notes* (London, 1964).
Jan Kott, *Theatre Notebook, 1947–67* (London, 1968).
R. Mander and J. Mitchenson, *The Theatres of London* (London, 1961).
Charles Marowitz, *The Act of Being* (London, 1978).
Allardyce Nicholl, *A History of English Drama, 1660–1900* (Cambridge, 1930).
——————, *A History of English Drama, 1900–1930* (Cambridge, 1973).
Hesketh Pearson, *The Last Actor Managers* (London, 1950).
G. B. Shaw, *Shaw on Shakespeare*, edited by Edwin Wilson (New York, 1961; Harmondsworth, 1969).
Constantin Stanislavski, *My Life in Art* (London, 1924).
J. L. Styan, *Drama, Stage and Audience* (Cambridge, 1975).
Howard Taubman, *The Making of the American Theater* (London, 1965).
John Russell Taylor, *Anger and After: A Guide to the New British Drama* (London, 1962).
——————, *The Second Wave: British Drama for the Seventies* (London, 1971).
J. C. Trewin, *The Edwardian Theatre* (Oxford, 1976).

Kenneth Tynan, *A View of the English Stage* (London, 1975).
——————, *The Sound of Two Hands Clapping* (London, 1975).
Irving Wardle, *The Theatres of George Devine* (London, 1978).
Arnold Wesker, *Fears of Fragmentation* (London, 1970).
John Willett (translator), *Brecht on Theatre* (London, 1964).
Raymond Williams, *Drama in Performance* (Harmondsworth, 1972).

PERIODICALS

Plays and Players
Theatre Quarterly

NOTES ON CONTRIBUTORS

JAMES AGATE (1877–1947): Dramatic critic, especially for the *Sunday Times* from 1923 until his death. He was always entertaining, though he refused to admit that any actor after Irving could be great. In addition to collections of theatre reviews, he published several autobiographical volumes (*Ego*).

WILLIAM ARCHER (1856–1924): Critic, editor and journalist, translations of Ibsen under his editorship appeared in 1890–91 and a revised edition was published in 11 volumes in 1906–8. A friend of G. B. Shaw and an enthusiastic supporter of the idea of a British National Theatre, he was dramatic critic of the *London Figaro* (1879–81), *World* (1884–1905), *Tribune* (1905–8) and *Nation* (1908–10).

JOHN ARDEN (b. 1930): English dramatist, although trained as an architect. His most famous play to date is *Serjeant Musgrave's Dance* (1956).

ARISTOTLE (384–322 BC): Greek philosopher, tutor to Alexander the Great. In *Poetics* (c.330 BC) he attempted to describe the form and function of tragedy and epic (and possibly, in a lost part, comedy). The work was intended to counter the views of Socrates and Plato about the role and work of the artist. Much of his influence in the sixteenth and seventeenth centuries (e.g., the famous Three Unities) was an elaboration of his ideas made known through Latin versions of commentaries on his works by the Arabic scholar Averroës. Aristotle is a good practical critic of a particular type of tragedy.

ST AUGUSTINE OF HIPPO (345–430): His *Confessions* (c.397) is a striking account of his early life before he was converted from Manichaeism to Christianity by St Ambrose, bishop of Milan.

ERIC BENTLEY (b. 1916): British-born American dramatic critic, he became Brander Matthews Professor of Dramatic Literature at Columbia University in 1954. He has espoused the cause of Brecht in America, and is the author of an excellent study of Bernard Shaw (1948).

MICHAEL BILLINGTON (b. 1939): Read English Literature at Oxford, and spent two years working in the theatre at Lincoln. Deputy drama critic of *The Times* from 1965 to 1971, he is currently drama critic of *The Guardian* and film critic of the *London Illustrated News* and *Birmingham Post*.

M. C. BRADBROOK (b. 1909): formerly Professor of English in the University of Cambridge and Mistress of Girton College. In addition to *Elizabethan Stage*

Conditions (1932) she has published many studies on Shakespeare and on Renaissance and Modern Drama.

PETER BROOK (b. 1925): A brilliant and inventive director, he was already directing Shakespeare productions at Stratford-upon-Avon in his early twenties. Since 1956 he has spent more and more of his time in France and has come increasingly under the influence of Artaud. In 1970 he opened an International Centre for Theatre Research in Paris for experimental work with an international company of actors.

JOHN RUSSELL BROWN (b. 1923): Professor of English in the University of Sussex, he was previously head of the Department of Drama and Theatre Arts in the University of Birmingham. In 1973 he was appointed an associate director of the National Theatre with special responsibility for scripts. In addition to *Theatre Language* (1972), his publications include *Shakespeare's Plays in Performance, Shakespeare's Dramatic Style, Free Shakespeare*, and *Effective Performance.* He is editor of the Casebooks on *Antony and Cleopatra* and *Much Ado About Nothing* with *As You Like It.*

BARRETT H. CLARK (1890–1953): American author and editor. His publications include *The Continental Drama of Today* (1914), *British and American Drama of Today* (1915), *Eugene O'Neill* (1926) and, with R. Sanborn, a biography of O'Neill (1931).

SAMUEL TAYLOR COLERIDGE (1772–1834): Poet, literary critic and philosopher. His play *Osorio*, written in 1797, was produced in 1813 with Byron's encouragement, but he is most remembered for his poetry of the imagination and use of the theory of imagination in literary criticism, which enabled him to see previous writers, and particularly Shakespeare, in a new light, and which appears in disconnected form in *Biographia Literaria* (1817) and the notes for his lectures on Shakespeare.

E. GORDON CRAIG (1872–1966): Son of Ellen Terry, the famous actress. After a brief career as an actor he took up direction in 1900, but after 1902 his name is associated with only four more productions. His demands – e.g., that a theatre should be closed for ten years while he rehearsed a play – were quite unrealistic, and it is clear that the practicalities of the theatre did not interest him. He is important as a theatrical prophet whose ideas on non-representational production and the use of dance and mime have become part of the vocabulary of the modern theatre.

JOHN DRYDEN (1631–1700): Poet Laureate, dramatist and literary critic. In his *Of Dramaticke Poesie* (1668) he reviewed the problems of dramatic art which had emerged since Shakespeare's death, particularly when compared with drama as practised in France and Spain on principles that were, theoretically, more reasonable and against which Shakespeare and Elizabethan-Jacobean drama generally had to be measured. Samuel Johnson described the essay as an 'epitome of excellence', and it is certainly a milestone in the development of dramatic criticism in England.

T. S. ELIOT (1888–1965): Poet, dramatist and literary critic. Although enjoying some success with his verse plays in the theatre, he will be remembered mainly as a poet and as the critic whose studies of the Elizabethan and Jacobean playwrights and poets have exerted a strong influence on modern literary appreciation.

JOHN ELSOM (b. 1934): Read English at Magdalene College, Cambridge and is currently theatre critic for the *Listener*. He spent six years in the script department of Paramount Pictures and has worked in drama in Adult Education in London. His publications include *Theatre Outside London* (1971), *Erotic Theatre* (1973), *Post-War British Theatre* (1976) and – with the late Nicholas Tomalin – the controversial *History of the National Theatre* (1978); and also, for the Liberal Party, *The Green Paper on the Arts* (1978).

HARLEY GRANVILLE-BARKER (1877–1946): Playwright, actor, theatre director and critic. An outstanding figure in the progressive theatre in the early twentieth century, his production of plays by Shaw, Euripides and other dramatists during the Barker-Vedrenne management of the Court Theatre (1904–7) established his reputation. His productions of Shakespeare at the Savoy theatre in 1913–14 were memorable, largely influenced by his association with William Poel. His later fame rests on the *Prefaces to Shakespeare* (five volumes, 1927–1947), which exerted a strong influence on English Shakespearean production.

SIR TYRONE GUTHRIE (1900–197): British theatre director. He started with the Scottish National Players, 1926–27, and was Director at the Old Vic theatre 1933–34, 1936–37 and 1951–52. In 1953 he founded the Shakespeare Festival at Stratford, Ontario. An inventive director – usually in the service of the play – most of his best work was with Shakespeare and the Elizabethan-Jacobean drama. He was knighted in 1961.

WILLIAM HAZLITT (1778–1830): Essayist, literary critic and political writer, between 1813 and 1818 he contributed dramatic criticism to the *Examiner*, *Morning Chronicle*, *Champion* and *The Times*; his articles and reviews were assembled in *A View of the English Stage* (1818). His essays in literary criticism – especially *The Characters of Shakespeare's Plays* (1817–18) – had a powerful influence on the development of popular appreciation of Shakespeare.

LEIGH HUNT (1784–1859): Poet, essayist, critic and political-writer. Among his many journalistic activities he wrote dramatic criticism for the *News* (1805–7), the *Examiner* (1808–13) and the *Tatler* (1830–32), the last two of which he also edited. In 1813 he was sentenced, with his brother John, to two years' imprisonment for publishing derogatory remarks about the Prince Regent. With Byron he edited at Pisa *The Liberal* magazine (1822). He was among the first to recognise the genius of Shelley and Keats. He produced editions of the plays of Sheridan, Wycherley, Congreve, Vanbrugh and Farquhar in 1840, and of Beaumont and Fletcher in 1855. His only play, *A Legend of Florence*, was performed at Covent Garden in 1840.

HENRIK IBSEN (1828–1906): Norwegian dramatist, generally regarded as the father of modern theatre. He moved from historical romantic drama to realistic studies of contemporary life and then to symbolic drama. His change from verse to prose for serious drama must be qualified by the recognition that his 'prose', however naturalistic, always carries symbolic resonances.

HENRY JAMES (1843–1916): American-born novelist, critic and novelist who settled in England in 1876 and took British nationality in 1914. He never worked as a dramatic critic but wrote articles on dramatic subjects, chiefly for American periodicals. Only three of his plays were produced in his lifetime and none was successful – though adaptations of his novels and short stories for stage, film and television have proved popular in recent years. Throughout most of his life he had aspirations to become a dramatist and he wrote extensively about the theatre.

SAMUEL JOHNSON (1709–84): Poet, novelist, critic, lexicographer, dramatist, and editor of the works of William Shakespeare (eight volumes) with the splendid Preface (1765).

ANDREW KENNEDY (b. 1931): Hungarian-born critic. Educated at Hertford Grammar School and Bristol University, he is currently Senior Lecturer in English Literature in the University of Bergen.

G. WILSON KNIGHT (b. 1897): Emeritus Professor of English, University of Leeds. His Shakespearean studies – especially *Myth and Miracle* (1929), *The Wheel of Fire* (1930), *The Imperial Theme* (1931), *The Shakespearean Tempest* (1932; 1953), *Shakespearean Production* (1936; 1964) and *The Crown of Life* (1947) – have had a strong influence on modern literary criticism and on performance-interpretations. He is the foremost exponent of the symbolic interpretation of Shakespeare.

GEORG CHRISTOPH LICHTENBERG (1742–99): German satirical writer and physicist. He lived for some time in England (whence his *Briefe aus England*, 1776–78) and among his works is a book about Hogarth's engravings.

CHARLES MAROWITZ (b. 1934): American-born theatre director who came to Britain in 1956. He worked with the Traverse Theatre Company in Edinburgh and in 1968 founded in London his own company, The Open Space. Well-known for his 'collage' versions of Shakespeare, starting with *Hamlet* in 1966, he was for a time joint-editor of the theatre magazine *Encore*. His publications include *The Method as Means, The Act of Being* (1978), the edited volumes of essays, *The 'Encore' Reader* 1965 and *Theatre at Work* 1967.

HENRY MORLEY (1837–94): Professor of Literature, University College, London (1865–78) and Queen's College, London (1878–90). He wrote on drama for the *Examiner*, and compiled the *Journal of a London Playgoer from 1850 to 1866* (published in 1891).

GEORGE JEAN NATHAN (1882–1958): American writer on theatre, one of the most famous and influential dramatic critics of his day. He became theatre critic of the *New York Herald* in 1905 and campaigned for a modern drama of ideas. He championed the cause of Ibsen and of Shaw, and was one of the first to recognise the merits of Eugene O'Neill.

WILLIAM SHAKESPEARE (1564–1616): English actor, dramatist and poet.

GEORGE BERNARD SHAW (1856–1950): Anglo-Irish dramatist and Fabian socialist. Dramatic critic of the *Saturday Review* (1895–98), his criticism was collected in three volumes, *Our Theatres in the Nineties* (1931). While a dramatic critic Shaw developed clear ideas on the stage and on how to put over ideas through plays. He received a strong impetus from Ibsen, whose cause he championed in England.

J. L. STYAN (b. 1923): Andrew Mellon Professor of English in the University of Pittsburgh. Previously he taught in the Department of Adult Education, University of Hull. His publications include *Dark Comedy* (1962), *Drama, Stage and Audience* (1975) and *The Shakespeare Revolution* (1977).

KENNETH TYNAN (b. 1927): English drama critic and author, he graduated from Oxford in 1949 with a degree in English Literature, and began a career as actor and director. His first book, *He That Plays the King* (1950), suggested what his best work would be, and he is still regarded as a leading post-war theatre critic (especially for his reviews in the *Observer*, 1954–58, 1960–63). As a critic he has moved from the enthusiastic approval of heroic acting to support for those plays that have a pronounced social purpose – though his collection, *The Sound of Two Hands Clapping* (1975) is also introduced as a book of enthusiasms. He was Literary Manager of the National Theatre from 1963 to 1973. In addition to the books already mentioned, his publications include *Curtains, Tynan Left and Right, A View of the English Stage* and an edition of Farquhar's *The Recruiting Officer*.

A. B. WALKLEY (1855–1926): English civil servant and drama critic. He reviewed theatre for *The Times* from 1900 to his death. In 1903 he published *Dramatic Criticism: Three Lectures*.

T. C. WORSLEY (1907–77): English literary critic and educationist, and a former literary editor of the *New Statesman*. He was its theatre critic between 1948 and 1952, when he joined the *Financial Times* to review theatre and subsequently, in 1965, became its television critic. His publications include two studies of English education and a collection of theatre reviews, *The Fugitive Art: Dramatic Commentaries, 1947–51* (1952).

KATHERINE J. WORTH (b. 1929): Reader in English at Royal Holloway College, University of London. She was previously lecturer in the History of Drama at the Central School of Speech and Drama, London. Her publications include *Revolutions in Modern English Drama* (1972).

INDEX

This index includes only significant or repeated references to plays, playwrights, players and critics.